THE AUSTRALIAN CENTURY

The Australian Century

Asher Judah

Second edition 2025

ISBN: 9781764034616

Cover design by James Hooper

Maps by SWIM Communications

For Mary, Joshua, Marcus,
Rachel & Anneliese

To the foreigner, at first, it is a different, unusual country. To the sane, healthy native-born, it is a mother of everlasting youth and beauty, and the freest, richest, happiest land on earth.

Edwin Brady

CONTENTS

Author's note

Despite being one of the world's most cohesive societies, occupying the world's richest island, located between the first and third most important oceans, situated farthest away from the globe's most intractable problems, Australia has resigned itself to remaining little more than a deferential 'middle power'.

Our willingness to accept this fate originates neither from our history as former British colonies, nor from our preference for comfort over influence. Rather, it derives from our culture's inherent apprehension about size, our risk averse nature and the lingering doubts we have about our full potential.

Australia is indeed a peculiarity.

As a large but thinly populated island beyond the south eastern tip of the Eurasian supercontinent, Australia sits physically and culturally isolated. Despite cordial relations with almost all our neighbours, and a history of genuine cooperation and support, Australians are nonetheless concerned about the large swathe of humanity which resides just beyond their northern borders.

To most observers, the numbers are indeed intimidating. Four billion people, across 42 nations, sprinkled upon both island and continent, all less than 8,000km away. Eastern Eurasia may not have been the birthplace of humanity, but today it is certainly its demographic heartland.

Australia exists in this region as a nation of 23 million people. Our largest neighbour, Indonesia, is home to 250 million people. In the minds of many Australians, this mismatch can only mean one thing – that Australia is the weaker of the two and will be forever destined to remain so. This conclusion is wrong.

If the last 500 years have taught us anything, it is that size, despite its capacity to intimidate, doesn't guarantee strength. During the age of discovery, a small island nation off the western coast of Eurasia looked enviously upon its regional rivals Spain and Portugal.[1] That nation was England. The Spanish and the Portuguese, originally minor powers themselves, had built vast overseas empires, and dwarfed the economic, military and technological capacity of the middle-ranked English nation.

However, with the benefit of circumstance, capacity, vision and luck, the English incrementally recast their place in the world by seeking to build something greater. By 1922, the English controlled the greatest empire known to humanity. England governed almost a quarter of the world's surface and over 458 million people (one quarter of the world's population at that time). In the space of three and a half centuries, the English used changing circumstances to create a new reality.

Australia too, is a nation with the opportunity to achieve great and remarkable things. Endowed with almost limitless capacity, near inextinguishable natural resources, defendable territory and limited social division, Australia has few reasons for keeping its ambitions small.

In this century, unlike any before, nations such as Australia will have a rare chance to use changing circumstances to create a new reality for themselves. One in which they can be envied by both the powerful and the powerless.

This book is about discovering Australia's full potential. It seeks to illustrate how the world really is, where it's headed, who we are within it and what opportunities lie before us. Importantly, it is also a call to action to all those who have often thought that this amazing country was destined for exceptional things.

The time has come for the Australian Century.

Overture:
An introduction to the Australian Century

Throughout modern history, only a few nations have had the chance to become truly exceptional.

To be exceptional, either regionally or globally, a nation must be capable of acting outside the behavioural norms of other nations. In doing so, it must conduct itself with a unique air of self determination; it must possess a special sense of identity; and it must demonstrate a consistent record of high achievement.

Exceptional nations also exercise power completely disproportionate to their size. By excelling in multiple fields of endeavour, exceptional nations not only dominate their peers, but they also invoke their respect, awe and envy.

The best example of exceptionalism today is the United States of America.

The United States is one of the most exceptional nations in human history.

Representing 4.5 per cent of the world's population, on 6.6 per cent of its land mass, the United States is responsible for 23 cents out of every dollar of global production.[2]

As the world's largest economy, its annual production exceeds that of the next three biggest nations combined.[3] The United States is home to the world's largest consumer market and leading industrial base, and it is the world's top importer and the third largest exporter.[4]

Like Australia, the United States is greatly endowed with natural wealth. Controlling some of the world's most extensive natural resource reserves, the United States is ranked first in coal production, third in oil and agriculture production and sixth in natural gas, fisheries and aquaculture production.[5, 6]

The United States also leads the world across a range of influential cultural fields such as scientific research, technological innovation, higher education, representative government, religious pluralism, sport, capitalism, environmental protection and popular entertainment. In addition to producing the world's highest number of Nobel laureates[7] and Summer Olympic medallists,[8] the United States is also home to 45 of the world's top 100 universities,[9] hundreds of distinct ethnic groups, and the world's largest film industry.

Underpinning all of this is the world's most powerful military, second largest nuclear arsenal, and most advanced space capability. Not only does the United States rule its continent and hemisphere unchallenged, it also dominates the world's oceans, trade routes and financial systems.

In 1947, it was said:

> America would soon bestride the world like a colossus. Neither Rome at the height of its power, nor Great Britain, in the period of its economic supremacy, enjoyed an influence so direct, so profound, so pervasive.[10]

For all of us who now live in the United States' shadow, this prediction of exceptionalism has come to pass.

Its influence is everywhere.

Even now, when its economy is struggling, its culture permeates our society, its military determines our security and its creativity shapes our lives.

Due to the full extent of its soft and hard power, today's United States epitomises the term 'exceptional'.

Becoming exceptional

Becoming exceptional is no simple feat. In fact, for a nation to become exceptional and undergo a period of exceptionalism, a number of elements must collide in its favour. These elements are: circumstance, capacity, vision and luck.

Circumstance occurs when the conditions beyond a nation's control shift decidedly in its favour. Often defined as a unique era in which the nation exists, these changes can relate to seismic shifts in global trading activity, technology, environment, geopolitical power structures or even the realisation of trade or territorial conquest.

Capacity, on the other hand, refers to a nation's ability for taking advantage of such shifts. This relates directly to a nation's internal qualities such as its economic, cultural and military strengths. In order for it to capitalise upon fortuitous circumstances, a nation must be built upon a foundation which is both stable and capable of reforming itself.

Vision is a nation's foresight and discipline to achieve bigger things. While almost all nations aspire for greater power, not all can see or manage a path to it. Nations which possess a unifying vision for the future are always better placed to seize opportunities whenever they arise. Conversely, nations without them rarely end up achieving their full potential.

Finally, there is the uncanny element of luck, which represents nothing more than the timely and lengthy intersection of the above three elements. Despite its random and incidental nature, the occurrence of luck helps determine whether the lofty ambitions of nations are ever going to be given their moment to arise.

Collisions of opportunity

Over the past four hundred years, collisions between the elements of exceptionalism have been extremely rare. However, when they have occurred, their ramifications have spanned generations.

The most important collision of the past 400 years occurred in Europe at the dawn of the age of discovery. At that time, five moderately developed, stable and centrally governed European nations, Portugal, Spain, the Netherlands, France and England, collided with several of the naturally rich, but technologically backward and underdeveloped peoples of the world.

Empowered with ocean capable vessels, gunpowder, organised government and imperial ambition, these previously modest nations slowly transformed themselves into globe dominating empires. This unique collision of capacity, circumstance, vision and luck unleashed an era many historians refer to as European exceptionalism – a period in which several small nations, in a singular geographic region, successively exercised disproportionate power around the globe.

Of course, European exceptionalism didn't last forever. Domestic political strife, unrest in their colonial holdings and devastating warfare on their home continent forced an eventual retreat back to more natural limits. But while this period lasted, these five nations enriched themselves immensely, creating long term economic and cultural legacies which echo around the world even today.

Fast forward to the beginning of the 18th century, and we arrive at the second greatest collision of the past five hundred years. In this case, America's vision of 'continentalism' collided with the capital needs of Europe. Through its sale of the Louisiana Territories, Napoleonic France single-handedly doubled the size of the United States and made the dream of American exceptionalism possible.

Within fifty years, America's continentalist vision had surged all the way to the Pacific Ocean. What was once just a modest nation hugging the eastern coast of North America had grown into a continental power of tremendous strength and capacity. Despite American exceptionalism being unleashed over 211 years ago, its legacy continues to this very day.

Moving to the aftermath of World War II, we arrive at one of the most unexpected collisions of modern times. In this case, it was the Japanese and German desire for economic, cultural and military recovery that collided with the containment policy requirements of the anti-communist alliance.

Aided significantly by the Marshall Plan, the Korean War, and favourable US trade and investment conditions, both of these nations recovered quickly. Within a few short decades, Japan and Germany transitioned from being economically devastated pariahs to being the world's third and fourth largest economies – each exceptional in their own right. Today, despite a minor slip in their respective global economic rankings, both nations continue to dominate their hemispheres across a variety of economic, technological and industrial fields.

Regrettably, not all nations that encounter collisions succeed in managing them. Indeed, from time to time, a nation can get so lost in the whirlwind of success, and be so overwhelmed by the challenges it poses, that they can unintentionally bring their opportunity to a close.

Perhaps the best example during the past century is Argentina.

In the early 20th century, Argentina was the most vibrant nation in South America. Riding high upon a surge of exports, immigration, declining mortality and European investment, the Argentine population grew fivefold and the economy 15-fold between 1880 and 1929.[11] To the casual observer, Argentina's future looked good.

Yet despite its tremendous wealth, strong prospects and regional leadership position, Argentina squandered its opportunity for exceptionalism by failing to master itself (genuine capacity). Over the next 80 years, rather than building upon its position of advantage, Argentina instead engaged in terrible self harm. Argentina became beset with problems such as burdensome debt, monetary uncertainty, excessive regulation, barriers to free trade, a weak rule of law, corruption, repeated coups, territorial aggression and a suffocating bureaucracy.[12] What was once the tenth wealthiest nation in the world (per capita),[13] fell backwards to become the 62nd by 2010[14] – the only wealthy nation to experience so great a reversal in recent history.[15] Despite being granted an opportunity for genuine exceptionalism, Argentina ended up squandering its chance.

Australia's collision

In Australia today, we find ourselves in a position similar to Argentina in the first quarter of the 20th century.

At the midway point of the present decade, we are a nation standing at the cusp of our own form of exceptionalism. One that, if recognised and nurtured correctly, has the potential to transform us from a deferential middle power into a truly exceptional one.

Australia's opportunity for greatness will not come about as a result of territorial conquest, land acquisition or even strategic necessity. Rather, it will manifest due to something far simpler – the rise of the global middle class.

The rise of the global middle class

According to the Asia-Pacific Economic Cooperation (APEC), the global middle class "consists of those who have scope for discretionary expenditure over and above the basic necessities of life such as food, clothing and shelter."[16] Globally, this commonly refers to any household whose income per person falls between $11 and $47 international dollars per day.[17,18]

Over the next 16 years, the size of the global middle class could increase from 1.8 billion people to 4.9 billion people.[19] Further, tens of millions more can also be expected to join the global rich.

This predicted rise in living standards is the direct result of sustained economic growth driving up disposable incomes throughout the developing world, but is also being fuelled by population growth in several advanced economies like the United States, the United Kingdom and Canada.

The near tripling of the global middle class represents one of history's most significant socioeconomic changes. And its impact upon the world economy will be profound.

One area which will be irrevocably changed will be that of global consumption. Here are some illuminating figures:

- By 2030, 60 per cent[20] of the world's 8.3 billion people[21] are forecast to be living in cities and towns, up on today's figures by over 1.4 billion people.[22] In order to facilitate this scale of urbanisation, hundreds of cities will need to be built, upgraded and expanded, with accompanying infrastructure to support them. In China alone, 22 new cities are presently being built every year, with 20-50,000 new skyscrapers forecast to be constructed over the coming decades.[23, 24] Global demand for the raw materials necessary to deliver this will see demand for copper, iron ore and steel rise by 122 per cent,[25] 100 per cent[26] and 80 per cent[27] respectively.
- Meeting the energy needs of these cities and the people living and working within them will require a massive increase in energy production. Global electricity demand is forecast to increase by more than 80 per cent between 2010 and 2040.[28] Furthermore, there will be an additional 225 million vehicles in use in China and India by 2030.[29] As a result, global demand for uranium, natural gas, steaming coal and oil is forecast to rise by 78 per cent,[30] 54 per cent,[31] 53 per cent[32] and 37 per cent[33] respectively.
- As the global middle class grows, demand for the services which address the educational, leisure and professional needs of a wealthier population will also rise. In 2010, there were approximately 150 million students enrolled in postsecondary education around the globe.[34] Within 15 years that number will have breached 262 million.[35] Moreover, within just six years worldwide tourism is forecast to increase 60 per cent to over 1.6 billion international tourist arrivals.[36] Similar increases in demand

for healthcare, wealth management and legal services are also predicted.

- Finally, the quantity and variety of global food consumption will soar. By 2030, overall demand is forecast to double,[37] shifting many nations from net exporters to net importers. In order to meet expected demand, world food production will need to rise by at least 50 per cent,[38] with meat production rising 135 per cent,[39] dairy production 100 per cent[40] and cereal production 43 per cent.[41]

Of course, these phenomenal consumption increases are just the tip of the iceberg. Demand for products and services in the transport, construction, mining services, telecommunications, recycling, research, farming, energy generation, water management, environmental sciences, information technology and waste mediation fields will all reach new heights as well. And the level of investment necessary to deliver them will be immense.

The impact on the world

Naturally, the rise of the global middle class will not take place without major implications for the world's many and varied nations. All will feel its impact.

Consequently, as this century unfolds, the world will splinter into two distinct groups.

- The developing world: those nations in which the bulk of the rise is occurring. The developing world will be in the unenviable position of requiring increased access to raw materials, energy, food, water and expertise at the same time as supply for each will be tightening. How their governments manage this challenge without unleashing social unrest and economic upheaval will determine whether this century truly becomes about them.

- The established world: those nations which are already developed. With the heavy lifting of nation building behind them, the established world will be focused upon managing their demography, securing trade access to foreign markets and reshaping their geopolitical power. How effectively their governments do so will determine whether they reach mid century in a stronger position than which they began it.

The impact on Australia

In 1851, the colony of Victoria experienced its first historic collision. Gold was discovered (circumstance).

The discovery of gold throughout regional Victoria unleashed a period of dramatic social and economic reform (capacity) which permanently changed the colony and its place within the Australian federation.

Within ten years, Victoria's population had increased sevenfold; its cities and towns had been radically transformed; and its economy had exploded in size. What was just five years earlier forecast to remain the smaller, weaker and poorer cousin of New South Wales, had decided to leapfrog its larger sibling to become Australia's biggest and most productive colony (vision).

For this generation of Australians, the rise of the global middle class represents its gold rush. However, this time the goldfields will exist in our cities, mines, gas wells and farms.

Just as the 1850s gold rush transformed Victoria into Australia's preeminent colony, this phenomenon has the potential to transform Australia into one of the world's most exceptional nations. Most importantly, it will do for Australia what the gold rush did for Victoria all those years ago – drive a socioeconomic revolution.

Through a combination of a surging economy, intense foreign investment, high employment, strong population growth and rapid technological change, Australia will finally be able to unlock its full potential. By harnessing the rise of the global middle class, Australia will be able to use changing circumstances to create a new reality for itself. Importantly, it will be able to do so at a time when much of the world will be struggling.

Seizing the moment

Opportunities for exceptionalism rarely visit a nation more than once, and in Australia's case, the most important century of its existence has finally arrived.

Australia's ability to rise to the occasion will succeed or fail based upon how it responds to this special opportunity. Indeed, it will pivot entirely upon whether the nation recognises what is before it, and if its people are hungry enough to change.

Australia has an amazing future ahead of it.

It's time to go and seize it.

1
The rise of the global middle class

Over the next two decades, the size of the global middle class is forecast to almost triple in size. An additional three billion middle class consumers are expected to emerge bringing the total number to 4.9 billion people, up from 1.8 billion today.

The global middle class "consists of those who have scope for discretionary expenditure over and above the basic necessities of life such as food, clothing and shelter."[42] This encapsulates any household whose income per person ranges between $11 and $47 international dollars per day.

This monumental rise in global living standards is the direct result of sustained economic growth driving up disposable incomes throughout the developing world as well as population growth within several developed economies like the United States, the United Kingdom, Canada and Australia.

The rise of the global middle class will be one of history's most significant socioeconomic changes.

What makes this change so significant is the scale and speed at which it is occurring.

During the first industrial revolution, the United Kingdom took 154 years to double its real per capita GDP (PPP) for nine million people. Over a century later, the United States accomplished the same result for 11 million people in a third of the time. A century after that, the Japanese did the same for 50 million people in just 33 years.

Today, nations like China and India are achieving the same result for over two billion people every 12-16 years.

In other words, the world's fastest growing economies are modernising themselves at ten times the speed of their predecessors for over 200 times the people.[43] These changes are without precedent. They are also widely misunderstood.

§

With over three billion additional consumers forecast to enter world markets in the next twenty years, the way the globe functions is set to change. Not only will the weight of global consumption decidedly shift from the west to the east and the south, but the geopolitics which shape how global trade and service provision occurs will change as well. Summarised below is an overview of how the internationally significant markets of raw materials, energy, services and food will be transformed by the rise of the global middle class.

Raw materials

The world will experience a sustained and long term surge in demand for raw materials as a result of rise related industrialisation, urbanisation and multifaceted infrastructure change.

Industrialisation

Industrialisation is the transition of a nation's economy from one dominated by rural based agricultural activity to one based upon urbanised industrial activity. In an industrialising nation, manufacturing slowly assumes a central place within the economy at the expense of agriculture with metallurgy and energy generation often playing key support roles. As this transition takes place, the total amount of raw materials consumed for capacity building, industrial operations and domestic consumption rises sharply.

Urbanisation

Urbanisation occurs alongside its transformative accomplice, industrialisation. Urbanisation is the process of relocating people from rural settings to urban environments such as cities. People in industrialising nations primarily move to urban centres to pursue a higher standard of living through better employment opportunities. This is nearly always because urban centres offer greater social mobility and improved odds of success.

Over the next 16 years, the world's population is forecast to increase to approximately 8.3 billion people.[44] During this growth spurt, 60 per cent of all people will choose to be urban dwellers[45] with five million people moving into cities each month.[46] In order to facilitate this shift, thousands of cities around the world will need to be built, upgraded or expanded. In China alone, over 200 cities with populations over one million people will be required by 2025,[47] necessitating the construction of three new cities the size of Sydney every year until 2030.[48] Similar construction will also be necessary across Asia, South America and much of Africa where urbanisation rates are also accelerating. In total, over the next three decades, almost 100,000 new skyscrapers will need to be built throughout the developing world – the high rise equivalent of 17 New Yorks!

Infrastructure

Complementing the physical development of the cities themselves will be the enormous support infrastructure necessary to facilitate their operation: "By 2040, there will be 2.8 billion households in the world, an increase of nearly 50 percent from 2010. These households will need energy for lighting, heating, cooking, hot water and refrigeration, as well as electricity to run everything from computers to air conditioners."[49] Their occupants will also need efficient transportation choices, a wide array of social services and a clean environment in which to live. As a result, these urban centres, both new and old, will require hospitals, universities and schools; mass transits; waste and sanitisation processing systems; water, electricity and gas generation and distribution networks and billions of kilometres of paved roads.[50] In total, over $40 trillion dollars will need to be spent globally during the coming decades just to provide basic levels of infrastructure.[51]

For the developing world to respond to the forces of industrialisation, urbanisation and infrastructure development, as well as source the inputs necessary to operate their societies effectively, access to a diverse and rapidly expanding array of raw materials will be necessary. Consequently, demand for a wide range of commodities will rise.

§

Over the next 50 years, the world will use five times the mineral supplies which have been extracted up to the year 2000.[52] Most importantly, the pace of global consumption will be unprecedented. Outlined below are some of the likely side-effects global consumers can expect to experience as a result.

Commodity source concentration

Commodity concentration is a major obstacle to supply responsiveness as fewer suppliers often result in weaker competition and higher prices. In the rare earths market for example, a commodity essential to the manufacturing of magnets and lasers, approximately 97 per cent of global production occurs in China.[53] Unfortunately, despite efforts to diversify, the number of suppliers has in fact declined in recent years. As a result, China is now in a position to control both the global supply and price of many rare earth elements. Similar levels of concentration exist in many other commodity markets, albeit mostly as oligopolies rather than monopolies.

Supply responsiveness

Another challenge which is often under reported is the capacity of suppliers to meet rising demand. Across all fields of extraction, a vast array of technological, financial, political, environmental and infrastructural obstacles make production increases complicated. In the case of iron ore, global demand has stayed well ahead of global supply for many years because miners could not increase production fast enough. As a result, prices hit record highs despite the commodity itself being common and its extraction practices being well established. A similar problem also exists with Australia's exportation of black coal. In recent years, coal carriers have had to wait off the coast for months before being loaded. The delay is not due to a shortage of coal. It is because the rail network and their related port facilities are both incapable of facilitating demand.[54] In other words, just because a commodity is technically available and plentiful in a developed nation, doesn't mean an effective supply chain exists. Financiers can change their minds, politicians can equivocate, environmentalists can stall and infrastructure can remain a blueprint. Consequently, it is more than just availability that matters when it comes to meeting demand.

Risk premiums

According to McKinsey, the geographic concentration risk associated with several of the raw materials essential for fuelling the growth of a middle class (coking coal, copper, bauxite, platinum, tin, rare earths, phosphate and potash) are rated as either medium or high.[55] What this means is that over the coming decades, raw materials sourced in these markets will continue to be traded at an elevated risk premium.

Export restrictions

Raw material consumers should also expect unpredictable disruptions throughout existing global supply chains. According to the World Trade Organisation (WTO), "from October 2010 to April 2011, China, India and Vietnam among other countries, imposed at least 30 export curbs on mineral resources, up from 25 during the previous 12 months."[56] Changes such as these are often driven by domestic shortages. Therefore, as global demand rises, these types of protectionist actions will probably become more common.

Extraction costs

Predictions are decidedly pessimistic regarding the cost of resource extraction. Despite rapid improvements in technology, the cost of resource extraction has become more expensive.[57] This is largely attributed to the cost of labour, machinery, rising environmental standards, related resource costs and the use of less productive and more complex locations.

Supply perceptions

Finally, in relation to economically recoverable reserves, coking coal, copper, gold, zinc, nickel, silver, lead and tin are each estimated to have less than 50 years supply left, with five estimated to have less than 24 years.[58,59] While estimates naturally fluctuate as a result of continued exploration, technology improvements, recycling and the creation of substitutes, market behaviour can still be expected to operate on the basis of perception. Put simply, as each commodity edges closer to its forecast supply limit, it is reasonable to assume that its price will rise. These rises will make the task of industrialisation and urbanisation much harder for nations incapable of absorbing higher input costs.

Energy

Massive increases in electricity demand, vehicle usage and industrial and agricultural production linked to the global rise will ensure the world's insatiable appetite for energy does not ease.

Between 2010 and 2030, primary energy demand is forecast to increase by 33 per cent - the equivalent of current US and European Organisation for Economic Co-operation and Development (OECD) member usage combined.[60] According to the International Energy Agency (IEA), the vast majority of this increase will be taking place in nations outside of the OECD. Non-OECD members are forecast to account for 90 per cent of energy demand growth over the period 2010 to 2035.[61]

Electricity demand

Electricity usage will be the single biggest driver of energy demand accounting for more than 40 per cent of global energy consumption.[62] Between 2010 and 2040, electricity demand will rise more than 80 per cent with industrial activity being the biggest driver representing 45 per cent, followed by residential activity at 30 per cent and commercial activity at 20 per cent.[63] The rise will be the main force behind these changes as billions discover non-agrarian employment, household electricity consumption and recreational activity. For example, by 2040, Chinese demand will more than double.[64]

Global transport

Large changes can also be expected within the global transport market with energy demand for transportation forecast to rise by nearly 45 per cent between 2010 and 2040.[65] By 2030, the global vehicle fleet is forecast to have doubled to 1.7 billion[66] with China's passenger fleet increasing from 58 million to 450 million[67] and India's from 15 million to 135 million (larger than France, Germany, Italy and the United Kingdom combined).[68] "By 2030, the world will use more fuel for trucks and other heavy duty vehicles than for all personal vehicles combined."[69] Demand for energy for commercial transportation is expected to rise by more than 70 percent[70] and over the next 30 years, hunger for aviation and marine fuel will almost double.[71]

Industrial and agricultural production

Creating the manufactured products necessary for urbanisation and industrial activity and will also play a major role in stimulating energy demand. Over the next 16 years, copper and steel demand alone is forecast to rise by 122 per cent and 80 per cent respectively in order to meet urban infrastructure, machinery, electrical wiring, roofing and plumbing requirements. Energy demand within the agriculture sector will also rise as energy intensive activities such as groundwater pumping, irrigation, desalinisation and long distance water distribution increase.

§

In order for the world economy to meet this huge upswing in energy demand, a massive increase in energy production will be required. At present, fossil fuels are responsible for approximately 86 per cent of global energy production with the remainder being generated by non-fossil sources.

In the twentieth century, fossil fuel use increased 16-fold.[72] During the first half of this century, fossil usage will need to increase substantially more just to meet minimum demand. In order to do so, revolutions in energy extraction, distribution and conversion will be required. Unfortunately, as par the course of all markets energy, a number of complex, costly and intractable challenges make the achievement of this objective a difficult one.

Oligopolistic suppliers

Purely by chance, the bulk of the world's economically recoverable primary energy supplies are located in approximately two dozen nations. In regard to crude oil, natural gas and coal production, just ten nations in each market account for 63.4, 66.7 and 89.7 per cent of global production.[73,74,75] Further, seven of those can claim top ten production status in at least two of these markets. This makes them amongst the most powerful and fortunate in our planet's energy lottery draw.

Not so lucky however, are their price-taking customers. Due to the relatively small number of nations with multi-decade energy reserves, most of the world's nations are forced to endure the oligopolistic behaviour of ruthless suppliers. Actions such as artificial price setting, profit maximisation, below capacity production and restrictive trade practices all contribute to higher market prices and distorted and reduced global trade. Even the United States, a champion for freer global markets, continues to flirt with natural gas export restrictions despite its reserves and production levels soaring in recent years. These factors will no doubt complicate future efforts to boost supply, attract investment and reduce prices.

Resource nationalism

Resource nationalism is policy action undertaken by governments seeking to assert control over their natural resources. Governments in resource rich nations seek to exercise higher levels of control for a number of different reasons, but the two most important relate to the perceived strategic or economic advantages of control. For example, by taking over existing production facilities, or seizing control of deposit licenses, governments are able to prioritise the sale of the commodity to their preferred customers or into their own domestic markets.

Over the past two decades, dozens of nations have engaged in some form of resource nationalism ranging from full nationalisation and local content requirements to regulatory and fiscal changes which have robbed investors of their investment. In each case, these interventions have severely disrupted the market. Despite the destabilising effect this has on a nation's sovereign risk and its global reverberations, this practice is definitely on the rise. According to Maplecroft, over the past year the risk of resource nationalism has increased in 15 per cent of nations.[76]

Political instability

The threat of political unrest within the world's leading energy nations also has the potential to disrupt global trade. The absence of democracy and liberty, as well as the presence of social repression, corruption and civil war can all contribute to major disruptions in global energy supplies, as occurred during the Libyan civil war (2011). Indeed, in the past decade alone, the Arab Spring and a variety of ethno-religious conflicts and succession challenges have contributed to higher energy prices and supply chain instability. With little prospect of political reform in many of these nations, a continuation of existing instability can be expected.

Poor infrastructure and transportation assets

Poor quality infrastructure and transportation assets will also undermine efforts to boost global supply. Issues such as limited rail, highway and port capacity, unfortunate resource location, outdated transport vehicles, poor storage facilities and inefficient power generation each contribute to supply side underperformance. According to the IEA, "cumulative investment of $37 trillion is needed in the world's energy supply system over 2012-2035."[77] This amounts to more than 1.5 per cent of global GDP (approximately US$1.5 trillion dollars) per year with 61 per cent required in non-OECD nations.[78] At present, the combined global infrastructure annual investment spend across all nations dedicated to meeting future demand for steel, water, agriculture and energy is approximately $2 trillion.[79] Therefore, it seems unlikely that this investment requirement will be met.

Rising environmental and health expectations

A number of complex environmental and health challenges also threaten to undermine efforts to boost global energy supplies. Environmental grievances about land clearing, the destruction of key ecological sites, impacts on groundwater supplies, carbon dioxide emissions and the irreversible consequences of hydropower generation are all major obstacles to increased energy production. Moreover, community apprehension about the health risks associated with the extraction and consumption of fossil and non-fossil fuels also poses a major threat (e.g. Hydraulic fracturing, tailings, dust, runoff and poor water management). As the developing world becomes more aware of these side-effects, the growth rate of global supply will be affected.

Competition for operational resources

Finally, one important obstacle which is often forgotten is access to operational resources. For steam-driven power generation and hydroelectricity, ongoing access to water will remain essential. However, water continues to remain a key ingredient of both agricultural and industrial activity, being essential to the processes of irrigation, food processing, heat exchange and cleaning. As the world economy expands, demand for water to facilitate these activities will inevitably rise. This will place them in direct competition with domestic energy generation priorities. Managing these competing interests will be an extremely complicated task, especially in areas where these diverse uses mix.

Services

Mass urbanisation, rapid industrialisation and rising levels of disposable income driven by the global rise will radically alter the size and nature of globally consumed services.

Mass urbanisation

Throughout the developing world, almost all urban areas will grow in size and complexity as a result of increased industrial development, commercial and infrastructural investment and population growth. Consequently, these centres will need to be dramatically expanded, redesigned, or at a minimum, economised in order to handle new demand pressures. This process will be particularly challenging in nations where cities were constructed before the advent of the automobile, and certainly in those built before the horse and cart. Odd as it may sound, almost all of the world's cities were founded before Henry Ford rolled out his first Model T.

Managing the challenges posed by growth, development and urbanisation will extremely difficult as few developing nations have home-grown expertise, especially at a cost effective price. As a result, in order to achieve the best outcome at the lowest cost, assistance is likely to be brought in from elsewhere. For example, in the lead up to the 2008 Beijing Olympics, China spent an estimated $40 billion dollars (USD)[80] upgrading its capital resulting in the importation of thousands of foreign experts and companies. Over the next four decades, trillions will be spent replicating a similar retrofitting task all across the globe. This massive uptick in demand represents an unprecedented opening for the globe's urban service providers: planners, architects and sustainability, waste management and transport design specialists.

Rapid industrialisation

A sharp rise in demand for business advisory services can also be expected. In addition to the obvious service delivery areas of investment, internet commercialisation and legal, accounting and capital raising advice, the developing world will also be seeking specialised expertise in a large variety of high technology fields: manufacturing, chemical processing, heavy industry, mining, energy, agriculture, information technology, biotechnology, pharmaceuticals, sustainability and waste disposal. As with the urban transformation challenge outlined above, the business community will want the most efficient and cost effective path to success.

Rising levels of disposable income

Over the next 16 years, average disposable income levels across the world will rise lifting billions into the global middle class. As incomes begin to enter the middle class income range, the proportion of household expenditure devoted to basic living expenses declines in favour of discretionary alternatives. This takes place as a result of the consumer's exposure to new ideas and concepts brought about by rising levels of wealth within their own lives and their community. When this occurs, the local population begins to demand new services such as higher education to improve their job prospects; better healthcare for increased longevity; dependable legal and financial services to protect rights and increase wealth, and greater access to new leisure and entertainment experiences.

Over the next six years, consumer spending in the best performing developing nations is forecast to exceed $20 trillion – twice current United States consumption levels.[81] A great deal of it will be in the area of service delivery. Below is a sample of what could be coming.

Education

Global place demand for higher education is projected to rise by 165 million people to over 262 million by 2025.[82] In India during the next decade alone, over 50 million skilled technicians and workers will be required just to meet its most basic economic growth needs. With its domestic training capacity at barely 10 per cent of this requirement, India's education problem is likely to become the service exporters' grand opportunity.

Healthcare

As income and education levels rise, demand for doctors, nurses, medical support staff, surgical tools and pharmaceuticals will surge. These increases will be driven both by rising expectations in the developing world and by ageing demography in the developed world. Based on current global training capacity, these targets are unlikely to be met. This too will trigger a large spike in international health service demand.

Legal services

Social change, government regulation and increasing personal and commercial wealth will amplify demand for legal services. As with healthcare, legal service provision is unlikely to be met by domestic supply alone. For example, "India has the second largest legal profession with more than 600,000 lawyers,"[83] but this only equates to "six lawyers per 10,000 people, which is far less than what is available in any of the developed nations".[84] The sheer number of professionals required to meet existing demand, let along future demand, is surreal. Similar skilled labour shortages in the professional services field exist throughout the developing world, including Africa and South East Asia.

Wealth management

Wealth management services also represent another exciting opportunity. At present, billions of the world's poor are presently defined as "unbanked". This means that they do not have access to basic financial services like savings accounts, loans or remittances. Over the decades ahead, the vast majority of these people will be seeking the ability to financial empower themselves. As with healthcare and legal service provision, meeting this demand will require a dramatic expansion of global service capacity.

Leisure and entertainment experiences

Finally, increased discretionary income and improved working conditions will allow millions of people to devote more time toward enjoying life, rather than simply surviving it. This change will manifest in increased demand for online and social entertainment, retail consumption, hospitality, domestic and global tourism, hotel accommodation and personal and professional air travel. Whichever way it is assessed, the scale of demand for new forms of leisure and entertainment will be huge.

§

With global demand for services forecast to rise dramatically across all of these areas, the opportunities for boosting living standards look limitless. However, while demand will undoubtedly be strong, not all nations will be eager to see services easily traded across their borders. Broadly speaking, there are two areas which could undermine the expansion of the world's $4.4 trillion global export service market.[85]

Trade barriers

Significant trade barriers restrict the entry of foreign businesses into specific service markets. Across the developing world, trade rules restricting market entry exist for retail businesses, legal services, healthcare and wealth management. Similar restrictions even exist in the developed world with Europe and Japan being particularly protective of their domestic service providers. While elements of the world's finance, internet and telecommunications sectors operate in highly liberalised markets, many foreign firms participating within them continue to be stifled by heavy handed regulation. As with trade barrier restrictions, these too present a challenge for meeting global service demand.

Self-imposed international treaties

International treaties, trade embargoes and restrictive technology transfer agreements also act as effective obstacles preventing service hungry markets from being satisfied. At present, self-imposed trade restrictions exist in several developing nations across multiple service markets including pharmaceuticals, nuclear technology, advanced manufacturing and defence patents. As economic opportunities grow across the developing world, internal pressure to change these restrictive policies will naturally rise. Nevertheless, at present, they remain effective barriers to service exporters seeking to fill international service delivery shortfalls.

Food

Increasing global wealth, population growth and hunger for alternative transport fuels associated with the rise will keep demand strong for food products throughout this century.

Rising wealth

As the world economy develops and income levels rise, dietary habits across the globe will change. At present, demand for a multitude of food products including meat, milk and eggs are already rapidly rising[86] as consumers seek out more calories, protein, new culinary choices, better quality products and governments work proactively to address health problems like vitamin and mineral deficiencies.[87] By 2050, global food demand is forecast to exceed $US9.1 trillion.[88]

Population growth

By 2030, the world will be home to over 8.3 billion people. In addition to the 1.1 billion additional mouths to feed, the vast majority of global population growth will be occurring in developing nations where technology, social and economic change will be lifting living standards, dietary intake and convenience foods. The end result of this will be a rise in global food demand of 50 per cent.[89] In China alone, meat consumption could rise by as much as 40 per cent.[90] For global producers to accommodate this tectonic shift in demand, a dramatic expansion of food production will be required.[91]

Alternative transport fuels

Widely used transport fuel alternatives such as ethanol regularly secure their key ingredients such as grains and sugar cane at the expense of global food supplies:

> The rapid increase in demand for and production of biofuels, particularly bioethanol from maize and sugarcane, has had a number of effects on grain supply-and-demand systems. Expanded production of ethanol from maize, in particular, has increased total demand for maize and shifted land area away from production of maize for food and feed.[92]

As strange as it sounds, rising food prices resulting from increased biofuel demand leads to larger volumes of food crops being shifted into biofuel production, rather than into food.[93] Factors such as these will undoubtedly cause major distributions to the global food trade.

§

At present, "30 crops provide 95 per cent of human food energy needs and just four of them – rice, wheat, maize and potatoes – provide more than 60 per cent."[94] Meat, dairy and seafood products also make large contributions helping to feed most, but not all of the globe's population.

In order to meet the long term demand forecasts outlined above, world food production will need to rise by at least 50 per cent,[95] meat production by 135 per cent,[96] dairy production by 100 per cent[97] and cereal production by 43 per cent.[98] Large production increases will also be required for seafood and oilseeds. Naturally, achieving increases of this magnitude will be no easy measure. Several significant obstacles exist.

Production ingredient shortages

Despite our much romanticised notions of farm life, agricultural production does not operate in isolation from global markets. Not only do farmers compete with their peers, but they also compete against unrelated industries which desire their essential business inputs. As the world economy develops over the decades ahead, competition for land, labour, water, energy and fertiliser will rapidly intensify.

According to McKinsey, as much as an additional 175m-220m hectares of cropland might be required to meet future demand by 2030.[99] Finding this and bringing it into production will be challenging. It is also worth noting that the ratio of total arable land per person is in long term decline. Since 1970, it has shrunk from 0.38 hectares per person to 0.23 hectares in 2000.[100] It is forecast to decline further to 0.15 hectares per person by 2050[101] due to population growth, degradation, urbanisation, industrialisation and climatic issues.

Major threats also exist in regard to access to labour. Throughout the developing world, much of the workforce is still engaged in agricultural activity. However, as nations industrialise, workers are increasingly migrating to the cities in pursuit of better opportunities. While mechanisation and technological improvements are helping to counterbalance these effects, in some regions, acute labour shortages are devastating production levels, especially during season sensitive harvests.

Competition for water is arguably the most vexing challenge facing efforts to boost global food production. Considered globally, a massive surge in demand is being driven by increasing irrigation, meat production, power generation, mining and municipal and industrial activity. Combined, these factors are placing intense pressure on water prices and available resources. Currently, 40 per cent of the world's population lives in water-scarce regions[102] with Libya, Saudi Arabia, Yemen and Egypt already operating as net water importers.[103] "By 2030, more than half of the world's population could live in regions that suffer from water scarcity."[104] How they strike an effective balance between their many water stakeholders will be extremely difficult. Sadly, food production tends to be the least profitable.

Rising energy costs also pose a threat to food production efforts because "energy accounts for 15 to 30 per cent of the cost of crop production"[105] and "roughly 70 per cent of the cost of groundwater."[106] Moreover, the agriculture sector is also a big consumer of transport fuels which are necessary for machinery operations, product storage, goods transportation, irrigation and water pumping. Over the next few decades, the price of electricity, diesel and petroleum are all forecast to rise.

Finally, access to key agricultural fertilisers like phosphate and potash will also present a major challenge. At present, "approximately 80 per cent of global phosphate reserves are located in and around Morocco",[107] placing them in a monopolistic trading position. This bodes poorly for international phosphate competition. Global potash supplies which are also vital to food production are somewhat less concentrated, but still share many of the same supply characteristics as phosphate. At present, eight nations produce approximately 90 per cent of the world's potash supplies.[108] While a global oligopoly is unlikely to form, the high concentration of producers is unlikely to result in intense product competition. Sadly for consumers of both commodities, there are few viable substitutes.[109]

Environmental challenges

Overharvesting, overfishing and pest epidemics also have the capacity to undermine agricultural productivity.

Overharvesting of farm land and grazing pastures represents a real threat to global food supplies. Overuse, loss of top soil, rising salinity, urbanisation and the misuse of fertilisers and pesticides has already contributed to the loss of productive farm land. According to FAO, approximately 33 per cent of the world's land resources are rated as degrade or moderately degraded.[110]

Overfishing also poses a risk. Overfishing takes place when fish stocks are fished down below the size that supports their long term sustainability. When this occurs, the ability of the fish population to replenish itself through reproduction is severely weakened. It also risks secondary problems like trophic cascades in which local food chains become unstable. According to FAO,[111] approximately 53 per cent of the world's marine fish resources are fully fished or fished to their maximum sustainable level while "another 32 per cent is overfished, depleted, or recovering from depletion".[112]

Pests such as weeds, fish, birds, mammals, insects, pathogens and microbes also threaten global food production. Many of these undermine production by directly threatening crop, livestock and commercial fish activity. In some regions, pests, pathogens and weeds can create production losses of up to 40 per cent.[113] "Among the 80 new infectious diseases identified since 1970, 70 per cent are of animal origin and pose a threat to food supplies across the globe."[114]

Trade protectionism

Increasing volatility in food prices combined with soaring demand has resulted in many nations taking protectionist measures to improve food security and/or reduce domestic prices.[115] During the past decade alone, over a dozen nations have enacted food-related trade protection measures. These have included eliminating export subsidies (China), raising export taxes (Argentina, Russia and Malaysia), introducing volumetric restrictions (Ukraine, India and Vietnam) and imposing export bans (Egypt, Cambodia, Vietnam, Indonesia and Kazakhstan).[116] In the vast majority of cases, these measures have only served to increase global prices and trigger retaliatory action.

Competitive demand for feed products

Despite widespread acknowledgement that cereals feed people more efficiently than meats, nearly half of the world's cereal production is used to produce animal feed. This is because meat production is a more profitable business proposition than cereals. According to the United States Department of Agriculture (USDA), it requires 2.6, 6.5 and seven pounds of feed to produce one pound of chicken, pork and beef respectively.[117] Over the next few decades, global demand for these three products is forecast to rise considerably. This will undoubtedly place pressure on global cereal supplies.

Demand for biofuels also has the potential to complicate food supply chains with an increasing share of grain production being used to produce biofuels. By 2030, demand for biofuels is forecast to rise to 350 billion litres from 110 billion litres in 2010.[118] Not only will this undermine global efforts to meet food demand, but it will also risk increased social instability due to rising commodity prices, as occurred with the Mexican Tortilla Riots in 2007.

Transport limitations

At present, vast tracts of arable land within Africa, South America and Asia remain commercially unviable for food production because of inadequate infrastructure. According to McKinsey, "more than 80 per cent of the remaining unused available arable land is in countries with insufficient infrastructure or political issues".[119] The absence of roads, railway lines and ports all contribute to the costs of bringing food to market. Moreover, the geographical realities of landlocked Africa and South America make the cost of rectifying these inadequacies extremely expensive. Much like deep water drilling, just because a process is technically possible, doesn't mean its economically viable.

The quality of government

Government incompetence and poor decision making can also undermine efforts to meet future food demand. While neither the developed nor developing world has a monopoly on incompetence, poor governance practices in the developing world remain far bigger obstacles to increasing global food supplies than those found elsewhere. Corruption, unstable governments, radical policy shifts, sovereign risk, civil wars and domestic unrest all undermine production improvement efforts.

Poor decision making can also threaten efforts to improve food production. At present, some of the most promising productivity breakthroughs such as genetically modified food are being held up by an avalanche of government obstacles including excessive farming regulations, anti-investment tax arrangements, technophobia, environmental obstructionism and political populism. For example, genetic modification technology has substantially increased soybean and maize production in the United States, yet it is illegal to grow such crops in dozens of other nations.

If global food demand is going to be met in the future, then decisions such as this will need to be revisited.

§

Frazier vs Ali

With so many competing forces cascading over the world as a result of the rise of the global middle class, it is easy to misunderstand what is truly going on.

To many, the rise represents a long overdue rectification of the global order. Through a comprehensive reduction in poverty, burgeoning service provision, industrialisation, mass urbanisation, the creation of a genuinely global consumer class and a sustained lift in demand for raw materials, energy, services and food, the rise is seen as being responsible for a reorganisation of world power, markets and economic influence along lines more reflective of today's global demography.

In many ways, this assessment is correct. A genuine and undeniable economic and geopolitical realignment is taking place. However, as with all forms of upheaval, not all of its side effects are beneficial. Much like Joseph Schumpeter's economic theory of "creative destruction", the rise is a complicated phenomenon which possesses both positive and negative traits.

Consider the following.

Over the next 16 years, the rise is forecast to trigger demand for an additional 392 million passenger vehicles in China. As a natural byproduct of this, global energy demand will rise. But, due to the inelasticity of global energy markets, the paucity of responsive supply chains, and the absence of viable alternatives, this increase will result in a rise in global energy prices. Consequently, as energy price inflation occurs, living standards, social stability and government budgets within China will be undermined.

In other words, at the same time that the rise is positively transforming China, it is also simultaneously sabotaging it. Like two boxers sparring in a ring, the true nature of the rise involves both a punch and a counterpunch. The punch catapults the nation forward, but the counterpunch sends it flying back. In essence, the rise is best understood as a multi-decade boxing match between two well matched opponents. The momentum always remains with the aggressor, but only if they can maintain their balance.

Interestingly, it is this process which is being played out in every nation in the world right now. And while many are continuing to move forward in terms of development and growth, several developing nations are starting to lose their footing. Outlined below are some of the most serious rise related dangers threatening to derail the world's most promising growth stories.

Market volatility

During the past decade alone, strategic resource volatility has reached an all time high.[120] Energy prices are up 190 percent, materials prices are up 135 per cent and food prices are up 135 per cent.[121] In fact, since the turn of the century, the average annual volatility of resource prices "has been more than three times that witnessed over the course of the 20th century and more 50 per cent higher than the 1980s".[122]

Market dynamics such as this are a problem for all nations seeking to improve living standards in an increasingly competitive world. Whether it is developing ones seeking to stimulate industrialisation and minimise socioeconomic disruption, or developed ones working to lift efficiency and reduce their cost base, market volatility is a plague upon all forms of economic development.

Consumer product inflation

In recent years, almost 100 nations have been significantly affected by food and energy inflation. "In 2007 and 2008, price increases triggered food protests and riots in 48 countries."[123] Food inflation also contributed to the downfall of governments in Indonesia (1998), Libya (2011) and Egypt (2011). Similar examples also exist in regard to rising energy and raw material prices.

Due to the close relationship between consumer product inflation and political instability, over $1.1 trillion is spent every year globally on subsidies.[124] In Indonesia for example,[125] concerns about social instability and slowing economic growth are so great that more money is spent on oil and coal subsidies than on health and education. Not only does this approach undermine Indonesia's long term development prospects, but it also makes its budget highly vulnerable to fluctuating oil and coal prices. In 2011, fuel subsidies accounted for 38 per cent of government expenditure.[126]

Throughout the entire world, similar stories exist of governments fearful of the inflation genie. Over the next few decades, the price of cereals, meats, seafood, dairy products, oil, coal, cooking oil, palm oil, tin, potash and magnesium are all forecast to rise. No doubt these increases will complicate the development paths for more nations than just Indonesia.

Insufficient production

In the 20th century, the world population quadrupled and economic output expanded approximately 20-fold.[127] Yet against this backdrop, prices fell. The reason this occurred was because soaring demand was offset by even faster rising production. In the 21st century, this process has yet to fully occur. Supplies suitable for economically viable development are declining, the cost of production (and extraction) is rising and real and perceived environmental concerns are undermining confidence, investment and policy settings. Troublingly, at a time when humanity's appetite has never been stronger, global supply lines have become less reliable.

The unfortunate reality of this change has been a rise in global unpredictability. As a result, spill-over effects are forcing many nations to change their patterns of behaviour leading to a further elevation of global tension. Rising protectionism, political upheaval, unexpected trade policy shifts and changing power dynamics are amongst the most obvious examples. Worryingly, internal competition for resources such as water in industrial and agricultural production is also becoming more fraught. On complex issues such as land and water use, nations are not only dividing against each other, they are also dividing against themselves (as with the Indian states of Tamil Nadu and Karnataka) over water.

Export-import reversals

In 2004-05, 131 out of the 196 nations in the world were net food importers.[128,129] Over the next few decades, the number of exporters catering to growing global demand for food is forecast to decline. This will result in the majority of the world's nations not being able to technically feed themselves.

A similar situation is also expected for the world's net energy importers.[130] By 2035, 80 per cent of oil consumed in non-OECD Asia will come from imports, up from just over half in 2010.[131] Europe and North America will also face similar dependency challenges. As a result, the majority of the world's nations will become completely dependent upon energy imports simply to function.

Driven by a permanent shift in domestic consumption levels, many of these "switching" nations can be expected to consider prioritising the needs of domestic growth ahead of the profitability of export markets. Consequently, globally traded supply can be expected to become more unreliable and government budgets less stable.

Uncontrolled population movements

As the effects of the rise wash over all nations, positive and negative forces within them will trigger planned and unplanned population movements. In nations like India and Pakistan, large scale urban drift powered by the pursuit of greater economic opportunity will result in cities like Mumbai and Karachi being overwhelmed by demand for employment, infrastructure and services far beyond their capacity to provide it. Equally, in places as dissimilar as the European Union, Malaysia and Turkey, governments will experience regional and financial destabilisation as a result of uncontrolled migration caused by self-selecting migrants and the genuine avoidance of social and economic unrest.

The potential of innovation

Of course, not all will be doom and gloom. As they say, necessity is the mother of invention and supply uncertainty will remain a powerful motivator for technological innovation. Historical breakthroughs such as the green revolution (cropping) and horizontal drilling (shale oil) both demonstrate how unexpected innovations can fundamentally alter resource production, supply and price levels. Over the decades ahead, similar breakthroughs in areas like computing, biotechnology, battery storage, energy efficiency, genetics, recycling, robotics and subsurface exploration and extraction will undoubtedly help ease market tensions. How quickly these benefits flow however, no one can truly be certain.

§

In summary, the rise is best understood as this century's greatest opportunity as well as its most significant threat. At the same time that it is unleashing the world's full potential, it is simultaneously undermining its capacity to cope. By mid-century, analysts predict that an additional 3.1 billion people will have joined the ranks of the global middle class. In order for such forecasts to eventuate and achieve permanence, all of the world's nations will need to have successfully overcome the challenges outlined above. With the future looking so decisively volatile, and the world's nations being so unevenly developed and led, it is unlikely that this outcome will eventuate as smoothly as many imagine. As a result, the rise of the global middle class should be relied upon to be unequally beneficial, temperamental, and in all likelihood, seriously destabilising.

2
The developing world: triumph and tragedy

One of the great misnomers in popular forecasting today is the near unshakeable belief that much of the developing world will one day join the established one as developmental equals. That some time soon, these nations will come to enjoy the same economic clout, institutional stability, social harmony and standard of living which presently define the world all Australians live in.

This kind of thinking is misguided.

Despite what many may wish to be true about the developing world's prospects, wilful blindness is never a good substitute for objective analysis.

For much of the developing world, maintaining progress amidst their innumerable internal and external challenges will be the real ambition that consumes their attention this century. Indeed for many developing nations, overcoming the handicaps of widespread poverty, ethnic division and geopolitical circumstance will be all consuming.

In an effort to demonstrate the scale of the challenge confronting the developing world and expose the remoteness of them becoming capable of achieving exceptionalism, let us first explore their current predicament.

Generally speaking, there are two kinds of developing nations: threshold and emerging. Within the category of emerging also exists two important subcategories: supergiants and atrophying. In this book we will explore all four.

Threshold nations

Threshold nations are those nations which have made solid progress towards becoming constituents of the established or developed world.

In a threshold nation, much of its primary infrastructure base has been built, a strong middle class has developed and the standard of living for the majority of its citizens has been rising for decades. Sometimes, this has been the result of a collision of opportunity working in its favour. Whatever the cause, threshold nations are considered to be the cream of the world's developing nations.

Threshold nations are different from other developing nations because of their advanced state of development. Factors such as established road and rail networks, modern ports and airports, sophisticated education and health services, a functioning judiciary, broadly competent national and subnational governments and a diversifying economy all tend to differentiate threshold nations from their less developed peers.

Threshold nations also tend to be more resilient to external shocks than less developed nations. Key internal factors such as high national incomes, strong domestic capital generation, growing consumer markets, a vibrant private sector, a stable demographic profile and established financial institutions all help maintain their internal stability. Moreover, internally corrosive elements such as inflation, corruption, crime, cronyism, income inequality, sovereign risk, overt reliance upon primary production, human rights abuses, secessionism, heavy market intervention, rapid population growth and environmental degradation all have a propensity to be in decline as a result of a thriving and increasingly engaged middle class.

Threshold nations derive their name from the fact that they are on the brink of achieving established nation status. The majority of their citizens enjoy moderate GDP per capita average annual incomes, their level of human development is high[132] and their overall poverty levels are in decline. They are nations such as Chile, Turkey and Malaysia.

Emerging nations

Emerging nations are those nations which are still in the early stages of transitioning between agrarian and industrialised society. An emerging nation is most easily identified by its poor infrastructure, widespread poverty and contrasting economic development.

Emerging nations are different from threshold nations in many ways. The development of national infrastructure such as roads, highways, railways, sewage systems and power and water distribution networks severely lags behind demand. Essential services like education, healthcare, and law and order are inadequate, and the public and private institutions which provide government, regulation, financial services and environmental protection are also generally very poor. Additionally, the economies of emerging nations are also fairly narrow with agriculture, natural resource and energy extraction, and tourism dominating their GDP. High value sectors like services and advanced manufacturing are underrepresented, domestic consumer markets are underdeveloped and the city-rural wealth divide is often a source of considerable political tension. Finally, corrosive developmental factors such corruption; cronyism and environmental degradation are seldom rare.

As a result of their weaker socioeconomic position, emerging nations are often vulnerable to internal and external shocks. Price spikes in food, energy and farming additives, ethnic tensions, changes in international trade rules, unstable capital flows, worsening unemployment and widening inequality each contribute to social and economic discord. In many cases, it is shocks like these that have brought down governments and even triggered civil wars.

Governments in emerging nations are also typically more authoritarian in nature. Human rights tend to be curtailed, the media controlled or censored, political participation restricted, the role of the military pervasive and community dissent suppressed. Faced with complex and deep-seated internal problems such as terrorism, secessionism, restive borderlands, private militias, large black markets and communal conflict, such measures are often considered to be the lesser of two evils. Governments in emerging nations also tend to assume a larger role in the economy by intervening in sensitive markets and controlling strategically vital sectors like manufacturing and resource extraction. While periodically these interventions can be politically useful, they invariable distort markets and undermine the development of sustainable solutions to the nation's modernisation challenges.

Emerging nations regularly face significant demographic pressures as well, often due to a mismatch between population and capital. As a result of a declining infant mortality rate, rising incomes and improvements in food production, almost all emerging nations have fast growing populations. Though population growth is not a negative in itself, a nation's economy and infrastructure must be able to maintain growth in employment, services and infrastructure in order to sustain rising living standards. In established and threshold nations, strong institutions and a large middle class each act as stabilising forces when such pressures arise. In emerging nations, these stabilising forces tend to be in short supply. Consequently, many emerging nations struggle to keep ahead of their own population challenges.

Notwithstanding these obstacles, there are many emerging nations which enjoy the highest economic growth rates in the world. Powered by foreign investment, rising incomes and soaring productivity, many have successfully reduced the level of poverty that exists within their borders.

Despite suffering a multitude of challenges, economic and social development is slowly changing these nations into more confident and stable entities. In almost all emerging nations, the majority of citizens experience low GDP per capita average annual incomes. However, their general level of human development is on the rise.[133]

The vast majority of emerging nations aspire to established nation status, but, in order to achieve this, they must first transition into self-sustaining threshold nations. Sadly, due to their unstable nature and endemic vulnerabilities, achieving this outcome is extremely difficult.

Some emerging nations include Indonesia, Vietnam and the Philippines.

Supergiant and atrophying nations

Within the category of emerging nations, there are two special subcategories worth mentioning – the supergiants and the atrophying. The supergiants are those nations whose populations, development challenges and forecasted appetites are so large that they dwarf all others. Within the world today, there are two nations which fall into that category, China and India. In the following chapter we will explore their prospects and challenges in more detail. Atrophying nations we shall discuss here.

Atrophying nations are those nations which are best characterised by social, economic and political failure. Often referred to as failed, failing or fragile states, atrophying states typically find themselves in such situations as a result of war, ethnic strife, physical isolation, poor governance and/or internal and external disaster.

Atrophying nations are different from other emerging nations because they are highly volatile. Issues such as civil war, social exclusion of ethnic/religious groups, involuntary migrations, brain drains, separatist agendas and cyclical conflict all complicate the task of achieving stable government and economic growth. Moreover, the absence of functioning infrastructure and institutions, a stable food supply, endemic corruption, debilitating unemployment, underdeveloped consumer markets and poor longevity all contribute to atrophying nations remaining in states of perpetual crisis.

Atrophying nations also suffer from very low standards of living combined with fast growing populations. Basic activities such as the distribution of life-sustaining resources, trade, capital generation and the provision of basic health and education services are often beyond them. As a result, many governments in atrophying nations are heavily reliant upon foreign aid simply to function. In Papua New Guinea for example, over 10 per cent of the nation's budget is comprised of foreign support.

Atrophying nations derive their name form the fact that they are in decline. While in some cases a particular nation's economy may be growing, social and economic development is often failing to keep pace with domestic demand. Under almost every comparable socioeconomic measure, atrophying nations rank amongst the worst in the world. The majority of their citizens experience GDP per capita average annual income at very low levels, their level of human development is poor[134] and their societies are riddled with extreme inequality.

According to the Fund for Peace's 2013 Failed States index rankings, there are 35 nations ranked on alert, high alert or very high alert.[135] In the majority of these cases, the nation was an atrophying or failing state ten years earlier. While much of the emerging world is on a slow upward trajectory of development, a large proportion of their poorer peers remain on the edge of unending collapse.

Zimbabwe and the Democratic Republic of the Congo are two examples of atrophying nations.

The management tightrope

As discussed in Chapter One, the rise of the global middle class represents the greatest challenge facing the developing world in the 21st century. Its sheer size, impact upon global markets and the pressure it will place upon developing nations is so significant that as well as offering a pathway to prosperity and stability, it also has the capacity to rip them apart.

During the next 30 years, approximately one billion people from the non Chinese/Indian developing world are forecast to join the global middle class. This increase has the potential to unleash tremendous benefits within the societies that house them. People could live longer, eat better, get paid more and enjoy a better education and experience a higher quality of health and welfare. Further still, for the first time millions may be able to enjoy new personal experiences such as individual savings, regular work hours, retirement, tourism and recreational activity.

However, in order for these beneficial changes to take place, the drivers responsible for their existence will need to continue growing. As a result, all developing nations will need to ensure that they are constantly improving, expanding and fortifying the foundations upon which their middle classes are being built.

Throughout human history, the predetermined fortunes of many nations have been dashed as a result of their inability to manage change and handle success. As highlighted earlier, Argentina is but one example of a nation which had every reason to prevail, but in the end, only succeeded at mastering self-harm.

The very same challenge confronts the entire developing world. If they cannot constantly improve the methods by which they operate, the benefits of the rise may never translate as popularly prophesised.

§

Malaysia and the Philippines are two developing nations which fall into the important categories of threshold and emerging respectively. Each is emblematic of their subcategory peers and is important to Australia's long term future. How these two nations manage their long term development in the face of intensifying global pressure will probably be the hardest challenge they will face this century. It will also largely determine if they ever develop the capacity to become exceptional nations.

So that we may fully appreciate the complexity of the task confronting these two nations, and through them, the bulk of the developing world, a major threat to each's developmental ambitions is analysed below:

Employing the Filipinos

Over the next 36 years, the Philippine population is forecast to soar from 98 million to over 157 million.[136] This increase will not only produce one of the world's largest workforces, but will also create one of the toughest development challenges a developing nation can face – the spectre of mass unemployment.

In established nations, mass unemployment is treated as a very serious socioeconomic issue. In developing ones, it can bring down institutional government. The reason the risk is so much greater in developing nations is because the side-effects associated with its presence: poverty, social instability, mass inequality, political tension, crime, debt, homelessness, xenophobia, religious tension, a culture of dependency and tax shortfalls, can lead to a devastating deterioration of the social and economic order. Whereas in established nations these consequences can be offset by a welfare system, competent institutions or even the stabilising influence of a large middle class, in developing ones, these forces are in short supply. As a result, the threat of mass unemployment to a developing nation's stability remains very real indeed.

For the Philippines to effectively satisfy the expectations of its future labour force, a key element in building a nation's capacity, it will need to improve its long term employment growth rate. This goal poses a major economic challenge for the Philippines Government.

In the past, the Philippines' employment growth rate has been periodically greater than its neighbours, yet in spite of this, its unemployment rate has stubbornly remained above them as well.[137] The reason this has been the case is because its population growth rate and labour force participation rate have always risen faster than its economy's job creating capacity.[138] As a result, despite a decent economic performance over multiple years, the Philippines has not been able to overcome its unemployment problem. If the Philippines is to handle the surge of new workers forecast to enter the workforce over the next four decades, it will need to find a way to defy its history.

In order to avoid this impending socioeconomic disaster, the Philippines will need to achieve something which has eluded it for as long as it has existed – strong, balanced and sustainable economic growth that creates employment. To overcome this developmental stumbling block, four key things must happen:

First, improve the quality of governance. Rather than being mired in corruption,[139] political assassinations, popular uprisings, coup attempts, presidential impeachments, communist insurgencies and religious separatism, the Philippines will need to host a clean, accountable, competent and representative government.

Second, embrace pro-business policies. Successive governments would not only need to become avowedly pro-commerce, but will also need to embrace foreign investment, wage restraint and laissez-faire economics, especially in the areas of fuel and energy.

Third, boost infrastructure investment. Historically, the Philippines has invested well below the regional norm. Moreover, its basic infrastructure base is one of South East Asia's worst.[140] Infrastructure investment must rise to a level closer to the South East Asian average, even against the backdrop of its Typhoon Haiyan recovery.

Finally, oversee balanced national development. Over the past 60 years, too much attention has been lavished upon the northern island of Luzon and its heartland of Metro Manila[141] at the expense of the southern two thirds of the nation. With 50 per cent of the population residing outside of these favoured regions, a fairer approach must be pioneered.

If the Philippines can accomplish these four things (something it has yet to achieve in 58 years of self-rule), it will be well on its way towards tackling its mass unemployment challenge.

Of course, what must not be forgotten when considering the Philippines' response is the role that the rise will play in undermining it (the counterpunch).

As the global middle class grows in size, its many side-effects have the potential to undermine any progress the nation makes towards solving one of its most pressing problems. For the Philippines, there will be two areas of particular concern – intensifying international competition and rising domestic expectations.

Intensifying international competition represents a direct challenge to the Philippines' ability to meet its mass unemployment challenge. As international trade increases and capital exchange becomes more fluid, developing nations will increasingly be pitted against one another as recipients for finite foreign investment. In the case of the Philippines, the nation's international reputation for sovereign risk, poor infrastructure, inefficient supply chains and corrupt and unstable institutions will undermine its ability to leverage a larger share. Further, its ability to compete with undemocratic and less developed nations on issues like wages, labour laws and environmental standards will also make its development task more complicated. Finding a way to secure increasing foreign investment with such an assortment of existing weaknesses will be a difficult task indeed.

The rise will also pose a challenge to the nation's development as a result of changing domestic expectations. As the wealth of the

Philippines grows and diversifies, a sizeable shift in public expectations will begin to occur. In all likelihood, this will manifest as its growing middle class demands a fairer distribution of political, social and economic power; opening up of government tenders; better labour conditions, wages and welfare; and changes in oligopolistic business arrangements. When such a change occurs in a developing nation, there is inevitably disruption. However, in a nation where the power has been entrenched since independence with a clan-based elite, this process can be counted on to be exceptionally complicated. Resolving these tensions without prolonged political instability will be a tremendous challenge. Nonetheless, navigating a successful pathway between the two camps will be essential if the nation is to overcome its growing unemployment problems.

Overall, if the Philippines is to gain control over its employment destiny, it will have to overcome its history as a slow growing, poorly governed and unevenly developed nation. Accomplishing this task in addition to its many other internal challenges will not come easily. Doing so against the backdrop of the rise will be even harder. This reality above all else makes the emergence of Filipino exceptionalism extremely unlikely.

Equalising Malaysian prosperity

Despite Malaysia's favourable prospects of becoming an established nation with exceptionalism capability, there is one major challenge which threatens to derail that outcome – diverging geographical opportunity.

Despite the dazzling allure of the Klang Valley conurbation (Malaysia's richest and most densely populated subregion) and a select few of its major corporate and industrial centres, all is not equitable in this developing South East Asian nation. Sharp differences exist in regard to the living standards, incomes, infrastructure, government services and economic opportunities between Malaysia's two greater geographical territories – peninsular Malaysia and eastern Malaysia.[142]

In the wealthier west (peninsular Malaysia), the vast majority of the population enjoys a standard of living which continues to rise rapidly, even in rural areas. Yet in the poorer east, where the historical advantages of Western investment and geography have always been weaker, millions still live in conditions similar to that experienced at the time of independence. Malaysia's eastern states of Sabah and Sarawak for instance continue to lag behind peninsular Malaysia averages:[143] "Many villages are still not connected by roads in Sabah and Sarawak and more than a quarter of households do not have access to electricity."[144] Moreover, 40 per cent do not have access to clean or treated water.[145]

As Malaysia's economic development continues over the decades ahead, it is likely that living standards in both of these territories will improve. However, while there are good reasons to be optimistic about overall improving living standards, there is one major reason why hopes of closer socioeconomic parity should be tempered – poor border control.

At present, eastern Malaysia shares a land border with its southern and poorer neighbour Indonesia and has a large coastline facing the less developed Philippine archipelago. Over the past two decades, as a result of weak borders and improving economic conditions, eastern Malaysia has been inundated with over a million illegal immigrants seeking to share in its success.[146,147] Importantly, due to the sheer size of this influx, the territory has suffered an erosion of living standards and a rise in crime, unemployment and social disharmony.

Where this becomes a major problem for Malaysia is not just that it cannot control its borders. It is the fact that its developmental success is causing the problem (the counterpunch). On one hand, the rise within its borders is lifting living standards and overall community prosperity. Yet on the other, it is this process which is attracting the forces of destabilisation. Success is creating instability and that instability is overwhelming taking place in a region already experiencing disadvantage.

The challenge facing Malaysia therefore is to find a way to secure its borders and mollify the negative side-effects of the rise before its geographical inequality becomes irreversible entrenched. One need only look to Malaysia's north (Thailand) to see how easily a developing nation's political and economic stability can be derailed when unresolved grievances become intractable.

If Malaysia can manage to resolve this problem without undermining the drivers behind its rise, then its long term development ambitions and capacity for exceptionalism may well be realised. If not, then its plans to become an established nation could land in jeopardy.

Navigating failure as a result of success

The final issue which must be considered in regard to the long term success of developing nations is whether they will be able to sustain their internal rises long enough to achieve established nation status.

Established nations are those nations which have advanced and diverse economies, quality service delivery, high material well-being and a reputable national infrastructure. Whilst standards naturally vary amongst established nations, these traits are the developmental fruits of long term precursor conditions such as economic growth, competent government, communal stability and strong investment (public, private and foreign). Consequently, in order for a developing nation to become an established one, it needs to create and sustain these conditions so that they can underwrite their socioeconomic transformation.

Where this becomes complicated for the developing world is that these conditions are rarely easy to achieve, sustain or even control. The very nature of development results in instability, invariably making these conditions harder to maintain. Moreover, the intractable realities of our globalised world mean that few nations, even established ones, have the ability to control the supply chains and cost structures necessary for preserving ideal development conditions. As a result, the ability of developing nations to astutely manage their transitions in the face of these obstacles remains difficult.

When considering the likelihood of their prospects, there are two important factors which must be kept in mind.

First, the geopolitical conditions in which the developing world seeks to modernise within remain fundamentally different from those enjoyed by existing established nations. Unlike old imperial Europe, the developing world does not have vast colonies which they can use to fund their development, nor do they have their ability to guarantee resource, food and energy supply. And unlike Japan and the Asian Tigers, only a very few will benefit from developmental advantages akin to subsidised peace, Cold War favouritism and geopolitical advantage. Finally, in contrast to the United States, Canada and Australia, only a couple will have large territories to exploit and lightly populated lands to expand into.

Despite public perceptions to the contrary, the world in which developing nations seek to modernise within will be harsher and considerably less amenable than that enjoyed by their wealthier and more developed peers. As a result, the likelihood of failure will be higher.

Second, the economic climate within which they are modernising will also be significantly more expensive. Whereas many established nations achieved established world status during a century where the production of raw materials and energy exploded yet costs didn't, the developing world is attempting to do the same thing during an era where costs are rising and supply lines are tightening. In fact, there is no better example of how these two situations differ than in regard to the price of oil:

> [D]eveloping countries which import oil are today facing prices in excess of $100 a barrel when at a comparable stage of economic development, many OECD countries faced an average oil price of around $22 a barrel.[148]

In other words, even if developing world growth rates are higher and global capital is more fluid, the costs associated with economic modernisation will still be higher than that experienced during humanity's most recently successful attempt. Consequently, the development goal itself will be all the more difficult to achieve.

§

Overall, the dilemma facing much of the developing world is this. In order to modernise and build capacity this century, developing nations will not only need to defy their history and conquer their worst internal weaknesses, but they will need to do so in a world in which accomplishing such transformations is becoming harder and more expensive.

In all likelihood, nations with much in common with Malaysia will become established before half this century is complete. Having accomplished the bulk of their heavy lifting under generally favourable conditions, they should be close enough to the finish line to triumph and be ready for any circumstantial shift which may arise.

For those with more in common with the Philippines, however, this century will likely turn out to be one defined by bitter tragedy. With so much hard work ahead of them, and global conditions souring with each passing day, many will find the development task too difficult to overcome.

3
The supergiants: too big to succeed

Of all the developing nations which exist in the world today, the supergiants are the two in which the largest number of people predict the highest probability of exceptionalism.

Much has been made of the progress of these two demographic titans. Indeed, many commentators, analysts and journalists routinely speculate about the day that China and India will reassume their natural places at the top of the world order.

Such predictions are overly optimistic.

While the international cities of Shanghai and Mumbai may work well as backdrops for the latest *Mission Impossible* films, they are not reflective of the entirety of their host nations. The bulk of China and the bulk of India exist inland, where the people are poor, life is harsh and the West's business media is absent. In essence, they reside in vast regions where the capacity for exceptionalism is entirely absent.

Therefore, if we are to attempt a prediction about the future of these two developing behemoths, we should begin by discussing what we know.

The dragon

China is home to one of the oldest civilisations in human history, reaching back over 5,000 years. During this time, it has been a place of high culture, scientific achievement, empowering religions, grand dynasties, vast empires, breathtaking beauty and unquestionable horror.

Despite being relatively peaceful for the last 40 years, throughout much of its history, China has pivoted between external warfare with its smaller neighbours and internal conflict with its rebellious provinces. During the 18th and 19th centuries, it endured a humiliating occupation at the hands of several European powers, and later in the 20th century, went through it again under the Japanese. Only since 1949 has the current incarnation of government, the People's Republic of China, been in power.

Ethnically, China is home to 56 different groups with the Han comprising the largest block (92 per cent). The core of the Han population resides along the coast and in the east with the bulk of China's ethnic minorities residing in the border regions of its buffer states. Despite the Han comprising the overwhelming majority of China's ethnicity, the nation's experience with weather, language, tradition and social isolation has helped create a very diverse society with many sub-regions engaging in uncommon and unfamiliar social and economic practices.

For almost its entire existence, China has also been a source of cultural, economic or political influence. As a result, it is responsible for one of the world's most geographically expansive communities. In today's world, few nations can claim to have never been touched by China's 50 million strong diaspora.

China is currently ruled by an authoritarian government which controls the populace, judiciary and the media through an efficient police state apparatus and large bureaucracy. Political dissent is not permitted, the military has a strong hand in government and violent crackdowns on civilians are common. Despite the abhorrent nature of China's political system, its commitment to improving living standards remains beyond doubt. Over the past 36 years, China has successfully dragged hundreds of millions of people out of poverty, lifted health and education standards and has reopened itself to the world. These successes have led many to refer to China's current political leaders as the "enlightened autocrats".

In area the fourth largest nation on earth, China has a highly diverse geography. A large portion of its land mass is mountainous steppe or dry unproductive desert, with the eastern third home to the bulk of its arable land. With some of the world's most fertile soils and best natural runoff, China is the largest agricultural producer on Earth. China is also home to many natural resources including the world's largest proven reserves of coal, rare earths, titanium and zinc. Importantly, the powerful Yangtze, Pearl and Yellow Rivers also play major roles in facilitating trade, transportation, industrial consumption and agricultural activity.

Economically, China has come a long way. Despite hosting one of the most advanced economies during the 18th century, China's failure to industrialise led to an economic decline which resulted in a multitude of misfortunes, one of them being the loss of national sovereignty. Muddling its way through the 19th and 20th centuries, China finally embraced a capitalist model for its economy in the late 1970s. Since then, its economy has grown 90 times over to become the world's second largest, its biggest exporter and home to some of the world's most assiduous investors and savers.

China's economy is dominated by export-orientated secondary industries which generate just under half its gross domestic product (GDP). At present, China's manufacturing capacity outstrips that of every nation bar the United States and Japan.[149] This achievement has earned it the reputation of being the "factory to the world". But it also means that it produces far more than it consumes – making it extremely vulnerable to economic downturns in its primary export markets – Europe, North-East Asia and North America.

In spite of all of its achievements, China still remains an extremely poor, imbalanced and underdeveloped economy. Over 362 million presently live on $2 a day or less.[150] It retains an unhealthy reliance upon fixed investment, high savings and overseas markets it cannot influence. Further, millions of its citizens remain unemployed and officially discriminated against by the government (hukou).[151] While tremendous progress has been made, and its weight in the global economy has expanded, China still has a long way to go before it can say its development task is complete.

Super organised, yet super vulnerable

As with all developing nations, China faces innumerable socioeconomic challenges. For a developing nation to evolve into an exceptional one, its ability to take advantage of favourable circumstances must be built upon solid foundations (capacity) such as a stable economy, social harmony, balanced growth, environmental sustainability and good governance. Presently, China faces many serious challenges to the achievement of these requirements. Outlined below are several of the most pressing.

Deficient infrastructure

Since mid last century, China has quadrupled its railway lines, developed a world renowned high speed rail network and constructed the world's longest expressway network. Yet despite these improvements, China's transport network still falls far short of what is required to service a population of 1.3 billion people. Large sections of the nation are still underdeveloped and logistic costs remain globally uncompetitive. For much of the past 20 years, transport spending has been focussed on regions showing the greatest economic promise (coastal regions and the major inland cities), leaving vast tracts of the inland and geographically challenging areas, lagging. As a result, China today is a nation where a businessman in Shanghai can catch a high speed train to the airport but an inland farmer must still ride an animal into town.

Similar problems also exist in regard to China's energy infrastructure. Even after its rapid construction timetable of power plants, several million Chinese still have no access to electricity and brown outs remain a regular occurrence. At present, China's energy efficiency is six times worse than Japan's and four times worse than the EU's. Despite the external appearance of a functioning advanced economy, China is still home to a power grid which struggles to service the entire populace without price controls and usage quotas.

When it comes to water, China's infrastructure network is in even worse shape. Two-thirds of its cities suffer water shortages.[152] 110 million people do not have access to improved water sources and 460 million cannot access improved sanitation.[153] As a result, over 500 million Chinese consume polluted water each day with tonnes of unprocessed sewage pouring into China's rivers every year. China's vast farming community also faces horrendous challenges when it comes to accessing reliable and unpolluted water. Huge regions of its agricultural producing areas are presently classified as water challenged and polluted. Put simply, while China's economic output may be growing day by day, its water crisis is worsening minute by minute.

According to World Economic Forum's 2011 Global Competitiveness Report, China's infrastructure base is ranked 74th worst in the world.[154] While much has been made of the improvements in China's high tech, coastal and major inland cities, vast tracks of its interior remain a mess. Consequently, China's desire to fully modernise continues to be plagued by the side-effects of an imbalanced and inadequate infrastructure base, food and energy inflation, inefficient transportation, unpredictable business and logistic costs, food insecurity, enduring poverty, mixed health outcomes and vast inequality.

Unless China's infrastructure can keep pace with baseline demand, sustainable economic development will not continue to take place. Worryingly, with China's population forecast to increase over the coming decades, the difficulty of overcoming its infrastructure deficiencies will intensify.

Inequality in income and economic development

China is presently home to the second largest impoverished population in the world. According to the World Bank, over 362 million Chinese live on $2 a day or less (more than the United States' entire population).

While there is much to celebrate in regards to China's progress in reducing poverty and boosting overall wealth, the benefits of economic growth have not been shared by all. Disposable income per capita in urban areas is more than double that in rural areas. In 12 of its 31 provinces, urban income is three times rural areas and in another four it is over four times. Despite decades of economic growth, hundreds of millions of Chinese still live like their grandparents – on the borderline of malnutrition in a poor and highly inequitable nation.

With over 300 million people still engaged in agricultural activity, these disparities should not come as a huge surprise. But oddly enough, they do. Too often when analysts look at China they only see its cities and miss the iceberg beneath the waves – the massive urban-rural divide. According to Michael Lipton:

> [T]he most important class conflict in the poor countries of the world today is not between labour and capital. Nor is it between foreign and national interests. It is between rural classes and urban classes.[155]

With China's 1.3 billion strong population evenly balanced between its urban and rural masses, its leaders remain permanently caught between two giant, competing interests.

Of course, one of the key reasons why Chinese equality is so imbalanced is because of its uneven development pattern. Over the past 30 years, the overwhelming proportion of China's economic development has taken place in its coastal cities. In China's four most productive (coastal) provinces, 36 per cent of national GDP is produced by 24 per cent of the population. Conversely, in its four largest inland provinces, just 15 per cent of national GDP is produced by 22 per cent of the population. As a result, China is now a nation in which the average GDP per capita in its major coastal provinces is the equivalent of European nations and its inland provinces are the equivalent of African nations. Whereas in the ancient past proximity to the Silk Road was a good determinant of a citizen's wealth and prosperity, today it is proximity to the coastline (and its ocean accessible rivers).

One reason for this divergence is due to the nation's unfortunate geography. China is presently home to the largest number of inland cities with populations over one million people in the world. Of these, dozens are located over a thousand kilometres from the world's most important transport network – the oceans. Prior to industrialisation, this settlement reality wasn't the harshest of challenges. But today, distance from world markets is a severe penalty which has profound implications for economic development.

For the majority of developing nations, the most common growth path has been through the creation of secondary industry products (manufacturing) for export. In order to build such sectors, developing nations have typically required three things: cheap labour, foreign capital and expertise, and efficient transport routes to market. Sadly, one of the greatest disadvantages facing China is the fact that a large proportion of its population resides far from the cheapest mode of transport. What this means is that despite China's ability to attract investment and provide cheap labour, its uncompetitive transport network remains a major disincentive to inland growth. This reality represents a significant barrier to China's ambition to become an established nation.

In essence, China remains a country with two very different futures. The first, a coastal one which appears purpose built for development, and the second, an inland one which seems permanently destined to remain disadvantaged.

Durability of its development model

The sustainability of China's economic growth model is also cause for serious concern, especially in the areas of wages and finance. According to former Premier Wen Jiabao, China's economy is dangerously "unbalanced, unstable, uncoordinated and unsustainable."[156]

Over the past 30 years, China has successfully positioned itself as the low cost factory to the world. This strategy has successfully attracted billions of dollars of foreign investment to its shores, lifting living standards, savings rates and domestic consumption levels. However, as living standards rise, wage pressures increase, and increase they have.

After thirty years of strong economic growth, wages are rising all over China, especially in urban areas (up 13.3 per cent in 2010, 14.4 in 2011 and 12 per cent in 2012).[157] "Current estimates suggest that factory wages in China are set to rise above those in Mexico and will overtake those in Brazil if current trends continue for the next few years."[158]

With the cost for food, energy and water forecast to rise over the coming decades, wage rises linked to cost of living pressures will be an absolute certainty. All of these factors mean that China's reputation as a low cost manufacturer is at risk.

For most developing nations, rising wages is a common road sign along the path to established nation status. As the middle class grows, the consumption economy follows, allowing workers to transition to higher paid jobs such as those which exist in the services industry. This has been the case for many former developing nations such as South Korea and Singapore where factory workers have evolved into service workers. But for China, this transition remains a long way off in the future. As highlighted above, much of China remains deeply impoverished and vast areas of its interior remain underdeveloped. Instead of being on the cusp of becoming a self-sustaining consumption economy where growth is driven by domestic demand, China is still a canvass incomplete. While its coastal cities appear ready for the development transition, vast regions of its interior are still waiting for their factories.

Consequently, the big risk facing China's continued development is the threat posed by other low wage nations. On one hand, it is dealing with wage pressure at home, but on the other, it is being challenged by those nations which offer the same investment incentives it does (Vietnam and Indonesia). China cannot stop wages rising without triggering social unrest, and it cannot hope to host a self-sustaining services sector without increasing wages. Consequently, it is caught in a developmental pincer. How China deals with this challenge will be critical to its ability to successfully develop its entire economy.

Demographic dilemmas

China's changing demographics also pose a serious challenge for its future development.[159] Much like the established world, China has a reproduction problem. However, whereas the established world is having fewer children because of lifestyle choices and the cost of raising children, China stopped having children because of its selectively enforced one child policy. For all intents and purposes, this draconian population control policy has achieved its aim. China's growth trajectory has slowed, but in doing so, it has paid a terrible price – China has shrunk its future workforce. This represents a major problem for China for two reasons.

The first is that it has triggered an early conclusion to the demographic dividend which helped propel its economy forward for the past few decades. Since the 1970s, China's economic growth has been boosted by an estimated 1.8 per cent annually as a result of its ample labour.[160] However, starting in 2013 China's labour force will begin shrinking[161] resulting in a workforce 11 percentage points smaller in 2050 than in 2010.[162] As a result, the demography of China mid-century will be nothing like that which facilitated its economic emergence last century.[163] This eventuality, combined with rising labour shortages and wage breakouts represent major threats to China's long term development.

The second problem relates to the fact that China has the economic profile of a developing nation but the demographic profile of an older, established one. According to the World Economic Forum, the number of elderly people in China is doubling at a speed four times faster than France and almost three times faster than the United States.[164] This is due to the fact that its older generations are numerically larger than its younger ones.

Where this will become a major problem for China is by how its society chooses to shoulder the cost of its ageing populace. At present, China's median age is 34.5 years, just 5.4 years below the European median. Back in 1980, China's median age was 22 years. If current demographic trends continue, by 2050, 26 per cent of China's population will be aged over 65.[165] This massive population cohort will place enormous pressure upon its public sector finances and social safety net. On one hand, the government will be under pressure to subsidise the ageing population's health and retirement, and on the other, the work force will want to pay lower taxes to maintain their Confucian commitment[166] to their parents. Finding a way to balance these competing interests will be fraught politically and economically destabilising, especially for a nation as large and inequitable as China.

Environmental degradation

In addition to China's many socioeconomic challenges, its environmental record serves as another major threat to its long term development ambitions.

At present, China is home to 16 of the world's 20 most polluted cities[167] with 70 per cent of its major waterways heavily polluted.[168] Over 30 per cent of its territory suffers from acid rain and its interior is home to the world's largest dustbowl.

Creating this mess is the practice of almost universal environmental degradation. Each year, billions of tonnes of untreated water pours into its waterways and ocean with waste water, ship contaminants and fertilisers and petrochemicals being amongst its worse components. In fact, the situation is so bad that the Yangzte River now only produces a fish catch half its 1960s size and the Yellow River is too polluted for irrigation use.[169] Indeed, China's major rivers are so degraded that 80 per cent of them no longer support fish of any kind with many containing ten times the bacteria from human waste as those found in the west.[170] With problems such as this, it comes as no surprise to learn that China's birth defect rate is 20 times the global average, 2.5 per cent of its soil is too polluted for agricultural use[171] and its air pollution is a globally renowned killer (resulting in pollution pay for expats!).[172]

According to Yale and Columbia University's 2012 Environmental Performance Index, China is ranked 116th out 132 nations assessed (across 22 performance indicators).[173] With demand for more food, water and energy resources set to intensify in the decades head, it is hard to see how China's already terrible environmental record is going to improve. How its ecology ultimately responds to this level of punishment will be critical to determining how sustainable its development ambitions end up becoming.

Authoritarianism and political reform

The last and perhaps most unpredictable issue threatening China's development ambitions is that of its system of government.

Modern day China is an authoritarian one party police state which has tight controls over all of its people's social and political freedoms. For several decades, this command and control approach has helped achieve remarkable economic growth, rising living standards and valuable strategic foresight. However, all of these accomplishments have come at a very high price. Free speech and large political gatherings are not tolerated (as with the 1989 Tiananmen Square protests), "show trials and foregone convictions"[174] are commonplace and the media and internet are highly censored. According to Reporters without Borders, China has more journalists in jails than any other nation in the world and is responsible for regular and brutal crackdowns in its ethnically diverse buffer states (Xianjian and Tibet).

Over the past few years, political and social freedom in China has waxed and waned. On one hand, democracy has been introduced at a grass roots level where citizens now have a greater say in electing their local officials, but on the other, the security services routinely exercise a firm grip over the populace as a result of their fear of Luan,[175] foreign organised Jasmine rallies and economic tensions caused by the Global Financial Crisis. Indeed, during 2010 alone, 280,000 mass incidents, petitions, demonstrations and strikes occurred in China, up from 87,000 in 2005.[176] As a nation with immense political diversity, unresolved ethnic grievances and increasingly varied economic fortunes, it is hard to see how an undemocratic system with no political outlets can successfully hold this assortment of contradictions together forever.

The elephant

Like China, India is home to one of the world's oldest civilisations. Dating back over 4,500 years, its long history has also given birth to many of the world's great religions and its soil has hosted several major empires.

One of the most defining characteristics of India is its tremendous diversity. Being located on the south central coast of the Eurasian supercontinent, its geographical position has resulted in the visitation of countless invasions, traders and proselytisers. These constant societal disruptions have given rise to one of the world's largest diasporas and the most complex and diverse civilisations on Earth. At present, India is home to dozens of religions, 1,632 languages and dialects and countless cultural traditions. Hinduism and Islam represent the largest religious blocs with Indo-Aryan and Dravidian representing the largest language families.

Prior to independence in 1947, India was dominated economically, culturally and militarily by a variety of European and non-European powers. Prior to that, India itself was not a united empire. Instead, the present day territories of India, Pakistan, Bangladesh, Sri Lanka, Nepal, Bhutan, Myanmar, Afghanistan and China were all ruled by a variety of competing kingdoms, dynasties and princely states with a shared cultural heritage over a common geographic area. This inability to coalesce around a dominant local power is one of the key reasons why India has been dominated so easily by foreign powers. Despite how it appears to the outside world, it is not a coherent entity. Rather, it is an assortment of distinctive nation states bound together by a common history of European colonialism.

India is also the world's biggest democracy and home to a Westminster parliamentary government. While it has periodically failed to live up to the highest of democratic standards,[177] India presently operates a vibrant multi-party democracy which supports civil rights, a free and unregulated press, a military serving under civilian rule and an independent judiciary which practices common law. India's highly decentralised federation is assisted by a vast bureaucracy which remains one of the most valuable legacies of British rule. As a result of this impressive record, India enjoys a global freedom index ranking above many of the world's developed nations, including Hungary.[178]

The vast majority of India's people reside throughout its northern plain and along its soil and water rich coastal regions. India's soils, monsoonal rains and plentiful river systems have allowed it to evolve into the world's second largest agriculture producer and third largest fish producer. Moreover, India's territories boast the seventh largest land territory, second largest arable land holdings, third largest water claims, fourth largest coal reserves and the world's greatest thorium supplies. Importantly, the Himalayas in the north, the Thar Desert in the west and its extensive nationwide river network all play critical roles in sustaining its economy, diversity and vibrancy.

India's economy has made impressive strides over the past 20 years, notwithstanding its early missteps. Despite being home to one of Asia's largest stock markets, a diversified resource base, more English speakers than the United States[179] and a well developed financial system,[180] India opted for a Soviet Union inspired state planning approach to managing itself after independence. This approach proved to be an unfortunate detour which led to the "Hindu rate of growth" – a multi-decade period of lacklustre economic development.[181]

During the 1970s, as a result of poor industrial progress, a worsening balance of payments and devastating oil shocks, an economic rethink too place. Starting with the removal of price controls and then the dismantling of the Licence Raj, higher levels of growth slowly became the norm. Since then, an internationally respected white collar workforce has emerged and the economy has expanded to become the tenth largest in the world.[182]

Yet even after such progress, the Indian economy remains a mixed bag. Tremendous numbers of its people remain exploited and unemployed. Presently, 840 million live on $2 a day or less.[183]

Despite the impressive strides India has made in recent decades, vast sections of its territory remain untouched by its statistical success.

Super free, but super messy

More so than its Asiatic cousin, India faces countless socioeconomic challenges to its capability for seizing opportunities for exceptionalism. Outlined below are several of its biggest obstacles.

Scarce infrastructure

India's poor infrastructure base is one of its greatest structural weaknesses.

In spite of having the world's fourth longest rail network, the third largest road network and the ninth most extensive inland waterways,[184] India's transport infrastructure remains decades behind China's and is well short of meeting existing demand.

While much has been made of India's national rail network, its many shortcomings far outweigh its over promoted strengths. Despite connecting all of its major cities, freight trains run below global speed averages and operate beyond their passenger safety limits. Each year, approximately 3,600 people die and over 4,000 people are injured due to overcrowding.[185] Further, only three railway lines traverse international borders.

India's road network is in even worse shape. Barely half of the nation's roads are paved, 40 per cent of its villages lack access to all-weather roads and average road transport speeds are half the worldwide average.[186] Worse still, after decades of investment, India still lacks a proper national highway system featuring four lane roads. In fact, India's roads are so bad that 1.7 per cent of them carry 40 per cent of its traffic.[187]

The side-effects of this transport situation are staggering. India's cities are rated amongst the most congested and dangerous in the world[188] As home to about one per cent of the world's cars (some 4.5 million), India still manages to kill over 100,000 people in traffic accidents each year (ten per cent of the world's traffic fatalities).[189] Rural Indians entrenched in agrarian lifestyles aren't spared the cost of poor infrastructure either: "Up to 40 per cent of farm produce is lost because it rots in the fields or spoils en route to consumers."[190]

India's waterway and coastal infrastructure also leave a lot to be desired. While over a third of its inland waterways are mechanised craft capable, total cargo transported on them is just 0.15 per cent of total inland traffic. This compares with 35 per cent in its poorer neighbour Bangladesh.[191] India's port productivity is also rated amongst the worst in the world with turnaround times six times slower in Mumbai than Shanghai.[192]

India's energy infrastructure position is not much better. Despite increasing its generation capacity by almost 300 per cent over the past two decades, over 400 million Indians still live without electricity and only seven of 30 states and territories enjoy power surpluses. Accessibility also differs across the urban-rural divide. Only 52 per cent of rural households enjoy access compared with 93 per cent in urban areas. Reliability is another challenge. Demand presently outstrips supply and scheduled and unscheduled blackouts are a regular occurrence. In August 2012, a power grid failure resulted in a blackout affecting 620 million people across 20 separate states.

India's water infrastructure is also in very poor condition. While India is now investing more aggressively in water infrastructure, its efforts still fall short of what is required. In regard to drinking water, 90 per cent of rural Indians and 97 per cent of urban Indians enjoy "improved access" to water.[193] While these figures sound promising, they are sharply balanced by the fact that supply can only be guaranteed for a few hours each day. At present, no major Indian city can maintain continuous supply.

Sewage treatment infrastructure is a problem as well with 66 per cent of Indians lacking access to improved sanitisation facilities.[194] While between 1980 and 2008 rural sanitisation levels lifted dramatically, improvement doesn't necessarily mean effective treatment. The Ganges River for instance, one of the holiest rivers in India, is also one of the dirtiest in the world. Despite being used by millions for bathing, drinking and washing, over 100 cities continue to dump untreated sewage and partially cremated bodies into it daily. The consequences have been devastating. In Varanasi for instance, "the coliform bacterial count is at least 3,000 times higher than the standard established as safe by the United Nations World Health Organisation".[195]

According to the World Economic Forum's 2011 Global Competitiveness Report, India's infrastructure base is ranked the 57th worst in the world.[196] While there are a few bright spots, Ahmedabad and Hyderabad in particular, India continues to remain a massively supply constrained economy. How India grapples with its infrastructure backlog against the backdrop of soaring demand will be one of the great developmental challenges of the 21st century.

Inconsistent government

Coherent and reliable government is another area which undermines India's efforts to modernise.

Contrary to popular belief, India operates more like 30 independent states rather than one coherent nation. There is no better example of this than in regard to how economic policy is conducted. As a consequence of its unique federalist structure, each of India's states enjoys a significant degree of autonomy when it comes to setting economy policy. In recent years, the failure of this approach has become evident through the central government's attempts to relax foreign investment restrictions in India's retail markets. As part of the reform process, every state was given veto rights over whether foreign owned retailers would be allowed to operate within their borders. Within hours of the announcement, Tamil Nadu stated its opposition to the policy. Following that, Delhi NCR, the largest retail market in the nation, instituted a ban on foreign access. For international companies seeking to invest in India, this process represents a huge red flag. Investors desire certainty above almost everything. They also crave consistency. India's approach to national economic policy sadly offers neither.

It goes without saying that this form of snakes and ladders democracy undermines India's ambition for balanced economic development. Yet this is exactly how the nation operates. States like Gujarat are racing ahead as a result of its pro-business philosophy and openness to foreign involvement. Conversely, states like Tripura remain steadfastly communist and continue to perform poorly. While India's federalist approach offers the subcontinent a model for maintaining national unity, it remains an albatross for its long term development.

Disparity in income and development

India's frightening poverty problem is another challenge which threatens its development ambitions.

As home to the largest impoverished population in the world, its territory hosts over 840 million people living on $2 a day or less. In fact, India's poverty situation is so bad that it has more poor people residing in its territory than the entire continent of Africa. As a result, the stability of Indian society remains highly vulnerable to price shocks affecting food staples like rice, onions, wheat, cooking oil and salt.

India is also a terribly divided nation when it comes to its internal income and wealth. This divide is no more obvious than in regard to wages where urban Indians earn on average up to four times more than their rural counterparts. In Mumbai for example, annual income per capita is over three times greater than the national average.[197] With over 50 per cent of the Indian workforce still engaged in agricultural activity, and 75 per cent of Indians still living in rural areas, this kind of disparity represents a serious challenge to India's internal stability.

Economic and social development in India is also highly varied depending on which part of the nation you are visiting. India's three main southern states produce 17 per cent of GDP but are home to just 14 per cent of the population. Conversely, its three main eastern states produce nine per cent of GDP but host 19 per cent of the population. Consequently, India's economy, much like China's, is highly imbalanced geographically. In fact, India's development is so varied that you can visit the southern state of Kerala and find a population which enjoys a bank in every village, a 99 per cent literacy rate and a life expectancy ten years above the national average. But travel 1,620km north east and you will find yourself in Orissa where 47 per cent live below the poverty line, literacy levels are 25 per cent below Kerala's and life expectancy is three years beneath the national average.

Bizarre as it may sound, India's regional successes are also a major cause of its development problems. Improved conditions attract internal migration. Internal migration destabilises communities. Destabilised communities experience social unrest and social unrest triggers living standard decline. Hence, India not only has trouble managing hardship, it also has trouble managing success. While this problem is clearly not unique to India, it is occurring on a scale unheard of throughout the developing world. In addition to its many other development challenges, this one is perhaps the most complicated.

Environmental tragedy

India's poor environmental health also poses a significant threat to its long term development.

As with China, India is the custodian of an environmental disaster in the making. At present, India is home to several of the world's dirtiest rivers and most polluted cities. In fact, the degradation of land and soil alone costs India an estimated 20 per cent of its agricultural output every year.[198]

One of the key causes is industrial and human waste. Many ground and tap water sources suffer from nickel, selenium, lead and cadmium contamination. Moreover, several waterways contain mercury, beta-endosulfan, pesticides, fertiliser and effluent run off from the nation's thousands of poorly regulated factories and mines. India's Yamuna River for example, the Ganges largest tributary river, has no freshwater for almost nine months a year.[199]

Air pollution throughout India is also worsening each day. In fact, air quality in its major cities is currently so bad that it is now well above the limit recommended by the World Health Organisation. The primary cause of this is the high diesel sulphur content used in its growing vehicle fleet. Presently, it is over 100 times that tolerated in Europe.

According to Yale and Columbia University's 2012 Environmental Performance Index, India's is ranked 125th out of 132 nations assessed.[200] With mass urbanisation and industrialisation set to continue, the pressures upon India's environment will undoubtedly grow. How this situation will affect its march towards modernisation is hard to predict, but it is difficult to see how it will be beneficial.

Unresolved geopolitical disputes

Another volatile challenge facing India's long term development is its complex and constantly resurfacing geopolitical disputes.

India is surrounded by six nations by land and four by sea. In each case, tension of varying degrees exists regarding resource claims, political responsibility, water rights, pollution impacts, cross border terrorism, illegal migration and even maritime control.

The bulk of these tensions derive from the fact that the political, cultural and religious borders of these nations have shifted regularly for several millennia. Present day demarcations, for example, have very little to do with the domains of the region's ancient empires, geographical barriers, trade routes or even river systems.

Over the decades ahead, India will be hard pressed to please all of the relevant stakeholders affected by these issues. The area is simply too complex, its resources too limited, the nations too unstable and the histories too tragic to remain manageable indefinitely. As a result, India will need a great deal of luck to ensure these periodic flare-ups do not undermine its long term goal of full modernisation. How India manages these problems will be a critical test of its ambition to be a global economic and social leader.

Cultural and political conflict

Underpinning India's territorial pressures are its tremendous internal cultural and political conflicts. In addition to there being no common national language, India is one of the most religiously and culturally diverse regions on Earth. It therefore comes as no surprise that in a nation with such diversity, massive underlying tensions exist.

Broadly speaking, India faces major internal conflict in three distinct forms: domestic and foreign terrorism, religious division and casteism.

Domestic terrorism is dominated by Naxalite activity which is currently active in half of India's 28 states. Naxalites are Maoist insurgents who are instilled with a communist ideology. They have the greatest presence in those areas where illiteracy, poverty, inequality, tribal hardship and population strains are their greatest. They also tend to be located in states where primary sector activity is strong and education and industrial development is weak. Over the past two decades, Naxalite activity has caused thousands of deaths and billions of dollars in economic damage. According to former Prime Minister Singh, the Naxalites are "the single biggest internal security challenge ever faced by our country".[201]

Outside of this major terrorist group, India also faces a number of threats from a variety of other sources. These include secessionist Sikhs in the Punjab; conflicts over finite water resources; independence, state division and greater autonomy claims in its isolated north eastern states; and of course, the militant groups linked to the Kashmir-Jammu territorial conflict. In each of these cases, instability, death and economic destruction are all threats to India's long term well being. How they are managed and/or defeated will be critical to India's ability to maintain a stable development environment.

Religious tension is the second major internal conflict which looms large above India's quest for stability. Historic disagreements between the region's major religions have been the cause of countless deaths and remain a key source of continuing strife within India's diverse communities. In the last 12 months alone, thousands of people have been killed in religion related violence and ongoing tensions remain one of the biggest obstacles to its economic development. Resolving these problems will be amongst its most trying of challenges.

The final area of internal conflict which threatens India's long term stability is its caste system and the practice of casteism (discrimination based upon caste). Entrenched in India to varying degrees for over a millennium, casteism is a key source of communal violence, human rights abuses, land disputes and discrimination against the poor, local tribes and dalits (untouchables).While efforts have been made to stamp it out, both politically and legally, widespread problems remain due to its deep entrenchment within the nation's culture. How India overcomes this form of ingrained discrimination will help determine its maximum potential as a nation. If managed well, India can unlock the creative and productive capacity of millions. If not, it risks condemning them to a lifetime of unrealised potential.

Growing pains

As highlighted above, both China and India face a number of complex challenges undermining their ability to become exceptional.

In isolation, each seems daunting. In combination, they appear almost insurmountable. Whatever the outcome in each case, none comes close to displacing the socioeconomic earthquake which has already begun to challenge the stability of their societies – the rise of the global middle class.

The rise of the global middle class represents the biggest challenge confronting the developing world and the supergiants will be no different.

China and India are the two most populated nations on Earth. The bulk of this century's socioeconomic upheaval will be taking place in their backyards. Over the next few decades, the middle classes of China and India are both forecast to grow by hundreds of millions of people.

One of the key side-effects of this increase will be the associated global rise in demand for personal, social and economic goods and services. As highlighted earlier, international demand for food is forecast to double, electricity demand is forecast to rise by 80 per cent and the key ingredients of industrialisation, iron ore and coking coal, are set to increase by 100 and 80 per cent respectively.

Over the next four decades, volatility in food, energy and the raw materials markets are forecast to increase as a result of tightening supply and soaring demand (the counterpunch). Two of the main contributors to this situation will be the increasing number of middle class Chinese and Indians. In every one of the above cases, either China or India is forecast to become one of the world's biggest inter national consumers.

In market environments such as these, securing access to strategically vital goods would be a challenge for any of the world's nations, not just the supergiants. Rich ones have the most options. They have the greatest capacity to absorb price rises and can often leverage their other strengths such as technology, foreign investment (and aid), military support and market access in order to secure supply. Poor nations however, have fewer options. Their economies are typically fragile, their populace can't easily absorb price rises and their negotiating position is generally weaker. As a result, when access to strategically vital goods is threatened, the risk it poses can quickly become a serious threat.

In the case of the supergiants, the risk of major supply disruptions poses a threat on a scale never before imagined.

Unprecedented demand, coupled with inadequate self-sufficiency and uncontrollable supply chains – all against the backdrop of simmering internal unrest. Sounds too pessimistic to be possible? Consider the following.

Feeding the Chinese

Despite being the world's largest producer of rice, wheat and seafood, China is one of the world's largest net importers of food. Due to its inability to achieve self-sufficiency, China is highly dependent upon access to global markets and is vulnerable to the prices which food commodities trade at.

Over the next four decades, China's appetite for food products is forecast to soar dramatically, with demand for rice, wheat, soybean, dairy products and beef expected to rise substantially. As a result, not only will China be a net importer of food, but a substantial number of its meals will be reliant upon another nation's exports.

For the Chinese Government, this exposure represents a tremendous risk. Take rice for example. Rice is presently the staple food for hundreds of millions of Chinese.

Approximately 93 per cent of globally produced rice is grown and consumed domestically.[202] This means that for all the nations of the world which must import rice to meet their domestic needs, they must compete for the remaining seven per cent of global supply.

At present, global rice markets are dominated by five players who produce 80 per cent of global exports (Thailand, Pakistan, Vietnam, India and the United States). Over the next 36 years, the populations of these five nations are forecast to increase by 543 million people. As this occurs, their internal demand for food will see some of them shift from being net rice exporters to net rice importers.

The risk this shift poses to China's food security is severe. At the same time that internal demand is increasing, the number of major global suppliers will be shrinking and the price of rice will be rising. These factors, combined with China's underdeveloped infrastructure, deteriorating land and water environment and low disposable income levels represents a major threat to its internal stability.

As highlighted above, China is home to 362 million people who live on $2 a day or less. Under such circumstances, how will China's poor afford to feed themselves when the price of rice is rising? What happens if Chinese rice production suffers an unforeseen environmental event brought about by its various water, pollution or land use problems? What if a major logistical or trade failure results in a critical food shipment delay? Further still, what happens if similar problems emerge in the other food production markets which China is dependent upon, such as soybeans? How do you guarantee food security to a population of 1.3 billion people when you are reliant upon markets you can't control and distribution systems which are semi-functional? How will China cope? How could any nation cope?

China presently spends over US$160 billion on food subsidies in order to alleviate the adverse effects of price spikes. In recent years it has even begun purchasing and leasing vast tracts of foreign farmland in an effort to improve supply chain control. As global demand for food grows over the decades ahead, the cost of maintaining both will intensify. How effectively China manages the task of feeding itself against the backdrop of its many vulnerabilities will certainly determine its capacity for exceptionalism.

Powering the Indians

This time let's look at India.

As one of the world's most rapidly industrialising economies, India has an insatiable appetite for energy. However, due to the scale of its demand, India remains dependent upon access to internationally traded energy commodities and vulnerable to the prices those commodities are exchanged at.

Over the next four decades, India's hunger for energy commodities will soar dramatically, with demand for coal, oil, natural gas, uranium and cooking oil each forecast to rise substantially. By 2035, this process will make India one of the world's top energy consumers and one of the world's largest energy importers. This dependence upon foreign sources of energy will place India's ongoing economic expansion and social stability in an extremely vulnerable position.

Take coal for instance.

Coal is the most important contributor to India's energy mix with coal-fired plants accounting for 56 per cent of installed electricity capacity.[203] Of this, only about 80 per cent of its present coal demand can be met through domestic production.[204] By 2030, this is forecast to decline to 70 per cent.[205]

At the same time as India's hunger for coal will be rising, the pressures which affect its price will also be increasing as well. These factors will have many serious and long term consequences for India's economic development and overall standard of living.

At present, over 300 million Indians do not have access to electricity, no Indians enjoy continuous supply and several hundred million do not even pay for the electricity they use, due to energy theft, inadequate metering and subsidies.

To date, the government has kept energy prices low by devoting a considerable amount of its public resources to pay for consumer and business related energy subsidies like coal pricing schemes. However, as the number of energy consumers rises, and the global price for coal appreciates, the cost of providing these subsidies will become increasingly unsustainable.

Like China, India is home to hundreds of millions of people who live on $2 or less day. Faced with such widespread poverty, how will India be able to fund the modernisation of its power grid when such a large share of its budget is spent on subsidising power to those who cannot afford it? How will India double electricity access for rural households when the price of doing so is more brown outs and fewer resources for building new assets? What happens to India's social fabric if the cost of modernising the whole nation in the long term is to continue ignoring parts of it in the medium term?

Sadly, there are no easy answers to any of these questions. The choice between economic growth and minimum human rights rarely offers the governments of developing nations any solace.

Despite India's best efforts to navigate this divide, living standards are not universally improving, infrastructure targets are not being met, foreign acquisitions have yet to deliver, private investment is continuing to underwhelm, tariff arrangements have not worked and the populace is losing patience.

As the nation's appetite for energy grows, decisions on these vexed choices will slowly become unavoidable. Historically, energy inflation in India has resulted in immediate social unrest and subsequent government back downs – leading to limited reform and only the postponement of failure. How India overcomes its history in this regard will definitely affect its potential for exceptionalism.

Building modernity

The final area worth mentioning is that of infrastructure. A modern infrastructure is a must for any nation aspiring to exceptionalism. In both supergiants' cases, the scale of the infrastructure challenge is enormous, and therefore, the cost of developing it will be as well.

Over the next 40 years, China and India will need to expend over 10 trillion dollars on infrastructure in order to lift their nations up to parity with the established world. This is the development equivalent of building the United State's entire infrastructure base several times over.

In order to facilitate this massive endeavour, enormous quantities of concrete, iron ore, aluminium, steal and coking coal will be necessary. Not to mention the energy and skilled labour necessary for design, materials processing and construction activity itself. Due to the very scale of the various inputs required, neither supergiant will be able to meet these needs entirely on their own. As a result, this will place them in a very delicate position.

Ponder this. Between 1750-1950, a few dozen nations with a combined population of less than two billion people began the process of modernising their infrastructure to standards which we can relate to today. At the same time that this process was happening, the remainder of the world's populations resided in nations where little or no such activity was occurring.

For those who were attempting to seriously modernise, the world was an entirely different place. Nations such as the United States, Canada and Australia had large, rich and underpopulated landmasses to exploit and help fuel their socioeconomic development. And those in Europe had vast global empires to drain to help them accomplish the same. In the case of those nations attempting to build humanity's first modern infrastructure, the environment was anything but unfavourable.

Today however, things are markedly different. Dozens of developing nations with a combined population of several billion people are attempting to accomplish that which their established neighbours have already achieved. Unfortunately for them, the conditions are now infinitely dissimilar. Global supplies are tighter, resource nationalism is increasing, the most accessible resources have already been consumed and competition for what remains is intensifying. It is into this cauldron of voracious demand and unpredictable supply which China and India find themselves.

At present, China and India combined are home to 218 cities with populations over one million people (165 in China and 53 in India). In the majority of cases, their infrastructure networks are in a woeful condition. Sanitation is semi-functional, electrical grids are unreliable, the water supply is polluted and transport networks are underdeveloped. According to the UN, China will need to build three cities the size of Sydney every year until 2030 in order to facilitate its drive towards urbanisation.[206] In India's case, an additional 500 million are forecast to move to their existing cities over the coming decades.

As these populations urbanise, the cost and complexity of this process will heighten considerably. As it does, their reliance upon foreign resources to do so will intensify. How either nation copes with a serious threat to their supply lines is extremely hard to predict. The optimist would suppose that the free market would engineer a timely and workable solution. The pessimist would refer him to world history.

§

In the end, the problem facing both supergiants is this. In order to possess the capacity for exceptionalism they must first become established nations. Yet they are attempting to do so for four times the population of Europe and America at four times the speed during an era where demand has never been greater, supply has never been tighter, and the costs of paying for it are almost always higher.

Not only is this a recipe for extreme disappointment, it is also being pursued at a time when they are being challenged by the greatest economic, governance, equity, demographic, environmental, cultural, social and geopolitical problems known to humanity.

Time will tell if either supergiant manages to overcome these tremendous odds. However, given the magnitude of the task and the enormity of the challenge, barrackers for their exceptionalism shouldn't hold their breath.

4
The established world: sunset and sunrise

So if the developing world is destined for less success than is commonly predicted, and the supergiants are up against near impossible odds to come anywhere near close to exceptionalism, then it is obvious that the 21st century belongs to those nations who have already achieved a position of global dominance.

Right? Wrong. And here's why.

There is a pervasive and subconscious belief within the populations of the established world that their long term prosperity is assured.

That while future social, economic and strategic challenges will undoubtedly arise, they will always be able to overcome them because the heavy lifting of nation building is complete.

Misplaced overconfidence such as this can be treacherous.

While it is true to say that established nations enjoy an unarguable degree of socioeconomic stability, this does not mean that the timely arrival of circumstance will grant them all a free ride to exceptionalism. Within the fabric of all nations are a series of unique characteristics which can change their prospects dramatically depending upon what pressures come their way.

As established nations navigate their way through this century, a variety of complex internal and external pressures will start to emerge. As these experiences occur, the various strengths and weaknesses of these nations will bring about a sharp divergence in their fortunes.

In an effort to understand how this process will unfold, let us begin by clarifying who we're talking about.

Generally speaking, there are two types of established nations: core and peripheridy.[207] Let's start with what they have in common.

Established nations

Established nations are generally recognised as possessing diverse economies, effective service delivery standards, established institutions, high material well-being and a well recognised national infrastructure. Often referred to as first world nations, established nations are considered to be the richest, most powerful and resilient on Earth.

What makes established nations different from developing ones is their advanced state of development. High value sectors such as services and knowledge based industries dominate their economies and domestic consumer markets represent the lion's share of their GDP. Key national infrastructure such as roads, highways, rail lines, ports, airports, and water, energy and sewage distribution systems have also all been constructed. Public services such as healthcare, education, welfare and the judiciary are provided at high standards, and the human rights of citizens tend to be well protected by legislation, long standing institutions and the presence of a free press. Flora and fauna also enjoys a protected place with established nations, with strong regulation and legislative protection governing the community's interaction with them.

Established nations are also socially and economically stable. High living standards, widespread prosperity, effective education systems, reasonable employment prospects, urbanisation and a large private sector all encourage popular support for the status quo. Further, the presence of long standing institutions, government accountability, high personal wealth and income, a welfare state, a wide tax base and a respect for the rule of law each help to stabilise the nation during times of adversity. Indeed, throughout established world history, the presence of a large middle class has traditionally acted as an effective check on self immolation.

Established nations derive their name from the fact that they are well known for their economic and social permanence. In the majority of cases, this has occurred as a result of favourable collisions of opportunity earlier in their development. The majority of citizens in established nations enjoy high GDP per capita level incomes and they no longer face the development challenges experienced by their less advanced peers. Importantly, almost all established nations have reproduction rates below population replacement levels. Established nations include France, South Korea and Singapore.

Core nations

Core nations are established nations which exist at the demographic and geographical core of human civilisation. Located throughout the Afro-Eurasian supercontinent, the world's 39 core nations exist upon land which birthed humanity's most powerful empires and is today home to nine per cent of its people and over 36 per cent of its economic production.[208] Combined with their developing world neighbours, core nations collectively represent the heartland of humanity.

Core nations differ from peripheridy nations in several complex ways.

For starters, core nations have dramatically lower population growth rates than their peripheridy peers. Indeed, their growth rates are so low that eleven of the 39 core nations are now in long term population decline with many of the remainder virtually stagnant.[209] Core nations are also significantly older than peripheridy nations having formed as nation states hundreds if not thousands of years earlier. As a result of their longer histories, core nations tend to more homogenous with more rigid cultures. This gifts them with tremendous self identification and tradition, but makes migrant integration challenging due to their near impossible cultural acceptance requirements.

Going hand in hand with their age are the scars long histories collect. Nearly all core nations have unresolved territorial claims with their neighbours. Moreover, dozens occupy restive borderlands which continue to be a source of cultural, religious, territorial and resource based conflict. Through human history, conflicts have been refought over all of these unresolved matters.[210] As a result, military conflict, post war reconstruction and the costly prevention of warfare features heavily in the histories of core nations.

Core nations also exist in close proximity to large foreign population centres, giving rise to a multitude of complex challenges. In addition to their neighbours hosting different cultures, religions, languages and levels of societal and economic development, many core nations exist close to unstable developing nations. Core nations in Europe and North East Asia each face the risk of large and uncontrolled population movements from North Africa, South East Asia and the Middle East.

The relatively small geographical size, resource depth and close proximity to other nation states also makes geopolitical challenges harder to manage. Issues like river utilisation, market access, international trade, resource extraction, pollution, water consumption, national defence and continental transport systems are infinitely more complicated. And unlike their peripheridy cousins, differences of opinion are spread amongst multiple nation states with no binding collective interests (as opposed to different sub national states within a cohesive and dominant national entity, for example, France and Belarus in the core vs California and New York in the peripheridy).

Overall, core nations are prosperous, stable and demographically mature. They are nations such as Italy, Japan and Germany.

Peripheridy nations

Peripheridy nations are established nations which exist at distance from humanity's heartland. Residing upon two continents beyond the shores of Afro-Eurasia, the world's peripheridy nations are home to five per cent of humanity and over 27 per of its economic production.[211]

What makes peripheridy nations different from all other nations is that they are home to the luckiest, most harmonious and richly endowed peoples in the world. In addition to their similar histories, demographics and cultures, peripheridy nations possess unquestionably large amounts of arable land, low population densities, the highest growth rates amongst established nations, expansive energy resources, a disproportionate food production capacity, almost unrestricted access to fresh water, an abundance of natural infrastructure, flat unobstructed land and some of the world's largest land, maritime and raw material claims in the world.

In addition to their natural world strengths, peripheridy nations also enjoy the benefits of coming to the nation state game late. As a result of their relatively late nationhood, peripheridy societies carry few of the cultural and historical burdens which plague the world's oldest civilisations. Unresolved territorial disputes, fractious religious divisions and restive borderlands are small or non-existent and all possess a deep and enduring commitment to the principles of freedom, pluralism, tolerance and democracy. Importantly, vast sections of their populations are comfortable with cultural and religious diversity as well as the concept of non-native citizenship. This attribute, in combination with the plasticity of their settler cultures, has helped them develop some of the world's largest and most effective immigration systems. It has also given them an important edge in the upcoming demographic battle to offset worsening labour and ageing challenges.

Existing at a great distance from the core of humanity, peripheridy nations also face few of the strategic challenges other nations do. They rarely experience the destructive consequences of sustained international warfare and enjoy the strategic insulation of vast and arguably impassable, oceans. Throughout recent history, this trait has gifted them the ability to develop economies and infrastructure without labouring under the costly threat of war or regional instability. Indeed, this reality has never been more evident than during the 20th century when no major city in Australia or North America required post-World War One or World War Two reconstruction.

Overall, peripheridy nations are unique because they enjoy the strengths of the established world's core nations but few of their weaknesses. As this century unfolds, these key strategic differences will place the peripheridy nations on a different and ultimately more prosperous development path. This eventuality will have significant implications for how future global affairs are conducted. It will do so by allowing them to more easily dominate their peers.

Peripheridy nations refer exclusively to the United States of America, Canada and Australia.

Geopolitical musical chairs

Like developing nations, the rise of the global middle class will pose many unique challenges to established ones.

Over the next 16 years, 3.1 billion people are forecast to enter the global middle class. As highlighted above, this explosion in consumers will unleash an unprecedented wave of global demand for products, services, resources and expertise.

For much of the established world, this boon represents an amazing opportunity for economic growth and wealth generation. However, just because the possibility of enrichment exists (circumstance), doesn't mean all nations will be capable of exploiting it (capacity). A variety of factors such as demography, geopolitical power, trade access and natural wealth will influence which nations are primed to benefit and which ones are not.

Throughout human history, there have been many nations which have conveyed an image of inextinguishable prosperity only to have external change and internal limitations bring them undone. England is one such nation which was seen to be unassailable during the 19th century only to spectacularly crash due to poor preparation for the 20th.

The very same challenge confronts the entire established world in this century.

Maintaining long term prosperity will be akin to a game of musical chairs.

The music won't suit everyone. And only those with the right capacity will end up securing a seat.

§

Germany and the United States are two established nations which fall into the important categories of core and peripheridy respectively. Each is representative of their subcategory peers and both presently play important roles in global affairs. How these two nations prepare for and manage change (circumstance) throughout this century will be a big determinant of how prosperous they will be in the future.

In order to fully appreciate the complexity of the challenges these two nations face, and through them, how their subcategory peers will be tested, a major yet common threat to each's long term future is discussed.

Averting Germany's decline

Despite Germany's astute reputation as Europe's bank, export house, economic engine room and former collision beneficiary, there is one major challenge which is slowly eroding its capacity to to take advantage of future circumstantial change – its deteriorating demography.

Like almost all core nations, Germany faces the daunting demographic dilemma of worsening fertility combined with an ageing population.

In Germany today, the fertility rate of the average woman is 39 per cent lower than what it was 54 years ago[212] having collapsed from 2.3 children per woman to 1.4 today (well below the replacement level of 2.1).[213] In 1960, about 1,251,600 children were born in Greater Germany.[214] In 2009, it was 651,000.[215] This is despite the population being 10 million people larger. On current trends, by 2050 Germany's population will have reverted in size back to its 1960s population.[216]

Today's average German is also rather old. At an average age of 44.6 years,[217] he is also over three years older than the average European.[218] Drained by the nation's long life expectancy and low fertility rates, by 2050 19 per cent of Germany's population will be older than the current retirement age.[219,220]

As Germany's population shrinks and ages, its economic prosperity, enviable living standards and capacity to seize future opportunities for exceptionalism will come under increasing pressure. This unfortunate change will occur as a result of two complex but interrelated problems – workforce decline and an unsustainable welfare budget.

Over the coming decades, the number of workers available to sustain Germany's economy will decrease. On current forecasts, the percentage of Germans aged 15-64 will decrease from more than two-thirds to 56 per cent.[221] While not entirely driven by low fertility rates, this eventuality will have massive implications for Germany's ability to sustain itself as an innovative and productive global service and manufacturing centre. Fewer workers will also have serious ramifications for keeping business costs under control. As German firms struggle to source workers, wage inflation is likely to result without the offsetting benefit of productivity gains. This outbreak will not only harm profitability, it will undermine export competitiveness as well.

An ageing population also threatens the vitality of Germany's workforce. For a number of years, the German workforce has been shrinking with recent studies predicting a workforce several million people smaller by 2030. This decline represents a triple hit to the German economy. In addition to the loss of net workers available for employment due to retirement, and those who choose to stay out of the workforce to care for new retirees, the younger workers who are entering employment are rarely as productive as the ones who are leaving it. Right across Germany for instance, 23-year-old graduates are slowly replacing 65-year-old veterans. While these graduates are entering workplaces with superb educations, they are simply no substitute for 40 years of work experience and training.

What all this means is that at the same time that Germany's workforce is "thinning out", it is also "skilling out". In combination, these two demographic changes represent the most serious challenge to German economic prosperity since their commencement of World War Two.

Germany's shrinking population will also have serious implications for its ability to maintain its generous welfare state. As home to one of Europe's most extensive welfare systems, the German state's ability to provide income support rests upon the vibrancy of its tax base. At present, 31.6 per cent of the national German budget is sourced from income taxes.[222] Over the next few decades, the number of workers contributing to income tax will decline. Further, by 2060, the ratio[223] of people aged over 65 to those aged 20-64 will rise from 34 per cent to 65 per cent.[224]

What makes this situation particularly bad for Germany is that at the very same time the number of taxpaying workers are declining in size and full time activity, the number of citizens drawing upon pensions, social security, health services and aged care will be rising – even more so if life expectancy improves. This situation will invariably put intense pressure upon the government to either reduce support levels or run heavy budget deficits – either of which is undesirable.

If Germany is to have any chance of avoiding the consequences of its deteriorating demography, it will need to reconsider the very structure of its long term development model. Much like the current GFC is forcing European states to re-examine the design of their welfare states, worsening demography will force Germany to re-examine how they manage population and ageing policy. In short, Germany has six options.

First, increase domestic reproduction levels. At present Germany spends over €200 billion[225] each year supporting and promoting families (almost two-thirds of its national budget). Despite this, German births have fallen 72,000 over the past decade[226] locking in its position as one of Europe's poorest breeders. Given Germany's failure in this sphere,[227] it is hard to see how more resourcing will change present reproductive decision making.

Second, lift the participation rate. As with domestic reproduction policy, Germany is already using changes to the pension age and tax and welfare incentives to attract retirees, semi-retired workers and casual and part time employees into the workforce with reasonable success. This approach will no doubt intensify over the years ahead. However, Germany will find the cost of doing so an increasing challenge as its workforce shrinks and its welfare bill grows.

Third, increase productivity through retraining. Since the painful structural reforms of the 1970s and 1980s, retraining existing and recently retrenched workers has been a major focus for established nations. However, despite the vast resources deployed, success has always been mixed. Retraining a 40-year car factory veteran to become an IT specialist has always been difficult. As all kinds of employment become increasingly complicated, retraining older workers will become ever more challenging.

Fourth, substitute human workers with technology and operational innovation. Germany is presently a world leader in the use of robotics with a robot density of 270 robots per 10,000 employees.[228] This enthusiastic embrace has partly eased labour shortages through substitution. Indeed, over the decades ahead, work substitution with machines, automation, voice recognition and better processes will play a key role in limiting labour shortages. Unfortunately, these advances do not represent a panacea to all of Germany's labour problems. With over 65 per cent of its workforce based in the services sector, non-human substitution will have its limits.

Fifth, outsourcing labour overseas. Germany is presently in the process of relocating a sizeable portion of its industrial activities to Russia and Poland. Much like its demographic twin in the Pacific, Japan has sought to alleviate its labour shortages by relocating its industrial base to China.[229] As with technological substitution, outsourcing provides solutions for some, but not all labour shortages. At best, outsourcing secondary industry will only free up workers for redeployment/retraining for Germany's tertiary industries and services.

Finally, use temporary foreign workers and/or replacement migration to increase the workforce. Historically, both have proven to be the most effective methods for easing Germanys' demographic and labour force challenges. In 2012 for example, over a million foreigners migrated to Germany. However, while this approach brings technical relief, in core nations it also brings its own set of challenges. Broadly speaking, there are two which make this approach a difficult one.

First, by virtue of their nature, permanent and temporary migration disrupts societies by introducing new elements which displace and challenge the status quo. In settler nations such as Australia, these side effects are milder because the concept of national identity is more fluid. However, in Europe and North East Asia, national identity is more closely tied to geographical and ethnic history.[230] As a result, successful integration and political will for using immigration as a tool for addressing demographic change is considerably harder to achieve.

Secondly, there are serious questions to be asked about the policy's long term effectiveness. For the past 40 years, the majority of German immigrants have come from other EU nations, often those less developed or in economic distress. In both cases, these immigrants have historically returned home once economic conditions have improved, rather than permanently resettling. A similar fate also follows that of non-EU immigrants, however, factors such as local discrimination and integration difficulties tend to also contribute in those cases. As a result, immigration policy in itself is not the fix-all solution it is often made out to be. In Germany's case, it tends to ease, rather than solve the challenge of finite labour.

There is one final factor worth mentioning in regard to the Germany's reliance upon foreign workers – their future availability.

As the demographic crunch bites across the established world, the race to secure foreign labour will intensify. In all likelihood, aggressive recruitment campaigns backed up by generous incentives will quickly become the norm. Whereas in today's world established nations are focussed on pre-empting self-selecting migration, in the future, government resources may well be deployed to help seek them out.

Undermining the established world's response amidst this migration scramble will be the complicating effects of the rise. As economies across the developing world modernise, demand for labour and the wages to keep them will increase. These changes will make the task of attracting foreign labour all the more difficult. Furthermore, as developing nations begin to experience their own version of labour shortages, they will likely commence their own global recruitment efforts, beginning with luring back their earliest diasporas.

In combination, these forces will make the global labour market an extremely competitive place to work. Nations with effective immigration systems, deep pockets, flexible employment regimes, innovative recruitment techniques and adaptable cultures will have a critical edge in this marketplace. Those which are slow or politically unwilling to respond, will not. Where Germany sits in this mix will be critical to its ability to use migration as a solution to its demographic problems.

Overall, Germany has several options available to it for addressing its deteriorating demography. If it can find a way to make these policies work more effectively, then Germany should be able to resecure the capacity to embrace positive circumstantial change. If not, than its risks losing its place as Europe's much envied "Economic Miracle".

Shaking America's complacency

When one looks at the varied strengths of the United States of America, it is hard to argue that it is not the luckiest nation on Earth. Equipped with a plethora of natural resources, deep financial, military and geopolitical power, a transcontinental political system, an adaptable culture and excellent long term growth prospects, the

United States possesses all the trademarks of an inevitable and long dominating global power.

Yet in spite of its multitude of advantages, this amazing nation faces one complex challenge which threatens to rob it of long term exceptionalism – complacency.

Like many peripheridy nations, the United States has long had the benefit of a large margin of error by virtue of its history of sound governance, advanced socioeconomic development and favourable natural and geographical features. Being rich, secure, stable and powerful, the United States has been able to effectively recover from a litany of financial failures, strategic miscalculations and periods of irresponsible self-satisfaction. However, in a century that will be defined by unprecedented economic expansion, destabilising social change and historical shifts in global power, the size of the net which the United States performs above is going to begin to shrink.

In recent decades, policy settings and the overall quality of debate in the United States has exposed a nation which doesn't really take its future seriously. Long term threats are ignored, strategic mistakes are rationalised and immediate problems routinely play second fiddle to less serious superficial ones.

At present, there is no better example of this process in practice than in regard to how the United States is handling its public finance crisis. With the exception of World War Two and its immediate aftermath, the United States has never been so indebted since 1792.[231] Currently, governments all across the country including the national government are plagued by unsustainable balance sheets as a result of underfunded pension and healthcare costs, careless spending and public borrowings.

According to Moody's, more than half of the United States' 50 largest local governments have liabilities from pension underfunding exceeding 100 per cent of their revenues[232] – a huge problem when you run a payas-you-go funding system! Further, as of 2009, 61 American cities with a population greater than 500,000 collectively had employee and retiree health liabilities of $118 billion, of which only six per cent had been set aside.[233] Put simply, American complacency in the area of financial management is out of control.

In response to this worsening crisis, both sides of politics have failed to act in a decisive or coherent manner. Rather than engaging in sensible budgetary surgery based on the undeniable facts of the problem, politicians have instead brought on confidence destroying government shutdowns, additional pump priming budgets, discredited trickledown economics, a scorched earth defence of unsustainable entitlements and harmful delays on social security and Farm Bill reform.

The United States' ineffective response goes to the heart of the challenge it is facing. Societal complacency has dug itself so deep into the national psyche that when the political elite are confronted by a problem with no easy solutions, they can easily get away without dealing with it. This indulgence of obfuscation, wilful ignorance, purposeful miscommunication and reckless overconfidence are all the signs of an ill-disciplined nation in which complacency has completely taken hold. Unless the United States can rediscover its focus and return to its more conservative fiscal nature, it not only risks its internal problems becoming worse, but it also jeopardises the chance to properly position itself (capacity) for this century's greatest economic opportunity (circumstance) – the rise of the global middle class.

Perhaps luckily for the United States, the solution to its complacency may well come from its next opening for exceptionalism – the rise driven shifts in global power. If there is any lesson to be learnt about American behaviour over the past 70 years, it is that when confronted with a challenge to its strategic interests, it quickly finds its focus. Whether it was the attack on Pearl Harbour, the launch of Sputnik or the September 11th terrorist strikes, once challenged, the nation gets serious very quickly. With global power shifting both East and South more with each passing year, the United States may well soon rediscover its former discipline.

Looking forward, the challenge for the United States this century is to learn the ability to find its focus proactively, rather than reactively. If it does, it will be much better able to take advantage of this century's global events. If it doesn't, it may well find that its exceptionalism is in decline.

Divergent fates

As the rise gathers momentum and spreads, the destinies of core and peripheridy nations will increasingly drift apart.

What once grouped established nations together by rising living standards, shared liberal values and common post war objectives will begin to give way to a sharp divergence of separate interests driven by differing capabilities for responding to internal and external circumstances.

Peripheridy nations will find themselves surging powered by burgeoning primary exports, expanding domestic markets, growing populations, rising tax revenues, a more manageable demographic crunch and less exposure to developing world spill over effects.

Conversely, core nations will find themselves wasting away. Burdened by declining workforces, ageing populations, out of sync tax and welfare policies, shrinking domestic consumer markets, limited natural wealth and closer proximity to global instability, core nations will be challenged on a range of fronts.

Perhaps the best way to illustrate the degree of divergence between the peripheridy and core nations is by better identifying how the rise will change their long term prospects.

Over the next 16 years, 3.1 billion people are forecast to join the global middle class. Of the 101 million additional people forecast to emerge within the borders of the world's three peripheridy nations,[234] the overwhelming majority will be considered middle class. Further, they can be expected to be joined by tens of millions of their fellow citizens who will be amongst the new class of growing global rich.[235]

Conversely, little more than 7.4 million additional people will appear across the 39 core nations with eleven experiencing a numerical decline.[236] In other words, at the same time that peripheridy nations are strengthening and core nations are weakening, each will also be experiencing markedly different levels of internal exposure to the biggest economic expansion in world history. As this process unfolds, the impacts on their economic vitality will be profound.

By 2050 at least four core nations previously in the global top 25 economies are forecast to fall outside of it. This contrasts with the prospects of the world's three peripheridy nations which will continue to remain firmly inside of it.

Demographically, their prospects will also sharply diverge.

By 2050, the populations of the United States, Canada and Australia will be 25, 28 and 43 per cent larger[237] as well as home to the third, twelfth and seventh lowest old age dependency ratios in the OECD.[238] Conversely, the populations of core nations like Portugal, Germany and Japan will be 7.5, 12 and 15 per cent smaller[239] with twelve core nations having age dependency ratios above the OECD average.[240] This demographic shift, amongst others, will give new meaning to the phrase "old world".

§

Overall, the challenge facing the established world is this. In order to maintain their position as leaders in geopolitical affairs, established nations will not only need to find a way to build a capacity for exceptionalism, but they will need to do so in the face of a punishing demographic decline.

In all likelihood, nations with much in common with Germany will struggle to stem the deep structural problems dogging their long term development. Unable to evolve substantially enough to starve off their demographic and geopolitical destinies, these nations will continue to remain established, albeit as stagnating versions of their former selves.

For those nations with more in common with the United States, the future will be one defined by ascension. Resourced to the hilt and equipped with the flexibility necessary to manage this century's toughest challenges, their potential will largely be determined by their own discipline and ambition.

Throughout human history, good fortune has often favoured some nations over others. In the age of antiquity, the rise of coastal trade allowed the Mediterranean city states to dominate their poorer landlocked neighbours. And in the age of empire, it was the power of organisation and technology which allowed Europe to systematically dominate the Americas, Africa and Asia.

In this century, circumstance will come to favour a new global grouping. They will be called the peripheridy.

5
Australia, the undiscovered country

Amongst the peripheridy there is one nation which is seldom recognised for the tremendous capacity that it possesses – Australia.

For hundreds of years, brave explorers, prospective colonists and successive citizens have routinely dismissed its innumerable possibilities. Often miscalculating its prospects based upon the common conventions of the time, rather than on what the future might make feasible, each group has succeeded in making a colossal error of judgment.

As Australia progresses through this century, the scale of these misjudgements will increasingly become obvious. Indeed, as a direct side effect of the most recent resources and energy booms, assessments about Australia's long term prospects are already beginning to be revised.

In order to avoid further misunderstandings, let us examine this nation which so many observers have spectacularly misjudged.

The Australian archipelago

Greatly endowed

For all of Australia's history, its landmass has been profoundly misunderstood.

As home to 23 million people, Australia has the greatest arable land endowment of any country in modern history. Measured by people per square kilometre of arable land, Australia has seven-and-a-half times more land per person than the world average.

In total, Australia has 69 times more arable land per person then South Korea, 26 times more than Indonesia, 22 times more than China and ten times more than Thailand. Put simply, Australia has more arable land for farming and urban expansion than Indonesia, Thailand, Philippines, Japan, Malaysia and Papua New Guinea combined – six nations with a total population of over 580 million people.[241]

Compared to the established world, Australia also boasts an impressive arable land advantage. Placed side by side against the United Kingdom, France and the United States, Australia has 25 times, 7.7 times and 4.1 times more arable land per person than each of these nations respectively.

Centralised living

In order to best understand how Australians live, a study of population density is essential. Outlined below is a map of Australia's population density. As the map demonstrates, Australians predominantly reside along the eastern, south eastern and south western coastlines closely reflecting the location of the continent's most habitable climate zones.

As one digs deeper into the Australian settlement pattern however, a less obvious demographic reality emerges. Despite Australia's preference for state-based identification, its strong farming history and its global reputation for being a nation with wide-open spaces, Australians live a distinctly concentrated existence. Aided by the economic importance of port and river access, city focussed industrial development and polycentric rail expansion, intense coastal settlement has long been a prominent feature of Australian life.

Australia's urban centres are home to 89 per cent of its population representing the nation's demographic backbone. Far from being common throughout the world, this demographic reality is not the global norm. Presently, approximately half of the world's population is classified as rural with developing nations such as India and China hosting over half of their populations outside urban areas. Even amongst the world's established nations, lower levels of urbanisation predominate. France, Germany, and

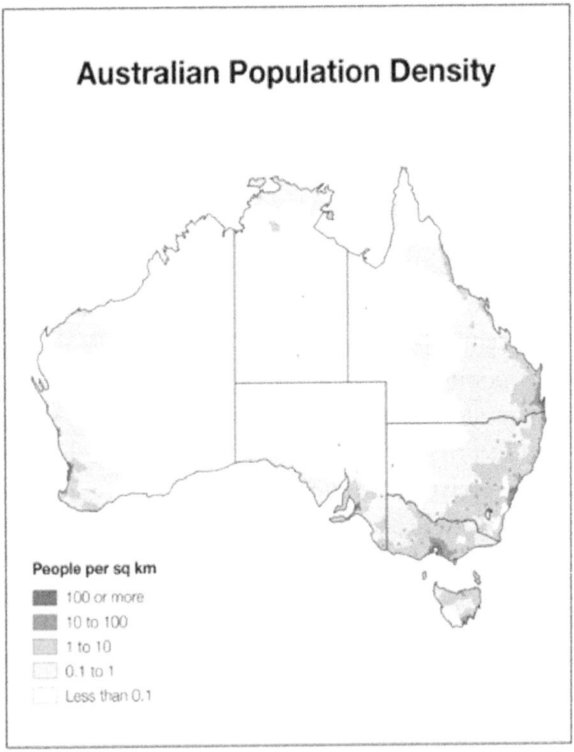

Source: ABS 3218.0, *Regional Population Growth, Australia, 2012-13*, Population Density by SA2, Australia – June 2013, 3 April 2014.

Japan all enjoy lower levels of urbanisation than Australia despite having just a fraction of our arable land resources.

Australians also have a hunger for life in large cities as well. Whereas comparable nations like Canada host 75 per cent of the population in 82 of its largest cities, Australia houses the same percentage in just ten. Even in regard to medium tier cities[242] Australia lags its peripheridy peer. Canada boasts 29 cities in this category whereas Australia claims only 14. These factors have combined to make Australia the most urbanised nation on Earth (excluding the city states like Singapore).[243]

Put simply, despite having the geographical freedom to live highly decentralised lives, Australians have demonstrated a consistent preference for the opposite.

Human lava

In Evangelista Torricelli's famous 11 June 1644 letter to Michelangelo Ricci, he reconceptualised humanity's place on Earth as being "submerged at the bottom of an ocean of air". By reimagining the atmosphere above sea level as an ocean of air rather than a continuation of steady atmospheric pressure, Torricelli changed the way his peers thought about the air around them. When attempting to understand where and how Australians live, it is useful to adopt a similarly unconventional approach.

Imagine that instead of Australia being a continental nation comprised of amalgamated states, it is instead an open ocean with a series of submarine volcanoes waiting to erupt. Now pretend that for every living person in Australia, an equal amount of lava spewed forth out of those volcanoes. Then, after the lava has cooled down, pretend that islands formed on the surface, with their size, shape and elevation determined by how large the eruptions were in each location. Now look at the map on the previous page again. What you are looking at is not a partially settled continental nation, but is instead an archipelago of population islands. This is, for all intents and purposes, how modern Australia actually exists.

While Australia is superficially referred to as a continental nation, upon closer scrutiny, it is in fact an archipelago.

Think about it. If we reconceptualise Australia's urban centres as islands, and redefine its unpopulated regions as the open sea, Australia's economic and social activity is exposed as functioning more like an archipelago than a continent.

In the Australian context, the nation's farms and mines do not operate as if they are conurbated businesses or primary exurbs connected to urban centres. Rather, they function more like offshore oil wells, producing valuable products, but at a great distance from their consumers. And Australia's freeways do not knit all urban centres together either. Instead, they operate more like bridges, linking the nation's workforces with workplaces and disparate population islands together as if they are all separated by water. Even our growth areas and growth centres exhibited island like characteristics. When a population centre expands its urban boundaries, it does so like a waterfront developer reclaiming the sea. In essence, growth areas exhibit all the traits of foreshores. When undeveloped they have periodic but limited interaction with the mainland (like the tide). But once fully urbanised, they become completely integrated – just like the land next to the foreshores they used to nestle.

By reimagining Australia in this fashion, we can glimpse a vision of Australian settlement not as it is politically organised, but how it actually exists. Put simply, we can dismiss the peripheral and elevate the tangible.

And by doing so, several previously invisible geopolitical entities start to emerge:

- the home islands;
- the secondary island chain; and
- the tertiary island chain

The home islands

Australia is home to five home (primary) islands which represent the core of the nation and bear the closest structural resemblance to those states found in continental Europe. In the absence of official names, we shall refer to them as:

- Cumberland (centred upon the Cumberland Plain in New South Wales);
- Yarra (encircling Port Phillip Bay in Victoria);
- Oxley (centred upon the south eastern coast of Queensland);
- Swan (centred upon the Swan Coastal Plain in Western Australia); and
- Vincent (centred upon the Torrens River in South Australia).

Home to millions of people, sizeable central business districts, decentralised urban centres, integrated transport networks and diversified economies, the boundaries of these islands are determined by conurbations, dominant commuter belts and their degree of economic independence and upper level service dependency. Importantly, they also radiate a considerable amount of political, economic, cultural and service provision influence upon the islets within their vicinity.

As key demographic and economic centres, each home island also hosts significant portions of Australia's artificial infrastructure such as roads, rail, ports, airports and public and private service delivery facilities. Highly urbanised and home to large educated workforces, they act as magnets for business, investment, capital generation and migration. Indeed, almost 60 per cent of Australia's population growth between 2001-2010 occurred in just four of these regions.[244] With the sole exception of Torrens, each of these five islands is forecast to grow by over one million people over the next 47 years, placing them amongst the largest growing regions in the nation.[245] Collectively, these five islands are home to 60 per cent of Australia's population and are responsible for producing 63 per cent of its GDP. Outlined below is a short summary of each one.

Cumberland Island is a coastal conurbation and exurb based upon the Cumberland Plain in New South Wales. It is comprised of two major interconnected urban centres, Greater Sydney and Gosford, which combined host 19.6 per cent of Australia's population (4.46 million people).[246]

Over the decades ahead, Cumberland's physical footprint is likely to expand westwards, south west and north west across the remainder of the Cumberland Plain. Cumberland and its other major exurb and neighbouring islet, Wollongong will also grow closer.

Yarra Island is a hooked shaped coastal conurbation and double exurb expanding outwards from Port Phillip Bay in Victoria. It is comprised of three major interconnected urban centres, Greater Melbourne, Melton and Sunbury which combined host 18.3 per cent of Australia's population (4.17 million people).[247]

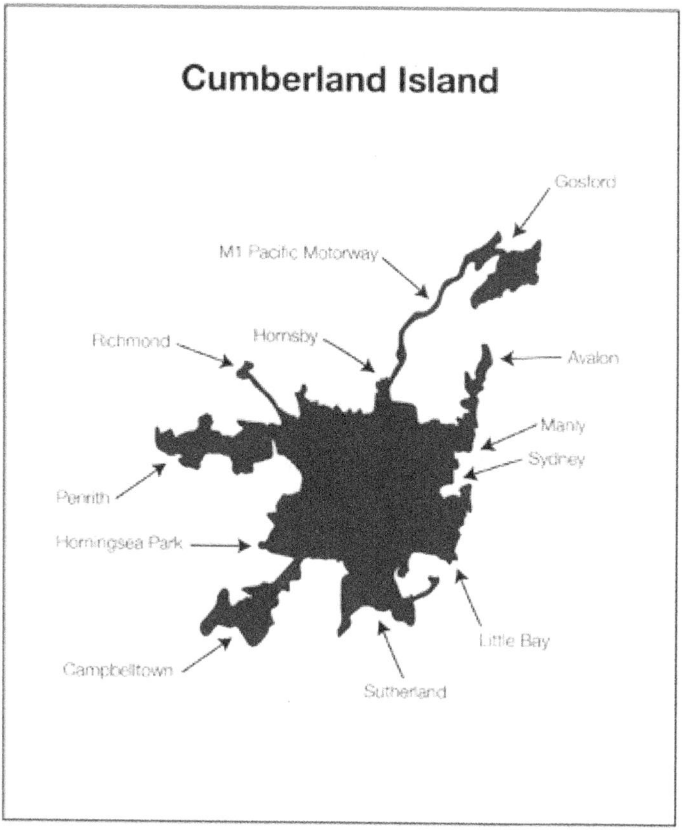

Sources: Department of Infrastructure and Transport (Major Cities Unit), State of Australian Cities 2011, Canberra, 2011, Figure 2.15, p. 34; ABS Census 2006; ABS Census 2011; Google Maps.

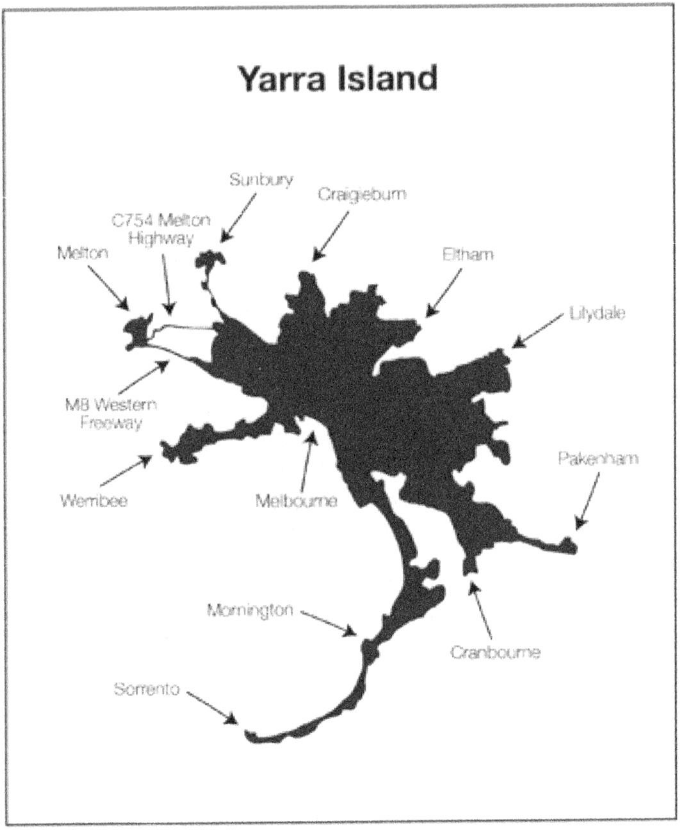

Sources: Department of Infrastructure and Transport (Major Cities Unit), State of Australian Cities 2011, Canberra, 2011, Figure 2.16, p. 35; ABS Census 2006; ABS Census 2011; Google Maps.

Due to the absence of any physical barriers to northern, western, south western and south eastern expansion, Yarra's physical footprint is likely to extend towards and in some cases, envelop its ring of growing exurbs as well as its neighbouring islets of Bacchus Marsh, Gisborne, Wallan and Geelong.

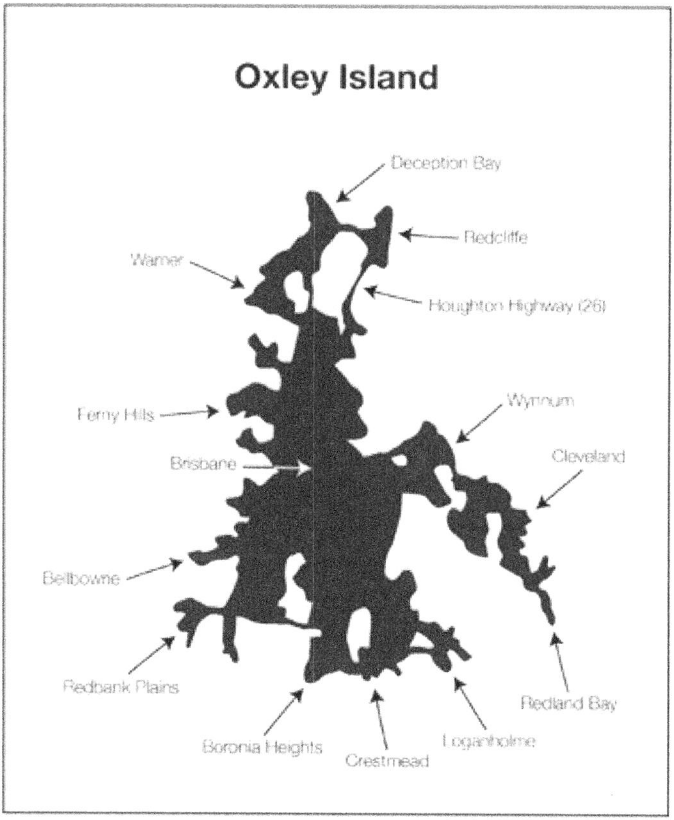

Sources: Department of Infrastructure and Transport (Major Cities Unit), State of Australian Cities 2011, Canberra, 2011, Figure 2.17, p. 36; ABS Census 2006; ABS Census 2011; Google Maps.

Oxley Island is a triangle shaped coastal conurbation located along the south eastern coast of Queensland. It is based upon the urban centre of Greater Brisbane and is home to the nation's third largest population centre hosting 9.2 per cent of Australia's population (2.1 million people).[248]

As a result of the economic and demographic gravity of Gold Coast-Tweed Heads and the Sunshine Coast, the absence of national and state parks in-between them and greater Brisbane, and the capacity for urban growth along Greater Brisbane's northern and southern approaches, Oxley's physical footprint is likely to expand towards each of these major islets as well as the minor islet of Jimboomba.[249] Over the decades ahead, this expansion will not only create Australia's largest physical conurbation (approximately 275km long), it will also be Australia's first major interstate one[250] (easily eclipsing Albury-Wodonga).

Swan Island is a coastal conurbation situated upon the Swan Coastal Plain in Western Australia. It is based upon the urban centre of Greater Perth and its neighbouring exurb Kwinana. Swan hosts 7.9 per cent of Australia's population (1.8 million people).[251]

Due to the absence of any physical barriers to northern and southern expansion, Swan's physical footprint is likely to expand north and south, envelop its growing exurb and eventually reach its neighbouring islet, Mandurah.[252]

Vincent Island is a hand shaped coastal conurbation and double exurb centred upon the Torrens River in South Australia. It is comprised of three major interconnected urban centres, Greater Adelaide, Gawler and Mount Barker which combined host 5.7 per cent of Australia's population (1.3 million people).[253]

Despite each urban centre's likely expansion over the decades ahead, physical conurbation between Greater Adelaide and Mount Barker is unlikely due to the presence of the Adelaide Hills. However, no physical obstacles exist in regard to Gawler eventually being enveloped by Greater Adelaide's long term northern expansion.[254]

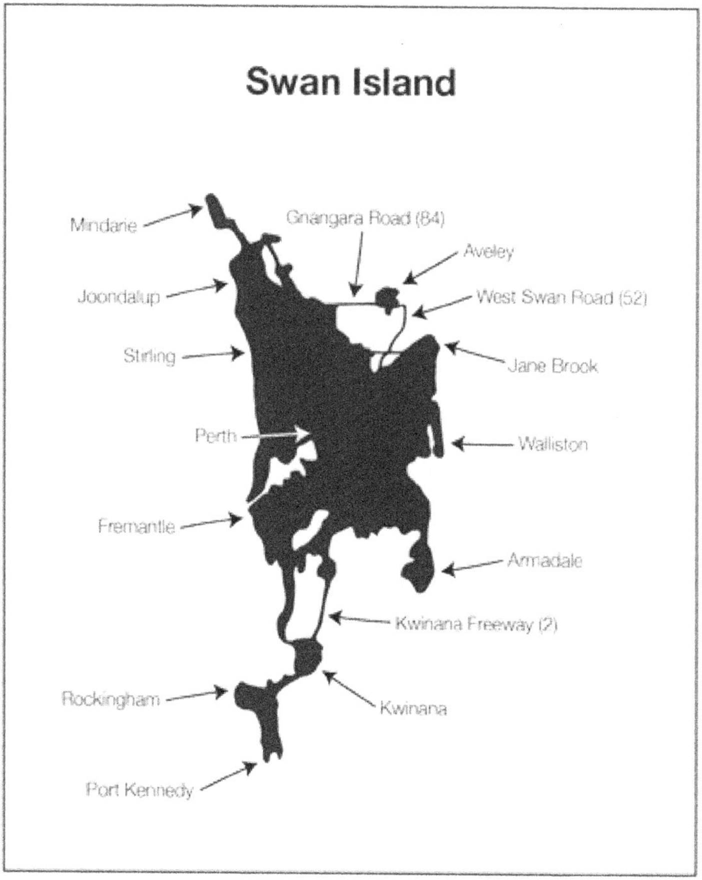

Sources: Department of Infrastructure and Transport (Major Cities Unit), State of Australian Cities 2011, Canberra, 2011, Figure 2.18, p. 37; ABS Census 2006; ABS Census 2011; Google Maps.

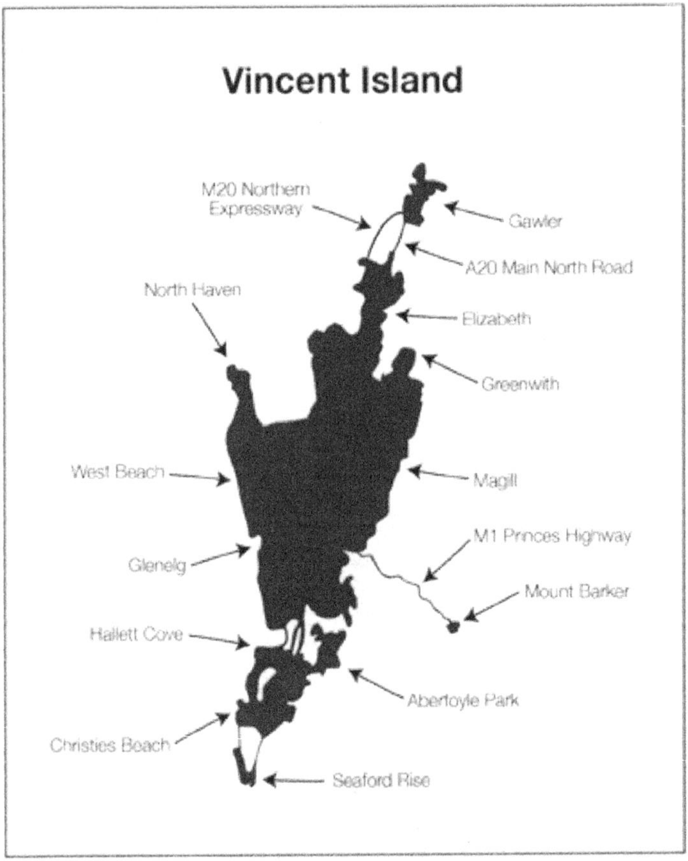

*Adelaide is equidistant between West Beach and Magill.

Sources: Department of Infrastructure and Transport (Major Cities Unit), State of Australian Cities 2011, Canberra, 2011, Figure 2.19, p. 38; ABS Census 2006; ABS Census 2011; Google Maps.

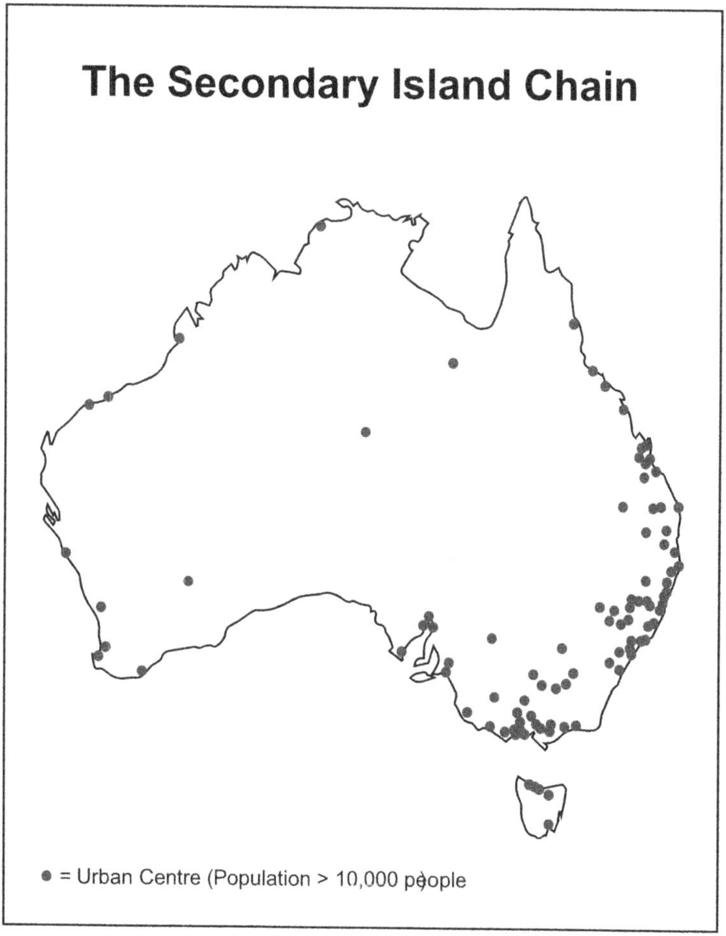

Sources: ABS 3218.0, *Regional Population Growth, Australia*, op. cit.; ABS 3218.0, *Regional Population Growth, Australia*, Table 1. Estimated Resident Population, Statistical Areas Level 2, New South Wales; Google Maps.

Australia's Secondary Island Chain is comprised of 95 urban centres (excluding the home islands) which host populations greater than 10,000 people. Combined, these islets are home to 24.6 per cent of Australia's population (5.6 million people)[255] with approximately half located within a two hour land commute of the five home islands.

Table 1: Urban Centres within the Secondary Island Chain[256]

Urban Centre	Population	Urban Centre	Population
Gold Coast - Tweed Heads	592,389	Wagga Wagga	54,093
Newcastle - Maitland	420,850	Hervey Bay	50,588
Canberra - Queanbeyan	412,049	Mildura - Wentworth	48,842
Sunshine Coast	286,497	Shepparton - Mooroopna	48,156
Wollongong	283,243	Gladstone - Tannum Sands	44,431
Hobart	205,557	Port Macquarie	43,733
Geelong	179,689	Traralgon - Morwell	40,815
Townsville	171,824	Tamworth	40,673
Wyong	155,063	Orange	38,471
Cairns	142,124	Geraldton	37,811
Darwin	116,215	Bowral - Mittagong	36,503
Toowoomba	110,855	Dubbo	35,675
Ballarat	95,240	Nowra-Bomaderry	34,823
Bendigo	88,827	Bathurst	34,158

Launceston	86,152	Warrnambool	33,291
Albury - Wodonga	84,983	Ellenbrook	33,042
Mackay	81,874	Kalgoorlie-Boulder	32,859
Rockhampton	77,613	Busselton	32,809
Bunbury	70,132	Albany	32,256
Bundaberg	69,929	Warragul - Drouin	31,257
Coffs Harbour	66,718	Devonport	30,479

Urban Centre	**Population**	**Urban Centre**	**Population**
Lismore	29,390	Yeppoon	17,457
Alice Springs	28,605	Murray Bridge	17, 321
Mount Gambier	28,439	Kurri Kurri-Wesron	16, 994
Burnie - Wynyard	28,001	Singleton	16,895
Maryborough	27,224	Moe - Newborough	16,759
Taree	26,374	Batemans Bay	16,349
Nelson Bay - Corlette	26,349	Camden Haven	16,287
Victor Harbor - Goolwa	24,783	Torquay	16,265
Ballina	24,592	Horsham	16,224
Armidale	23,568	Port Lincoln	15,741

Ocean Grove - Point Lonsdale	23,254	Warwick	15,194
Morisset - Cooranbong	22,776	Port Hedland	14,867
Whyalla	22,620	Ulladulla	14,848
Goulburn	22,493	Ulverstone	14,743
Mount Isa	21,945	Sale	14,527
Cessnock	21,206	Emerald	14,362
Gympie	20,370	Port Pirie	14,321
Forster - Tuncurry	20,329	Port Augusta	14,097
Echuca - Moama	19,798	Broome	13,752
Broken Hill	19,103	Bairnsdale	13,606
Grafton	19,070	St Georges Basin - Sanctuary Point	13,145
Gisborne - Macedon	18,917	Lithgow	12,799
Griffith	18,780	Muswellbrook	12,488
Wangaratta	18,051	Colac	12,018
Bacchus Marsh	18,034	Drysdale - Clifton Springs	11,851
Karratha	17,892	Parkes	11,408
Highfields	17,566		

Australia's secondary island chain is a collection of exurbs, isolated cities and semi-conurbated regional towns which have developed as a result of raw material or energy discovery, agricultural production, government sponsored industrial development, logistical support, public service delivery, tourism or military value. In the majority of cases, they are located near Australia's ports, productive arable land, renewable water resources and natural resource and energy wealth. To varying degrees, they also represent the outer borders of Australia's economic and social influence. Just under half are located along Australia's coastline.

Where these islets differ with Australia's home islands is through their similarity with the true island nations of the world. Hosting comparably smaller populations, narrower economies and smaller political clout, these urban centres are unable to generate enough capital to be self sufficient and tend to be overtly reliant upon central government support (instead of international aid), favourable commodity prices, large private enterprise and foreign direct investment. Due to their unique isolation, they are also more vulnerable to fluctuating government subsidies, transport costs, labour shortages, large enterprise withdrawal and disruptions in international trade.

Many of Australia's islets act as centres of political authority and/ or major regional service delivery. The urban centres of Darwin, Alice Springs, Cairns, Townsville, Mackay, Mt Isa, Kalgoorlie-Boulder, Albany and Launceston in particular act as major regional hubs. This comes about as a result of their relative size and isolation in comparison to neighbouring population centres. Consequently, several of these urban centres have an above average number of public sector employees across the government administration, service delivery and defence fields. As a result, they also tend to be mendicant in nature, meaning they are unhealthily reliant upon government funding.

Fly-in-fly-out (FIFO) labour also plays a major role in the demographics of Australia's most isolated communities. Due to their remoteness and challenging climate, many urban centres find that their local populations fluctuate sharply and on a regular basis. Interestingly, large regional urban centres also experience these fluctuations when their local population departs for labour activities on even more remote extraction sites.

Whilst sharing commonality in regard to their isolation, these islets enjoy very different growth paths for very different reasons. Whereas some are in the midst of a prolonged mining and energy boom, transforming previously modest regional centres into rapidly expanding urban hubs, others are growing as a result of regional population drift. Others still are in terminal decline, with their demographic booms long distant. The Sunshine Coast, Toowoomba, Mackay, Geelong and Townsville are all forecast to grow by over 70 per cent by 2030.[257] These five urban centres represent some of Australia's fastest growing secondary islands.

The Tertiary Island Chain

The remaining 15.4 per cent of Australia's population resides in a Tertiary Island Chain comprised of minor urban centres, regional businesses, research stations and military outposts which are scattered across the remainder of Australian territory. While many of these islets can credibly claim disproportionate economic and cultural significance, none boast a population greater than 10,000 people.

§

Overall, while Australia does a great impression of being a continental nation, it is in fact, an efficiently organised and arable archipelago. By settling in the regions offering only the best of economic returns, Australia's occupants have studiously avoided the costs of managing a continent far beyond their present means of faculty.

A cornucopian bounty

Poor press

Despite popular opinion to the contrary, Australia is one of the most self-sufficient nations on Earth.

Occupying territory greater than 97 per cent of the world's countries, and a maritime economic exclusion zone (EEZ) larger than its land holdings, Australia controls the natural resources of a superpower.

Yet in spite of the inherent strength of its position, it is not uncommon to hear Australians speculate on the timing of their next food, water, energy or natural resource crisis. For as long as Europeans have known of Australia, the continent has almost always been held in low regard.

One of Australia's earliest explorers, William Dampier, wrote several books which heavily influenced the enduring view of Australia's poor prospects.[258] His assessment, combined with similar views shared by his successors helped create a near permanent judgment that Australia remains a mixed development prospect at best.

But if we look beyond the clichéd headlines of nutrient poor soils, debilitating drought and dwindling natural resources, one actually uncovers a cornucopia which early explorers and subsequent settlers ignorantly and irresponsibly misjudged.

Abundant abundance

Food

In a productive season, Australia's farmers produce enough food to feed over 60 million people.[259] In fact, Australian farmers, commercial fisherman and aquaculturalists produce enough food to meet 93 per cent of our daily domestic food supply.[260] Australia is the world's ninth largest agricultural producer and 52nd largest seafood producer by volume. In total, Australia has the third largest fishing zone, greater than 60 per cent of its landmass is engaged in agricultural activity and over 2.1 million hectares of its land is in irrigated land use (an area slightly smaller than Sicily).[261] In fact, Australia's productivity is so proficient that it is a global leader in the production of wheat, sheep meat, wine, sugar cane, canola (rapeseed), barley, oats, lupins, goat meat, sunflower seeds, dry broad beans, lentils, hops, nut nes, triticale, chick-peas, horse meat, vetches, dry peas, persimmons, sorghum and grapes.

During 2011, the gross value of Australian farm production (at farmgate) was valued at over $48 billion.[262] Indeed, as a result of Australia's tremendous production capacity, it is rated as one of the world's most prolific agricultural exporters. It is also well regarded as a supplier of high quality produce. In total, Australia enjoys a net food surplus position of approximately $4.3 billion per year. Importantly, its self-sufficiency sits in direct contrast to 131 other nations which depend upon imports to meet their minimum dietary needs.

Despite rumours of encroaching food shortages, Australia's food production capabilities remain anything but insecure. Indeed, as the only middle-sized nation on Earth capable of producing enough food to feed a population over three times its size, Australians can argue they are the most food secure citizenry on the planet.

Water

Australian territory is home to some of the largest, most renewable and cleanest water resources in the world.

According to the Nation Water Commission, "Australia's water resources are highly variable, and range from heavily regulated working rivers and groundwater resources, through to rivers and aquifers in almost pristine condition."[263] Australia's rainfall is also extremely diverse with precipitation varying from location to location, year to year and season to season.[264]

Overall, Australia's water resources are spread out amongst three core sources: natural replenishment (rainfall),[265] water in store (dams and aquifers) and unnatural replenishment (desalination and reuse). In total, Australia's daily water availability per capita is 51,000 litres per day.[266] This is amongst the highest in the world.

Table 2. Water availability per capita per day[267]

Nation	Indonesia	United States	China	United Kingdom
Water per capita per day (lt)	33,540	24,000	6,000	3,000

Plentiful rainfall in the right locations is a key reason for Australia's water wealth.

Sydney, Melbourne and Perth for example receive more rainfall than London.[268] One of the main reasons such figures may come as a surprise is because most commentary about Australia's rainfall is bastardised by irrelevant and misleading averages. For example, Australia is technically the driest continent on Earth with an undeniably high evapotranspiration rate.[269] However, if the more temperate Tasmanian and Victorian rainfalls were assessed as a singular nation, then that nation would receive a combined annual rainfall greater than Germany, the United Kingdom, France and Italy.[270] As a result, when one considers that Australians live on just a fraction of their official territory, the importance of continental averages is rendered relatively meaningless. Instead, rather than accepting that Australia is the driest continent on Earth, it would be more accurate to label it as a disparately wet archipelago.

Australia's extensive network of supersized dams also play a major role in helping maintain the nations water edge. With over 500 large dams[272,273] and more than two million farm dams,[274] Australia "has the highest per capita surface water storage capacity of any country in the world".[275] These dams combined with Australia's highly variable rainfall both play a major role in ensuring its citizens enjoy a world leading water usage standard.[276] Further, they also ensure that the nation's food producing districts can conduct irrigation activity throughout their local growing seasons.

Table 3. Large dam storage by jurisdiction in Australia (as at 30 June 2005)[277, 278]

State	ACT	NSW	NT	QLD	SA	TAS	VIC	WA	Aust.
Volume (GL)	120	24,629	280	10,657	258	23,652	12,109	12,148	83,853

Australia's vast groundwater reserves (aquifers) also dwarf the water resources of several small countries. Comprised of a mixture of alluvial, coastal, fractured rock, sedimentary, palaeovalley and karst aquifers, Australia's total groundwater resources represent "approximately 17 per cent of accessible water resources and over 30 per cent of water consumption".[279] Australia's largest aquifer, the Great Artesian Basin, is up to 3,000 metres deep and is larger than France, Spain, Italy and the United Kingdom combined.[280] Overall, it contains an estimated 8.7 million gigalitres of water.[281] The equivalent of 129,800 Sydney harbours.[282]

As a result of technological breakthroughs and shifting community attitudes about water harvesting, Australia has also developed a respectable water creation capability. Total desalination and reuse capacity is approximately 450GL[283] and 414GL[284] respectively. Over the years ahead, this capacity is expected to grow.

In regard to water consumption, during 2011-12, 74,925 gigalitres of water was extracted from the environment and used within the Australian economy.[285] Of this, approximately 85 per cent was returned to the environment as regulated discharge, for example, after use in hydroelectricity generation, with the remainder (16,019GL[286]) consumed as follows:

- Agriculture: 9,417 gigalitres (59 per cent of consumption).
- Aquaculture, forestry, logging, fishing, hunting, trapping and agriculture, forestry and fishing support services: 169 gigalitres (one per cent of consumption).
- Water supply (sewage and drainage): 2,029 gigalitres (13 per cent of consumption).
- Households: 1,715 gigalitres (11 per cent of consumption).
- Mining: 677 gigalitres (four per cent of consumption).
- Manufacturing: 557 gigalitres (three per cent of consumption).
- Electricity and gas supply: 385 gigalitres (two per cent of consumption).

- Waste collection, treatment and disposal services: 7 gigalitres (0.04 per cent of consumption).
- Other industries: 1,063 gigalitres (seven per cent of consumption).[287]

As these figures show, the water consumption habits of the Australian farmer continue to define the reality of water consumption. Despite 60 per cent of runoff occurring in northern Australia, 50 per cent of water is consumed in the Murray Darling Basin in the south east – the nation's food bowl. In spite of considerable government and media attention on the thirst of our urban centres, household, sewage and drainage usage represents less than 25 per cent of total consumption.[288]

Overall, despite constant rumours about Australia running out of its most "precious resource", Australia's water future remains secure. Indeed, if there is any water related shortage Australia genuinely suffers from, it is one based upon information, management, infrastructure, distribution and investment. Luckily for all Australians, not one of these requires the goodwill of Mother Nature. Each of them rests entirely in its citizenry's hands.

Natural environment

Australia is also home to one of the world's most geographically gifted, cost effectively located and development friendly nations on the planet.

Topographically, Australia is the world's flattest continent. This lends Australia the tremendous advantage of having permanently lower building and infrastructure costs, making the capital outlays required for the development of our cities, offices, homes, roads and rail lines substantially lower than experienced elsewhere in the world. In contrast to the topographically challenged nations of

Brazil and Greece where mountainous features permanently inflate development costs and undermine capital generation, Australia faces no such handicap.

Being located at the centre of the Australian tectonic plate is also a useful advantage. Although Australia is periodically troubled by earthquakes,[289] no Australia city rests upon a major fault line. Consequently, unlike San Francisco (1906), Qayen (1997), Christchurch (2011) and Tohoku (2011), Australia has only infrequently had to contend with the cost of risk management, design, safety and rebuild and recovery issues resulting from earthquake hazard.

Volcano risk is also low throughout Australian territory with no activity taking place during the last 8,000 years. If volcanoes erupt often, the risk they pose heavily complicates settlement, planning, agriculture, infrastructure and insurance matters. While the concept remains foreign in Australia, volcano risk remains an everyday reality in Indonesia, New Zealand, Japan, Mexico and the United States as well as many other nations.

Australia's global location and isolation are two other important advantages the nation holds. With over four billion people located less than 8,000kms away, the opportunities for trade and cultural exchange are enormous. Whether it is the commercial advantage of transport times, operating in similar time zones or the ability to access growing markets quickly, Australia's location grants it a competitive edge few other nations hold. Additionally, its global isolation and the natural barrier of the sea both lend themselves favourably to improved defensibility, better customs control and illegal migration deterrence.

Australia's unique environment has also been of immense value to the nation's development. Its dry climate and cool winters have helped immune the populace from the spread of devastating insect diseases such as malaria, its modest rainfall and warm seasons have kept the cost and maintenance of infrastructure low, and the near absence of snowfall, blizzards, ice and monsoons has helped make sure weather costs have been kept to a minimum. Put simply, with the exception of periodically devastating bushfires and cyclones, Australians reside in some of the most development friendly climate zones on Earth.

Australia also enjoys an uninhibited and cost effective transport route to the global economy through the existence of dozens of warm water ports, many of which are rated amongst the best natural and deep water ports in the world. Routinely underappreciated, this is a critical advantage 48 other nations do not share. As the author of *The Bottom Billion* writes, "If you are coastal, you serve the world; if you are landlocked, you serve your neighbours."[290] As a nation with unrestricted access to three separate oceans and no volatile physically abutting neighbours, Australia enjoys the envied position of simply needing to serve itself.

Conversely, Australia's river systems leave a lot to be desired. While none suffer the inconvenience of the winter freezes common in the northern hemisphere, all are plagued by poor draft, natural barriers and narrow widths rendering them of little value to bulk commodity export or domestic trade. This has resulted in Australia being capital intensive, vulnerable to oil prices and highly dependent upon more costly road and rail based transport. It has also resulted in the absence of any major inland cities, making the continent unique amongst the world's great landmasses.

Overall, Australia's natural environment represents an amazing mixture of extraordinary advantage, modest weakness and unrealised potential.

Resource and energy wealth

One fact which has never really been in dispute is the scale of Australia's natural resource endowment.

Not including Australia's 5,896,000sq km Antarctic land claim, the nation's extensive land and maritime territories contain some of the largest and most diversified energy and non-energy resources in the world. According to Geoscience Australia, Australia has the world's largest uranium resources, second largest brown coal resources, fifth largest black coal resources, two per cent of global natural gas resources and 0.3 per cent of the world's oil reserves.[291] Consequently, Australia enjoys a position of incredible flexibility in regard to how it develops and manages its national energy strategy.

In regard to Australia's non-energy resources, the nation is equally blessed. It is home to the world's highest known economically demonstrated resources (EDR) quantities of lead, nickel, zinc, silver, rutile and zircon. Moreover, it has the second highest known EDR quantities of iron ore, copper, bauxite, gold, tantalum, ilmenite and niobium. Undeniably, these extensive natural resources have helped make Australia considerably richer and more powerful.

Indeed, in contrast to many of the world's nations which are heavily dependent upon resources they do not control and often, cannot afford, Australia has no such problem. During 2012 over $145 billion[292] of Australia's natural resource wealth was exported, predominantly to those countries with limited self-sufficiency.

For much of its history, Australia has also been reliant upon the importation of a few natural resources. Each year Australia imports approximately $37 billion of crude petroleum and refined petroleum[293] and 75 per cent of the nation's rock phosphate fertiliser needs.[294] Outside of this, a few natural rarities such as processed gold and wood products are imported as well.

Put simply, despite the nation's dependence upon a few select raw materials, Australia very much hosts a natural resource smorgasbord which feeds much of the world.

§

Former Australian Prime Minister Paul Keating once famously remarked, "For a nation to be successful, it has got to know itself, its strengths and weaknesses."[295] As a nation with the natural resources of a superpower, coming to grips with that reality will be critical if Australia is to realise its full potential.

An economic heavyweight in the making

Dynamic and wealthy

Australia hosts one of the most dynamic and affluent economies in the world.

With just 0.33 per cent of the global population, Australia hosts the world's 12th largest economy and ninth largest stock exchange.

Australia also has a strong presence internationally as a major exporter and importer and foreign investment source and recipient. Each year, Australia engages in $483 billion of international trade, and invests and receives over $1.2 and $2.1 trillion overseas respectively.[296] Further, over 45,000 Australian businesses are presently engaged in exporting activity. In combination, all of these activities have contributed to Australia's currency becoming the fifth most traded on the planet.

Over 70 per cent of Australia's GDP is produced in its vast services sector, with manufacturing, mining and agriculture, forestry and fishing rounding out the remainder. With over 80 per cent of Australia's twelve million strong workforce[297] employed in services,[298] this sector definitely represents the nation's economic backbone.

One of the great economic threats facing Australia will be its shifting participation and labour force growth rates brought about by the staggered retirement of the baby boomers. By 2036, more Australians will be retiring from the labour force than entering it.[299] Indeed "without immigration, labour force growth will almost cease within the next decade".[300] This represents a major threat to its long term prosperity.

Outside of paid work, Australia is also home to a 6.2 million strong volunteer workforce who helps subsidise its living standards, personal care, immigration programmes and welfare state. Furthermore, 493,000 people raise children and manage households for no income at all.[301]

Unsurprisingly, Australia is also a leader in personal wealth with its GDP per capita the highest in the Asia Pacific and the fifth globally.[302] According to the ABS, Australia's total net worth is $8.01 trillion[303] and the nation is home to the highest wealth per adult in the world (median).[304] Moreover, it also hosts the highest proportion of people with net wealth over $USD100,000 – eight times the world average.[305] These factors, combined with its high disposable incomes have contributed to the creation of one of the world's top 20 consumer markets. Put simply; Australia hosts one of the most impressive economies in the world.

Exceptional development

While there are numerous minor contributing factors to Australia's economic success, three major ones must be noted.

First, Australia has been extremely well managed for much of its history. As a result of its inherited cultural institutions, respect for property rights, democratic rule, stable tax base, strong emphasis on economic freedom and open minded attitude to new ideas, Australia's leaders have collectively forged a diverse and prosperous economy.

Second, by being isolated from the bulk of humanity, human history and global trading routes, Australia has enjoyed and developed many unique traits which have helped it establish its prosperity. The first is its historic good fortune at avoiding devastating wars on home soil. With the exception of Darwin and Townsville (minor cities at the time), no major Australian city has suffered the physical effects of modern warfare – a claim few nations can make. This has allowed Australia's cities to grow organically and uninterrupted. Australia has also been lucky to avoid the natural disasters which periodically devastate and destabilise other nations. Problems like famine, flood and prolonged drought have never reached proportions in which Australia's economic or social fabric has become highly destabilised. Nor has it suffered the burden of large scale foreign population movement which such events often create. As a result, Australia's economic expansion has remained largely uninterrupted since European settlement.

Of course, Australia's isolation has also made it strategically dependent upon the wider world. Inputs such as capital, labour, energy and farming products and specific processed and hi-tech goods have routinely been sourced from overseas. Whilst this dependency has its obvious weaknesses, especially during times of restricted trade (war or high protectionism), Australia's long term experience with foreign labour, goods and services has made its culture more open to the benefits of international trade, foreign investment, overseas travel, immigration and the influx of new ideas – all of which have helped its economy thrive.

Third, Australia's intrinsic natural wealth has helped set it up for highly probable success. Richly endowed with innumerable fruits of the earth, Australia has long enjoyed the financial and strategic benefits of being a major supplier to global markets. Best understood as an historic aberration, never before has so much been available for so few for so long.

The urban aorta

As with Australia's demography, broad statistical overviews only provide a superficial summary of its economy. While Australia may well be a continental nation on paper, it is nothing of the sort on the ground. Much like its archipelagic settlement pattern, Australia's economy is also highly dislocated.

Despite Australia being a major exporter of agricultural, energy and natural resource products sourced from a multitude of non-urban areas, economic activity still overwhelmingly occurs in its major cities. Australia's 18 largest cities produce around 80 per cent of its GDP and employ 75 per cent of its workforce.[306] Approximately 50 per cent of economic activity occurs in Sydney, Melbourne and Brisbane alone, with Perth and Adelaide contributing a further 12.5 per cent. Australia's major cities are also the principal location for approximately 70 per cent of Australia's businesses. Nearly two-thirds of its small and medium-sized businesses, almost 80 per cent of its large corporations[307] and the vast bulk of public service delivery organisations are based in these regions. In other words, Australia's cities collectively represent the heartbeat of the national economy.

Australia's economic heartland

Unlike the vast majority of the world's nations, Australia lacks an economic heartland. Whereas most nations have regions where economic activity is nationally dominant, as with the UK's Greater London or Pakistan's Karachi, Australia's disparate settlement pattern and evenly balanced economic centres have resulted in no one region gaining unquestioned dominance over all others. Consequently, Australia is unique in the world in that it has several definitive economic cores, rather than just one all powerful one.

Unsurprisingly, Australia's economic heartland is split across its five home islands.

Cumberland

Based upon the urban centres of Greater Sydney and Gosford, Cumberland is Australia's largest economic region generating approximately 23 per cent of output ($325 billion)[308,309] – the equivalent of the nation of Malaysia.

As Australia's corporate and financial capital, Cumberland hosts the Australian Stock Exchange, the Futures Exchange, the Reserve Bank of Australia, 32 per cent of Australia's commercial office space, 80 per cent of Australia's deposit-taking banks and approximately 60 per cent of all Asia Pacific regional headquarters in Australia.

In total, over 65 per cent of Australia's financial activity takes place in Cumberland with the total number of sector employees (pre-GFC) equal to nearly half of London's and more than 40 per cent of New York City's (both of which are their continents' leading financial centres).[310] Cumberland also hosts Australia's greatest concentration of private sector businesses, including the largest proportion of Australia's workforce with Sydney being home to the nation's highest level of labour productivity.[311] Cumberland is also home to the biggest proportion of Australia's industrial base, one-third of legal firm employment, 70 per cent of property and business services regional offices and almost 75 per cent of Australian ICT regional headquarters. Importantly, Cumberland is also Australia's largest consumer market, its top international tourist drawcard, home to its busiest airport, second largest container port and second largest suburban rail and freeway networks.

Yarra

Based upon the urban centres of Melbourne, Melton and Sunbury, Yarra is Australia's second largest economic region generating approximately 18.1 per cent of output ($263 billion)[312,313,314] – the equivalent of the nation of Egypt.

Yarra is considered to be Australia's industrial, superannuation, logistics, education and sporting capital. It is home to 40 per cent of Australia's superannuation funds and 65 per cent of industry superfunds.

Yarra's strategic location and the Port of Melbourne have helped make it south eastern Australia's most important transport node, facilitating international trade for the economic centres of Adelaide, Geelong, Tasmania and the NSW Riverina. Handling 39 per cent of container trade, Melbourne Port is Australia's busiest container port and the southern hemisphere's fifth. Yarra also hosts Australia's largest and densest freeway network, its second busiest airport, its largest suburban rail network and the world's fourth best university city.[315]

As well as featuring the nation's second largest corporate centre, consumer market, tourism market, workforce and private business sector, Yarra is also home to 22 per cent of Australia's commercial office space, the Australian Council of Trade Unions, the Productivity Commission, the Australian Securities and Investments Commission, the Australian Open Tennis Championships, the world's oldest Chinatown, the Melbourne Cup and Spring Racing Carnival, the Formula One Australian Grand Prix and Australia's largest sports and entertainment precinct.

Oxley

Based upon the urban centre of Brisbane, Oxley is Australia's third largest economic region generating approximately nine per cent of output ($132 billion)[316] – the equivalent of the nation of Hungary.

As the administrative centre of a major energy and resource state, Oxley is the corporate headquarters for Australia's coal, aluminium, alumina and bauxite operations. Combined, these industries power almost one-quarter of Oxley's economy.

Oxley is also the most important economic centre in northern Australia and the largest economic hub between Sydney and Singapore. It is presently home to nearly 14 per cent of Australia's commercial office space. However, unlike its resource and energy rival Swan, the Oxley economy is considerably more diversified with tourism and retail making up large segments.

Swan

Based upon the urban centres of Perth and Kwinana, Swan is Australia's fourth largest economic region generating approximately 8.3 per cent of output ($120 billion)[317,318] – the equivalent of the nation of Bangladesh.

As Australia's energy and resource capital,[319] Swan is home to Australia's largest oil refinery, half of the ASX's listed energy companies, 63 of Australia's top 300 companies[320] and "more listed companies per capita than any other Australian capital".[321] As a result of its role as the region's administrative centre, and the intense concentration of industry talent and expertise this attracts, Swan is also Australia's leading centre for research and development of oil, gas, uranium, geothermal and other new energy sources. Consequently, it is home to Australia's best scientists, engineers, specialists and strategic thinkers in the energy and resource extraction fields.

As one of the world's most isolated economic regions, being closer to Jakata than either Melbourne or Brisbane, Swan is also home to a strong entrepreneurial, FIFO and self reliant culture. Combined with its concentration of energy and resource extraction businesses, these factors have helped Swan become Australia's third most powerful corporate city with eight per cent of the nation's commercial office space and the second highest personal incomes levels in the nation.[322]

Vincent

Based upon the urban centres of Adelaide, Gawler and Mount Barker, Vincent is Australia's fifth largest economic region generating approximately 4.75 per cent of output ($69 billion)[323,324,325] – the equivalent of the nation of Cuba.

Vincent is the home of Australia's defence industry with 25 per cent of the defence industry located there[326] as well as the government's Defence Science and Technology Organisation. Vincent is also well known for its manufacturing output which, despite being smaller than Sydney and Melbourne, is a major local employer.

Despite its central position along the southern coast and its well planned city, Vincent's economy is in the midst of a long term decline. While Adelaide is home to over six per cent of Australia's commercial office space, approximately 50 per cent of the Adelaide CBD is filled with public sector tenants. Further, in most years its economy grows more slowly than Australia's and its labour productivity performs below all other state capitals.[327] This poor record of performance is due to its heavy dependence upon public sector activity and government subsidies for growth, as well as its lack of higher productivity industries.[328] Vincent is also ageing faster than Australia's other cities.[329] In spite of Vincent acting as a major economic centre in Australia, for all intents and purposes, it is Australia's premier mendicant region.

Secondary economic hubs

Australia's secondary island chain also makes a modest contribution to national economic output, although most remain highly dependent upon redistributed taxes to maintain living standards. Five major secondary islets are worth mentioning – Canberra-Queanbeyan, Gold Coast-Tweed Heads, Newcastle-Maitland, Geelong and Townsville. Together, these islets generate between one and three per cent of economic activity each with a combined total equivalent to Vincent Island.

As Australia's largest inland islet, Canberra-Queanbeyan, is home to nine per cent of the nation's commercial office space. Importantly, it hosts the bulk of the Commonwealth Government's administrative infrastructure including the Federal Parliament, the High Court and the Australian Defence Force Academy. Canberra-Queanbeyan's 412,000 people are also amongst the nation's most educated.

The non-capital cross border conurbation of Gold Coast-Tweed Heads is a major tourism destination. It presently dedicates over 25 per cent of its workforce to the ten million tourists who visit it each year. Gold Coast-Tweed Heads is presently home to 592,000 people and is the nation's fastest growing islet expanding at almost three times the national growth rate.

The world's largest coal export hub of Newcastle-Maitland is home to 420,000 people. As the main islet in the coal rich Hunter Valley, Newcastle-Mailtand also acts as an important regional healthcare, education and financial service hub. Worryingly, it is also highly mendicant with its major employers being either government owned or government subsidised.

The port and manufacturing islet of Geelong hosts 179,000 people. Much like Newcastle, Geelong is an important regional administration hub as well as a vital logistics, research and food processing centre. Geelong also has mendicant tendencies.

Over 171,000 people reside in the northern regional islet of Townsville. Unlike most isolated islets however, Townsville enjoys a diverse economic base with agriculture, mining, defence, tourism and public services all contributing to its vitality. Townsville also acts an important regional administration hub.

Economic districts

The Murray Darling Basin is one Australia's most valuable decentralised economic districts generating approximately eight per cent of GDP, one third of Australia's gross value agricultural production and over 900,000 jobs. This one million square kilometre economic district is separated from eastern Australia's major economic centres by the Great Dividing Range even though it envelops the ACT, three-quarters of NSW, over half of Victoria and large parts of Queensland and South Australia.

Currently, more than two million people live within this region, primarily in the secondary islets of Canberra-Queanbeyan, Toowoomba, Bendigo, Albury-Wodonga, Tamworth, Dubbo,

Orange, Wagga Wagga and Shepparton-Mooroopna. Australia's three longest rivers, the Darling, Murray and Murrumbidgee each flow through the region helping to generate Australia's rice, cotton, cereal, fruit, vegetables and irrigated crops and pastures. Globally, it is the world's third largest catchment.

After the Murray Darling Basin, the Pilbara resource and energy district is Australia's most important decentralised economic region. The Pilbara is responsible for generating approximately 5.5 per cent of Australia's GDP[330] and is one of the nation's most important export hubs. This district currently produces 90 per cent of Australia's iron ore, 85 per cent of its liquid natural gas and 80 per cent of its crude oil and condensate.[331] Approximately 63,000 people live in the region[332] with much of the workforce consisting of FIFO labourers from Perth, Darwin and regional Western Australia.

Australia's energy districts are also key sources of economic activity producing energy commodities for both domestic consumption and export markets. The Bowen Basin in Queensland, the Sydney Basin in NSW and the Latrobe Valley in Victoria are amongst the nation's largest, richest, EDR and most active coal producing regions. Further, Australia is also home to many large scale EDR crude oil, condensate, LPG and sales gas basins, including Browse and Bonaparte (based in the Pilbara resource and energy district), Carnarvon and Gippsland.[333]

Finally, Australia is also home to a large number of smaller, but nonetheless productive economic districts and activities. Queensland's Sunshine Coast and the Great Barrier Reef; Western Australia's wheatbelt, Kimberley, and Goldfield-Esperance; NSW's Riverina and the Snowy Mountains; Victoria's Western District and Great Ocean Road; South Australia's Barossa Valley; Tasmania's

Sydney to Hobart Yacht Race and the Northern Territory's Uluru and Kakadu each play important roles in generating economic activity and employment generation. Like most large nations, these isolated economic districts operate like a string of pearls lacing up the broad Australian continent.

§

Sophisticated, robust and incongruent, Australia seemingly possesses all the world's economic strengths with few of its obvious weaknesses. By combining the stability and economic maturity of the established world, with the vibrancy and economic dynamism of the developing world, Australia's full economic story has only just begun.

The West's cultural time-keeper

Family trees

In spite of repeated self-doubts about its alleged cultural cringe and neighbourhood claims about being the white trash of Asia, Australia is in fact host to one of the most leveraged and enviable cultures on Earth. The easiest way to understand this is by looking upon the world's nations as if they are families or individuals, rather than just a collection of unrelated independent nation states.

Under such a scenario, Australia is best defined as the youngest of four children sired by the British Empire. Its elder brothers would be the United States, New Zealand and Canada (which is partly sired by France). In many circles, this grouping is referred to as the Anglosphere which describes those nations where the English language and its culture is dominant. Naturally, several other similar groupings also exist such as the Francophone and Panhispania.

As in everyday life, family connections matter. Just as influential parents can smooth the paths of their children's future lives, their absence can have the opposite effect.

As a member of one of humanity's most influential cultural families, Australia enjoys advantages other nations can only dream of. Within her family tree is a parent who was once a superpower and a brother who currently is one. By virtue of Australia's shared cultural heritage, history, religions and language, it has enjoyed a significantly leveraged place in global affairs as a result of the legacies and successes accomplished by these two family members.

For everyday Australians, this leverage exists in the form of an ascendant[334] language (used globally for commerce, science, politics, computing, travel and the internet), a common law legal system followed by over a billion people, a Gregorian calendar in use across the world, a shared technological prowess which dominates the globe, democratic and accountable institutions, involvement with the world's largest entertainment industry, a dominant world religion and culture and an array of military alliances with the most powerful nations on Earth. By existing within the same cultural vein as two of the world's most important historical powers, Australia simultaneously rides on the coattails of its eldest brother whilst benefiting from the cultural legacy of its mother.

Despite lingering self-doubts about Australia's cultural depth as a settler society, few nations can claim a heritage so globally significant.

Congruent happenstance

Unlike most of the world's nations, Australia enjoys the highly strategic advantage of being culturally congruent. 92 per cent of

Australians have a high sense of identification with their country and 87 per cent indicate pride in the Australian way of life.[335]

Uniquely, Australia is not an amalgam of former nations or colonies like the United States, an occupying power like China, a multinational state like Russia, a bicultural state like Canada, a coerced entity like the former Yugoslavia, an artificial nation like Belgium or part of a former nation which has been split up like most of Asia, the Middle East and Africa. Instead, Australia is the amalgamation of six former colonies all sourced from the one colonial parent. Consequently, she possesses an internal unity and cohesion which most other nations cannot claim.

Australia also enjoys the complete absence of borderlands.

Borderlands are defined as the meeting points of different cultures and religions and involve those areas where cultural and political boundaries do not effectively match up.[336] Over the ages, thousands of wars have been fought over these regions, with many simply repeated efforts to regain control of land lost in previous borderland conflicts.[337]

At present, the world is filled with thousands of borderlands with the largest concentration on the Afro-Eurasian supercontinent. Despite almost 70 years of near global peace, borderlands remain one of the largest sources of global violence and communal tension. Indeed, every year thousands of people die within them.

Without a single borderland with its territory, Australia has never been burdened by these problems. Moreover, its history has remained absent of highly organised independence or reunification movements, sectarian political parties, rebel armies or unresolved territorial claims.

Combined with its deeply engrained cultural congruence, Australia is one of the most stable nations on Earth.

Institutional legitimacy and entrenched pluralism

An abiding respect for institutions and a deep affinity for freedom are also vital traits which help make Australia's culture special.

Australia operates one of the most stable, accountable and peaceful governments in the world. Its elections are held without social unrest and their results are always accepted without serious dissent. In fact, these features represent two of Australia's most important cultural virtues – its inherent flexibility and the ability to absorb disagreement. Within Australian society, as long as proper process is seen to have been followed, its society is capable of changing directions without public convulsion.

Australian society also operates under the rule of law. Throughout its territory, civil, property and economic rights enjoy strong protection and its people accept the authority of officials charged with overseeing them. Competing sources of authority such as religion and foreign powers are also largely absent. This sits in contrast to many of the world's other nations where the rule of law is absent (Venezuela), foreign decrees override national sovereignty (Ukraine) and religious edicts matter more than civilian rule (Iraq).

The role and value of Australia's public and religious institutions must not be underestimated either. Australia's healthcare system provides some of the highest quality outcomes in the world and its education system successfully educates millions. Overseeing these two areas, in addition to a multitude of others, is Australia's large, broadly competent and clean public sector bureaucracy. Working for elected politicians at all levels, Australia's public sector institutions play a key role in underpinning continuity of government and essential service delivery. Alongside them stands Australia's major religious institutions. In addition to providing a wide range of community services such as education, welfare and healthcare, they also provide valuable spiritual enrichment and social engagement.

Civilian control over the legitimate use of violence is another important feature which adds to Australia's cultural distinctiveness. While this may seem trite, many governments around the world cannot boast the same advantage. In Egypt for example, the military runs bakeries, in China they operate large businesses and in Pakistan they routinely veto civilian initiated foreign policy. In each of these cases, non-civilian sources exercise a degree of unaccountable authority. In some nations, they are the only authority. Australia's civilian monopoly over the legitimate exercise of violence ensures that its public can operate without fear of unaccountable institutional state action.

Freedom, pluralism, individualism and ethnic diversity also play a key role in shaping Australia's unique culture. Much like the other nations in its family line, Australia is an open society with a long tradition of promoting civil liberties, minority views, freedom of conscious, free trade, open borders and high rates of immigration.[338] Nowhere are the traits more obvious than in its capital cities. Sydney and Melbourne in particular are key hubs of tolerance and diversity, as well as bustling centres of commerce, trade and ideas exchange. Much like the culturally diverse mega cities of London and New York, Australia's major cities welcome all comers. In contrast, many of the world's cities are distinctly insular, reflecting their own complicated histories, religions and cultures. Few places in Australia remain untouched by the cacophony of creativity and ingenuity which these exchanges have unleashed. As a result, Australian culture is highly adaptive.

Australian manufacturing

One of the key reasons Australian culture is so versatile is due to its long term relationship with immigration. Unlike most nations, Australia has a symbiotic relationship with imported labour[339] which stretches all the way back to its original founding.

For as long as Australia has existed, immigration has been an essential component of its economic development and national ethos. Whereas most nations have commonly seen the arrival of foreigners upon their shores as a threat to national culture, Australians have has always adopted a different view. As Hirst explains:

> [I]t is inconceivable that boatloads of Italians arriving at Dover in the 1950s would have been called "New Englanders". In Australia, on the other hand, it was government policy to refer to the migrant Lithuanians, Italians and Greeks as "New Australians".[340]

Two of the key side-effects of this process have been Australia's capacity to adopt foreign business cultures without feeling compromised, and the art of migrant metabolisation. In regard to the first, Australians are more than happy to adapt their business styles to that of their trading partners if it will advantage their business interests. In regard to the later, Australia's metabolisation capacity is best captured by Charles Darwin: "What Australia does best is convert vagabonds into active citizens."[341]

In each case, Australia enjoys a tremendous strategic and cultural advantage.

A tolerant leader

Oddly enough, plenty of Australians believe their nation has a problem with diversity.

Despite some regrettable missteps in the distant past, Australia has an exemplary record when it comes to accepting, tolerating and protecting diversity.

As home to over six million "New Australians" and the third most culturally diverse nation on Earth, Australia has a multigenerational record of offering all comers a "fair go" and a fresh start. According to the CIS, "Australians are more likely to live in mixed neighbourhoods than their British, Canadian, and in particular, American counterparts."[342] Further, they have a higher chance of engaging in interracial and interreligious marriage.

While Australia receives a disproportionate amount of negative press about it's so-called racial and religious "intolerance", its record in these areas is pretty clear. Put simply, Australia has far more to teach the world about tolerance and diversity than it has to learn from it.

Living standards

For those who have visited, worked or lived in Australia, it goes without saying that it is one of the most pleasant places on Earth to live. While many nations attempt to claim this title, and in all seriousness believe it to be true, few can truly justify their claims in terms of their habitability, lifestyle and living standards.

Australia's natural environment is arguably the envy of the world. While the nation markets itself endlessly as a continental desert covered in farms, mines and native brush,[343] most Australians actually live in the most comfortable and productive climate zones on the planet. Over half of the population lives in Earth's temperate zone and a further 30 per cent reside in its subtropical zone. Combined with Australia's long daylight hours, these zones are considered to be Earth's most habitable making Australia one of the easiest and healthiest places for humanity to reside.

The Australian lifestyle is also one to be experienced. Whereas Americans value success and the Germans value precision, Australians on the whole, value recreation. In addition to its pleasant climate, clean environment, warm beaches, large sporting fields, natural heritage, generous annual leave arrangements, low crime rate, liberal welfare system, a perpetually climbing standard of living and infrequently interrupted social harmony, Australia's main holiday period is also universal. Unlike the northern hemisphere where the Christmas break is split from the mid-year summer shutdown, Australia's major public holidays and holidaying weather line up perfectly. Consequently, when the Australia summer-Christmas holiday season arrives almost the entire country takes a break. As a holidaying phenomenon unique throughout most of the advanced world, this practice helps cement Australia's reputation as a nation a fun and leisure.

Australia also has a well deserved reputation for high living standards. As home to an under five mortality rate of 4.9 per 1,000 births, a 99 per cent literacy rate and an 82-year life expectancy, Australia stands out globally amongst its advanced world peers. Further, all Australians have access to electricity, improved water sources and enjoy one of the highest internet penetration rates in the world (even better than the United States).[344] While Australia may be a disparate nation geographically, this has not stopped its leaders building a standard of living which is globally envied.

§

As a result of its special and varied traits, Australia has developed one of the most impressive and desirable cultures on Earth. Rated as one of the world's most tolerant, prosperous and liveable,[345]

Australia enjoys a standard of living to which the entire globe aspires.

§

For much of its existence, Australia's full capacity has been routinely dismissed as not being worth the world's time or investment. Located far from humanity's demographic and economic core, Australia's weaknesses have long been seen to outweigh its peculiar strengths.

Yet as the nation has developed, its economy matured and its technological base blossomed, the harsher judgements about its potential have become obsolete.

Like a country newly discovered, Australia is no longer the marginal backwater it once was. Rather, it is a nation bursting with potential just waiting to kick start the next stage of its evolution.

Home to an efficient settlement pattern, a rich land mass, a dynamic economy and an exceptional culture, Australia truly is a charmed country waiting for its moment to shine.

6
The Australian Century

The Australia in the Asian Century White Paper which was launched with much fanfare in October 2012 epitomises everything that is wrong about how Australia thinks about its future.

The rise of the global middle class will be the most significant socioeconomic event to occur on our planet this century, yet as part of the former Government's response to it, they chose to ignore 34 per cent of those taking part in it[346] (not to mention the world's non Asia Pacific rich). For some inexplicable reason, the disproportionate spending habits of North America and Western Europe, as well as the unrealised benefits of socioeconomic development in South America, Eastern Europe, Africa and the Middle East, were all deemed irrelevant to Australia's future when devising the brief.

This omission represents an unforgivable lapse in government thinking. It also reveals how badly our leaders are mishandling this century.

In the decades to come, it will not be the momentum of continental Asia which holds the attention of the global community. Nor will it be the lack of it within continental Europe. Rather, it will be the relentless and upward surge of Australia.

Much like how the world marvelled at Australia's ability to sail through the GFC without experiencing recession, during this century, Australia's unique identity, capacity for growth, inherent flexibility and seemingly limitless potential will be what truly impresses the world.

The gold rush reprise

In 1851, the discovery of gold in Victoria transformed Australia's weakest colony into the continent's pre-eminent one.

Within 10 years of it commencing, the colony's population had increased sevenfold; its cities and regional towns had been revolutionised and its economy had exploded in size.

What was just five years earlier destined to remain a minor colonial player had leapfrogged its more promising rivals to become the continent's biggest and most productive colony.

In this century, the rise of the global middle class will have the same circumstantial effect on Australia. But instead of this process being driven by a dozen isolated and landlocked goldfields, this reprise will be powered by a continent of world class mines, gas wells, farms and vibrant coastal metropolises.

For the raw materials, energy and food product industries, the rise will be responsible for unleashing a sustained increase in demand for nearly every product they produce. With the demand cycles associated with the rise lasting decades, perhaps even forever, vast geographical regions and industry related cities will be energised as a result of increased capital inflows, labour force movements and logistical infrastructure development. Indeed, for as long as the rise continues, Australia's primary economy, terms of trade and strategic importance in foreign affairs will be overwhelming and positively enhanced.

Australia's industries with expertise in technology, service delivery and wealth and information management will also greatly benefit. Through a combination of Australia's time zone happenstance and its multi-century experience with urbanisation, city planning, healthcare, retailing, education, financial management, mining, agriculture, infrastructure, utility generation, distribution grids, recycling, sustainability and professional governance, millions of gifted workers and savvy business people will find success and opportunity in an increasingly service hungry world. As with the global commodity export boom, the global services boom will have a transformative effect upon Australia. However, in the cases of the tertiary and quaternary economy, it will be the most dynamic service centres which enjoy the greatest uplift.

In tandem, the swelling of these two economic areas will bring about a golden age in Australian society. Through a combination of a surging economy, booming exports, intense foreign investment, high employment, rising corporate tax revenue, strong population growth and rapid technological change, the rise will not only enrich the broader Australian community, it will create a strong sense of momentum which will define the nation's international reputation for decades.

Unleashing an archipelagic powerhouse

With community affluence rising and self-confidence growing, national attention will increasingly become focussed upon tackling Australia's weaknesses and enhancing its natural strengths.

A surging economy and a growing immigration quota will help revitalise the nation's rapidly dating infrastructure and offset the consequences of its ageing and fertility challenges. Similar to how the original gold rushes in Victorian and Western Australia helped power each state's early development, soaring revenue and a growing influx of highly trained immigrants will assist with the funding and retrofitting of Australia's underperforming population islands.

The rise will also enable Australia to build upon its innate yet unreleased capabilities. Rapid technological change and rising foreign capital flows will increasingly unlock vast sections of Australian territory to economically viable development. Just as electricity and refrigeration opened up whole regions to greater settlement and employment, new resource extraction methods, automated transport systems and hardier food crops will revolutionise regional economic activity.

Interestingly, it will be these very side-effects which will help set Australia apart from much of the world during this century. As weaker nations wrestle with the economic disruptions that the rise causes, Australia's disparate economy will be growing into it. As they grapple with the social upheavals it creates, Australia's immigration programme will be gorging upon their instability. And as they struggle to feed, power, resource and service themselves, Australia's natural resource and service exporters will be making a fortune.

In other words, whereas the rise represents a combination of risk and reward for much of the global community, in Australia's case, it offers something else entirely: the chance to act outside the behaviour norms of other nations; the chance to become exceptional.

The great Mo

In Mark Roeder's instructive book about momentum,[347] Roeder detailed the findings of a study conducted by academics at the London Business School. In their exhaustive study, the researchers sought "to understand why share prices tended to continue in the same direction, and why, in the short run, you could make money simply by backing winners and selling losers".[348] What they found was that "once a stock gained positive traction (momentum) over a certain time period, it would continue to outperform well into the next time period".[349] Put another way, what they discovered was that once momentum was achieved, it not only had the capacity to generate exceptional future achievement, but if perpetuated, it also had the potential to create the perception of exceptionalism itself.

When considering the possibilities of Australia's long term future, it is this point which deserves the utmost attention.

As the established and developing worlds struggle with the perils of negative momentum, Australia will be experiencing the opposite. Bolstered by successive waves of positive momentum and a consistent record of high achievement, Australia will find itself in the position of being able to recast its place in the world as an exceptional nation on the rise. Whether it chooses to do so will boil down to how it responds to this opportunity. If it acts with the confidence of self-determination, Australia will be able to assume its place alongside history's greatest exceptional nations. If it conducts itself in the manner which has so far come to define it, it risks following the path of the world's wealthy, but ultimately dispensable, middle powers.

Obstacles to momentum

In spite of Australia's strong prospects of success, maintaining long term momentum is no easy thing. As much of the established world has demonstrated over the past century, careless or carefree management can easily evolve into a record of consistent incompetence, obliterating hard earned international reputations.

To ensure a similar fate doesn't become Australia's destiny, the nation's leaders will need to act proactively on the challenges which pose the greatest threat to its ability to establish and sustain momentum. Waiting "for the traditional spur of economic crisis to provide the impulse"[350] to act will not cut it if Australia desires the greater reward of exceptionalism. By acting before strategic obstacles manifest endemically, Australia can avoid being bogged down with their burdensome consequences later.

The greatest obstacles to Australia's ability to develop and sustain momentum this century will be:

- overcoming demographic weakness;
- avoiding a productivity slump;
- reversing the decline of responsive government;
- administering population growth; and
- managing its population islands.

In isolation, each of these interconnected obstacles has the potential to derail Australia's momentum this century. In combination, they could be far more devastating. As a result, if Australia wants to maximise its capacity for achievement before this century has concluded, each of these obstacles will need to be overcome.

Overcoming demographic weakness

The single greatest threat to Australia's momentum this century will be its weakening demography.

Historically, Australia has always been plagued by a mismatch between labour and opportunity. This has made the challenge of developing its territory a difficult one resulting in a heavy reliance upon foreign labour (immigration) to offset local shortages.

During this century, Australia's demographic dependency upon foreign labour will not disappear. In fact, it will intensify. The reason this will be the case is because Australia's population is ageing, demand for skilled and unskilled labour is rising, its fertility rate remains below replacement levels and its potential for population growth is expanding.

To ensure Australia manages these threats and opportunities successfully, it will need to make certain its demographic relief valves are functioning at full capacity. This will require continued community support for:

- organised and responsive global talent recruitment programmes;
- helping new Australians to become as productive as possible as soon as possible; and
- an immigration and settlement policy which is highly responsive to labour force needs.

Despite Australia's migration programme being an irreplaceable component of the nation's response to its demographic disadvantages, present community support for it remains unenthusiastic. Through a combination of declining liveability, elevated geopolitical tensions, the rise of self-selecting migrants and increasingly complicated integration challenges, public support for Australia's migration regime has begun to wane. While public support currently remains at manageable levels, a further decline could trigger a collapse in bipartisan support as has been the case overseas. Were this to occur, Australian efforts to sustain and build momentum would be severely jeopardised.

Even with an effective immigration programme in place, Australia's leaders can't deliver demographic mastery without a replenishing supply of aspiring citizens. As global migration demand intensifies as result of similar demographic challenges abroad, Australia will find its ability to attract and retain the world's most talented migrants under increasing pressure. Consequently, pioneering new ways to retain Australia's existing edge will be crucial.

Australia will also need to develop new ways to boost the productivity of the migrants it successfully attracts. A secondary side-effect of intensifying competition for migrants will be a decline in the productive value of the migrants which are sourced. With the wealthiest nations effectively bidding for those with the best technical and language skills, it is inevitable that the under-bidders will end up with migrants with productivity limitations. Whether it is substandard and unusable language skills, non-transferable education or the absence of higher learning, boosting their working capacity will be vital. As a result, nations such as Australia will need to devise new methods to improve migrant productivity.

Finally, Australia's immigration institutions will need to do a better job of serving the nations diverse and often divergent local economic, labour and demographic needs. Despite being a unified political entity, current migration policy favours the social and economic preferences of Australia's major economic centres over the unique needs of its less dominant regional centres. If Australia is to enable all of its economic regions to operate at their maximum capacity, the nation will need to devise a migration policy which has geographical flexibility at its heart.

Avoiding a productivity slump

Subpar or reversing productivity (especially multifactor productivity) also risks Australia's ability to build momentum this century.

There is an oft quoted saying:

> Productivity isn't everything, but in the long run it is almost everything. A country's ability to improve its standard of living over time depends almost entirely on its ability to raise its output per worker.[351]

In Australia's case, this insight holds special meaning due to the fateful mismatch between its economic potential and the modest size of its workforce. If Australia is to avoid missing this century's best economic opportunities, it will need to motivate the productive best out of every one of its potential workers. In order to achieve this Australia will need to:

- strategically improve its skills base;
- lift its participation rate; and
- empower its business class.

The rise offers countless opportunities for Australian businesses to export products and services and pursue dynamic careers. Yet just because the opportunity exists, doesn't mean Australians will be successful at securing them. In addition to Australia's natural investment hesitancy for non-Western markets, overseas consumer markets can also be notoriously hard to crack. Issues such as local customs, cultures, religions, domestic parochialism, trade access, politics and marketing can often scuttle the plans of a great Australian business man or woman. Overcoming the knowledge gap will be crucial for creating a "can do" culture and meeting expectations about Australia's export potential.

The failure to maximise Australia's participation rate also risks stalling the nation's momentum. With so many opportunities to grow Australia's economic and productive potential, the pressure upon employers to source sufficient labour will be extreme. To avoid wage outbreaks, skilled labour shortages and missed investment opportunities, efforts will need to be made to increase the overall size of the workforce and its operative potential.

Obliterating the one-size-fits-all approach to business policy will also be critical. As international trade expands and Australia's society increasingly transitions to global standards, Australian businesses will find themselves under intense pressure to compete and meet rising cost and service delivery expectations. Ensuring they have ultimate flexibility and authority to respond to these pressures will be paramount to their ability to maximise growth opportunities.

Reversing the decline of responsive government

Unresponsive government also threatens to undermine Australia's momentum this century.

While it is true to say that Australia has nearly always been well governed, it is not correct to state that it has been done so in a market sensitive, efficient or cost effective manner. Australia's present form of government is:

- outmoded;
- ineffectively structured; and
- underperforming.

Consequently, the nation as a whole is not primed to manage, let alone take advantage of, socioeconomic change this century. If the government sector is to avoid becoming Australia's most burdensome handicap, the way it presently operates will need to dramatically change.

In terms of being outmoded, Australia's sub-national borders are the problem. Whether we realise it or not, borders matter more than people think. As arbitrary lines dividing the Australian nation up, borders create complexity, entrench parochialism and encourage the provision of incentives which undermine the natural integration and growth of markets and communities. Accordingly, how effectively a nation's borders are laid out and how regularly they are updated to reflect changing markets plays a major role in determining how efficiently that nation is governed.

The ineffectiveness of Australia's local government structures is also preventing the nation from reaching its full potential. Whether it is the speed of planning approvals, the quality of urban design, the soundness of infrastructure investment or the efficiency of waste and rate collection, almost every municipality struggles to deliver a consistent quality of service. One of the key reasons for this is the fact that almost every municipality attempts to do these things in isolation, rather than pooling their resources for a more professional, better resourced and more cost effective outcome. Finding a way to improve performance will be vital to lifting service delivery outcomes and value for money.

Improving the ability of state governments to better manage their unique demographic and geographic qualities will also be necessary. Australia has one of the highest urbanisation rates in the world and its governmental institutions were never designed for managing this reality across an archipelagic settlement pattern. In order to maximise the nation's full socioeconomic potential, existing governmental structures will need to be reformed.

Administering population growth

If population growth isn't administered effectively, it will most certainly derail Australia's momentum.

According to the ABS, Australia is forecast to have a population between 36.8 and 48.3 million people by 2061.[352] Of the 13-25 million additional people forecast, the majority are expected to settle in Australia's five largest cities. This huge influx of new residents (foreign and domestic), commuters, workers and consumers will dramatically lift the economic capacity of Australia. However, it will also place enormous pressure on governments at all levels to maintain existing liveability standards, severely testing public support for population growth. How effectively governments meet community expectations against the scale of these changes will play a key role in determining whether population growth works as a positive or a negative influence on Australia's long term momentum.

Generally speaking, Australia faces two key tests in regard to its successful administration of population growth:

- effective infrastructure provision; and
- maintaining contemporary capital cities.

While there is naturally a multitude of other challenges, a successful response to these two challenges in particular will be essential for retaining public support for Australia's population growth model.

Funding infrastructure is a massive challenge due to the sheer costs involved. As no nation in the world has found a way to substantially reduce the cost of hard and soft infrastructure, its provision perpetually lags demand. Governments throughout Australia will not only need to adopt new ways to design and manage infrastructure provision, they will also need to pioneer new methods for funding and financing it.

Complicating this challenge of course will be the structural reality of Australia's cities. Having been built and designed in the 19th and 20th centuries, few former planners forecast the urban footprints and population densities which presently define Australia's cities. As a result, in order to maintain operational standards against the backdrop of rising population growth and rapid technological change, all of Australia's major cities will need to be retrofitted.

Managing its population islands

The final challenge which poses a serious threat to Australia's ability to sustain momentum this century is the complex management of its population islands.

Unlike Europe and North America, Australia's settlement pattern is not continental, it is archipelagic. As a result, maximising the full potential of its component parts as well as the linkages between them will require an entirely new way of thinking, governing and investing.

In addition to many of the above mentioned reforms, three additional policy innovations will be required:

- new performance evaluation tools;
- the empowerment of regional development; and
- innovative urban systems.

As demand for finite public and private resources intensifies over the decades ahead, decision makers will increasingly be interested in the operational performance of Australia's many and varied population islands. At present, information about these islands is of mixed quality with very little data available in comparable form. In order to fill this vacuum, new benchmarking tools which routinely compare and evaluate the performance of Australia's demographic and economic clusters will need to be developed. By pioneering this new method of data collection, Australia's investors and governmental decision makers will be better placed to identify, manage and engage with the nation's high achievers and mendicant underperformers.

Empowering Australia's various economic regions will also be vital to maintaining nationwide momentum. With so many population islands of differing need spread across such a vast distance, unique empowerment tools will need to be considered so that each island can meet its unique growth needs. Whether it is the development of geographically sensitive investment conditions, revised governance arrangements or the accelerated adoption of new technology, a bolder and more empowering approach to regional development will be required.

Finally, Australia will need to develop new management systems for administering the physical expansion and optimisation of its population islands. Land use change, soaring tourist numbers and population growth will each pose increasingly difficult governance and liveability challenges. As a result, innovative reforms to existing management systems will be required.

Forster's forecast

In 1786, Georg Forster a former passenger on board Captain James Cook's *Resolution* voyage corresponded about the future prospects of Australia. He surmised:

> New Holland, an island of enormous extent or it might be said, a third continent, is the future homeland of a new civilized society which, however mean its beginning may seem to be, nevertheless promises within a short time to become very important.[353]

Without knowing it, Forster's forecast about Australia's potential was prescient.

Over the 228 years which has followed, the tough prospect which Australia appeared to be has slowly transitioned to become one of the happiest, healthiest, freest, most tolerant, inclusive, peaceful and wealthiest nations on Earth. In a little over two centuries, a territory which was once judged to be the least habitable place for humanity has evolved to become one with the greatest lessons to teach it. As Forster boldly predicted, Australia has indeed become something "very important".

§

At the beginning of this book I discussed how the nation of England used its collision of opportunity to transform itself from a position of mediocrity to one of global hegemony. During its Imperial Century (1815-1914), England came to dominate nations like India and China with far larger populations and economies[354] simply by being smarter, luckier, better organised and more determined.

In this century, the Australian Century, Australia will also have an opportunity to achieve extraordinary feats. Whilst the pursuit of empire is definitely not the message of this book, the goal of Australia exercising disproportionate global influence is. Just as the United States dominates world affairs with less than five per cent of the global population, Australia too can make a lasting impression with its own limited demographics.

The rise of the global middle class is Australia's pathway to exceptionalism this century. The elements of circumstance, capacity and luck have fortuitously given it the opportunity to be bold. It now only needs the vision, organisation and motivation to see its full potential become a reality.

This century is our century. It's time to go and seize it.

7
A reform agenda for the Australian Century

Over the following pages are 15 essays illustrating the key reforms Australia must undertake in order to sustain momentum and build capacity in this Australian Century.

They discuss what we should do in order to successfully manage our greatest weaknesses as well as magnify our most important strengths.

Importantly, they encourage Australia's decision makers to be bold. They do so because exceptional nations cannot afford to be anything but.

As the rise of the global middle class washes over our wonderful country, I hope that our leaders will consider these ideas thoughtfully, debate them sensibly, and perhaps with good fortune, implement them quickly.

Best wishes

Asher Judah

Haussmann cities

Despite hosting Australia's greatest concentration of business and political leaders, deepest financial resources and highest concentration of urban planners, Yarra (Greater Melbourne) and Cumberland (Greater Sydney) are two population islands struggling to cope in the era of mass urbanisation.

Bedevilled by the complex challenges of population growth, rapid technological evolution and unrelenting socioeconomic change, each island is succumbing to the weight of rising transport demand and a worsening transport deficit.

Unless this situation is turned around soon, both risk losing their reputations as two of the world's most attractive and liveable places on Earth.

The transport conundrum in the era of mass urbanisation

Let's start with Yarra.

Yarra is Australia's second largest population island and is home to 4.17 million people living on a transport infrastructure base which has barely changed in the past 30 years. Currently serviced by a rail system which boasts more than 837km of track and over 218 stations, Yarra's railway network is the largest in Australia.[355] However, notwithstanding this impressive infrastructure platform, Yarra's network has barely grown during the past 50 years despite the population doubling and its physical boundaries exploding.

As a result of this mismatch between infrastructure investment and population growth, Yarra is now plagued with a capacity constrained rail network, overcrowded trains, lengthening commute times and the absence of rail services to the dozens of new suburbs springing up on its suburban fringe. Whereas decades ago Yarra's rail network was the envy of Australia, today it is considered to be last among equals.

Yarra's roads aren't much better either. Over the past four decades, billions have been spent on major projects like CityLink, East Link, Peninsula Link, the Ring Road and several freeway and arterial road upgrades, but city-wide congestion has worsened dramatically. In 2001, the average commute time in Melbourne was 27.2 minutes.[356] By 2006 it had risen to 30 minutes[357] and then three years later, it had jumped further to 36 minutes.[358] Through a mixture of under-funding, poor planning and inadequate attention to bottleneck management, the roads which service Yarra's major employment districts are amongst the nation's worst.

With Yarra's rail and road network struggling to keep pace with demand, it is evident that the island is facing a crisis. Without including funding for critical public works or disaster recovery, Victoria's infrastructure requirements up until 2024 are estimated to be approximately $70 billion,[359] a figure 40 per cent larger than the 2013-14 State Budget and more than eleven times the government's annual major infrastructure spend.[360] Therefore, in order to meet Victoria's major infrastructure needs in the medium term, the government will need to maintain infrastructure expenditure at a rate 27 per cent higher than the 2002-2012 average against the backdrop of rising road and bridge construction cost[361] and increasing demand for health, education, transport and law and order services. The simple fact is, this is not going to happen.

Sadly, Cumberland is in even worse shape.

Boasting a population of over 4.46 million people, Cumberland suffers from many of the same afflictions frustrating Yarra. Hosting fewer stations over a slightly smaller network,[362] Cumberland's train lines have also barely grown during the past 50 years despite its physical boundaries expanding like Yarra's and its population doubling. Complicating matters further is the fact that the land necessary for train line extensions into Cumberland's new communities has not been successfully reserved. As a result, the families moving into these areas can never expect to enjoy rail services.

With Cumberland's rail system in such anaemic shape, and its CBD positioned upon a harbour with limited access points, its road network has become increasingly important. Unfortunately, this is where the real tragedy rests for Cumberland. Poor design, combined with a systemic underinvestment in major roads, has resulted in a freeway system which cannot handle existing demand. Two lanes exist where four are required, the legacy road network is overused and space for road widening has not been set aside. Consequently, Sydney is now rated the seventh most congested city out of 123 studied across Australia, New Zealand, Europe, Russia, North America and South Africa.[363] Even travelling to Sydney's major employment hubs is a nightmare. Congestion on roads such as the M4, M5 and Eastern Distributor is no longer a peak-only phenomenon,[364] with the hours of congestion totally 13, 13.3 and 13.5 each day.[365] Disturbingly, "the morning peak on the M5 East now starts to build from 5am".[366]

Like Yarra, Cumberland's road and rail infrastructure network has failed to keep pace with demand. Unfortunately, unlike Yarra, Cumberland does not enjoy the benefit of long term land reservation. As a result, the cost of fixing Cumberland's infrastructure is higher and the task is much more politically complicated.

The diabolical transport dilemma

Over the next 47 years, Yarra's population is forecast to rise to 8.6 million people and Cumberland's to over 8.5 million.[367] These projections are based on current fertility and immigration forecasts which, in all likelihood, will change on the upside as a result of the nation's ageing demographic profile and tightening labour market outlook. Consequently, Australia's two largest population islands face a diabolical dilemma.

If they have no hope of affording the solutions to present day transport needs, and increased population growth and rising tourism visitations will result in even greater transport demand, how can either of these two islands expect to cope?

This is one of the great development challenges facing the established world today. How do modern population islands overcome multi-decade transport infrastructure deficits in the face of growing demand, finite finances and inadequate long term planning?

Oddly enough, the answer to this problem is simple, if not unconventional and controversial.

In order to fix the future, the world's major population islands must delve into the past.

Paris, 1852

During the early stages of Europe's industrial revolution, Paris was a mess. Having been ruled for centuries by leaders who did not value urban planning and infrastructure investment, Paris was ill suited to handle the dramatic technological, economic and social changes going on around it.

Each month, thousands of people migrated there to seek out new opportunities, and with each month that passed, Paris became further overwhelmed by the era's by-products of overcrowding. Crime increased, disease spread, living standards declined, and insurrection brewed. In short, Paris started to sink under the weight of its mass, and its foundations were incapable of preventing it from doing so.

Recognising that Paris' urban design was the source of its problems, Napoleon III appointed civic planner Georges-Eugène Haussmann to rectify Paris's situation. Haussmann was tasked with the responsibility of modernising the infrastructure base of Paris so that it would be able to function as a modern European city. With the full power of an authoritarian state behind him, and access to the funding necessary to address the city's problems, Haussmann was instructed to prepare Paris for the age of the railroad, gas lamp and residential toilet. In essence, Haussmann's job was to not only to help Paris cope with its current demands, but to prepare it for the economic and technological challenges its leaders could see coming.

Over the course of two decades, Haussmann achieved the seemingly impossible. Recognising that Paris was a medieval city struggling to function in an industrial era, he instituted the largest urban transformation since the Great Fire of London in 1666. During his tenure, Haussmann replaced 20,000 houses with 40,000, split and revolutionised the city's water and sewer systems, widened the streets to traffic, established multiple boulevards, constructed extra bridges to cross the Seine, built expansive gardens and grand public works, planted thousands of trees, and introduced new height limits to accommodate demand. At no time during his reign did he enjoy widespread community support. But when the job was complete and his vision realised, the people's faith was restored. Rather than being remembered as the destroyer of Paris (as many considered him to be at the time), he is now regarded as its saviour.[368]

By putting the city's long term future ahead of short term interests, Haussmann lifted living standards, improved mobility and connectivity, lessened the smell, improved airflow and lighting, eased overcrowding and congestion, lowered the disease threat and reduced city-wide violence. In short, he rebuilt the city's foundations to satisfy the demands of an era it was never designed to meet.

Today, Paris is the crown jewel of Europe and the world's most popular tourist destination. It is also one of Europe's best designed, with Haussmann's boulevards making the city accessible to both pedestrian and automobile alike. Put simply, Haussmann's visionary reforms made Paris' present day success possible. By ignoring the city's sacred cows and by focussing on the importance of utilitarian necessity, Haussmann saved Paris from its shortcomings by creating it a grand new future.

For modern day Australia, its two greatest islands sit at a similar crossroads. Whereas Paris was a medieval city which needed to evolve in order to survive the challenges of industrialisation, Yarra and Cumberland are two industrial era islands which must change in order to cope with the realities of mass urbanisation. In the absence of a natural tabula rasa or a gold meteorite landing on top of their states' respective treasury buildings, there is only one way either can hope to cope with their unwieldy transport conundrum – Haussmannisation.

Haussmannisation

In much the same way that Napoleon III resolved to clinically and controversially provide for the future needs of his community, so too must Yarra and Cumberland's leaders do the same for theirs.

No longer can each island afford to limp on with intermittent upgrades to a 19th century design model. Instead, they must both be re-imagined as futuristic regions capable of functioning on a level compliant with a 21st century vision. In order to accomplish such a change, an evolutionary leap in urban planning will be required.

Starting immediately, the sacred cows which have long been the bane of creative problem solving should be abandoned. Specifically, the community-wide benefits of compulsory acquisition and building demolition should be elevated beyond their present place as options of last resort to ones of first and most practical choice. Moreover, a more balanced revaluation of heritage policy around each island's many infrastructure chokepoints will also be necessary. By undertaking such reforms, both islands can begin the task of reconceptualising their road and rail networks beyond their current prism of immovable community infrastructure. While this approach is undoubtedly controversial, leaders in both islands must dedicate the time required to convince the public that there is simply no alternative to coping with the dilemma of mass urbanisation.

Through a mixture of compulsory acquisition (eminent domain) and building demolitions, both islands should seek to turn their inadequate road and rail corridors into the transport routes necessary to revitalise themselves. Where critical transport corridors are clogged or are deemed too narrow for the forecast demand of buses, trams, trains, trucks and private vehicles, they should be redesigned, widened, and if necessary, replaced. Much like the grand boulevards which allowed central Paris to blossom as an employment, residential and tourism magnet, Yarra and Cumberland should attempt to accomplish the same with their own. By combining the practicality of utilitarianism with the wisdom of modern urban design, both can rejuvenate their ageing transport networks whilst preserving that which has always made them great – good mobility.

§

For the Australian islands of Yarra and Cumberland, the challenge of how to respond to population growth, rapid technological evolution and unrelenting socioeconomic change goes to the heart of their current transport dilemmas.

On one hand, they can continue on their present trajectories and hope that good fortune will cut them a favourable break. Or, they can learn from history and give a bold and daring solution a chance to work.

21st century Australia is far from 18th century France, and its system of government is certainly no French autocracy. But whether or not Australia's are prepared to admit it, the problems their two major islands face today are no different to those faced by Paris 160 years earlier.

Napoleon III had the courage to concede that something radical had to be done and he made the decision to do it. Consequently, modern day Paris has his leadership to thank for setting them up for the success and liveability that they presently enjoy. Time will tell whether the same can be said for any of Australia's major island leaders. Let us hope, for our sake, that it can.

Embracing the latest Columbian exchange

When Christopher Columbus first visited the Americas in 1492, he had no idea he would end up triggering one of the greatest ecological events in human history. Entitled the Columbian Exchange, Columbus began a global transference which saw the biological commodities of two hemispheres exchanged on a scale and at a speed never before experienced. Animals, plants and new farming methods moved in both directions, and each hemisphere underwent several revolutionary changes.

Potatoes from Peru lifted living standards in Ireland;[370] capsicums from Mesoamerica improved vitamin and mineral intake in Asia;[371] cassava from the Caribbean transformed African diets; livestock, horses and grain crops revolutionised farming and mobility in the Americas; Asian sugar cane produced in South America lifted welfare standards in England;[372] and even tobacco from the Americas changed local currency exchange. Put simply, the Columbian Exchange transformed both hemispheres so fundamentally that they would never be the same again.

Of course, not all of these transformations were positive. Horrible diseases and involuntary migrations killed millions, and forced labour destroyed entire cultures. Moreover, the spread of pests undermined the benefits of the exchange with organisms like brown rats, zebra mussels and tumbleweeds devastating communities, economies and ecologies.

Yet despite these calamities, the socioeconomic changes brought about by the Columbian Exchange were profound. The rapid embrace of the unknown transformed the entire known world and the long term prospects for humanity forever.

In Australia's case, the results were also significant. By the time our part of the world was discovered, much of the biological transference had already occurred. As a result, a wide variety of crops and livestock were available to Australia's European settlers seeking to prosper in their new home. The suitability of the Australian landscape for sheep, cattle, wheat and sugar cane enabled the settlers to build one of the wealthiest trading nations on Earth.

At the turn of last century, Australia had one of the highest standards of living in the world. This is largely attributed to the enthusiasm that the nation had for incorporating foreign products into the Australian environment. If it were not for Australia's willingness to embrace the unfamiliar, it would never have been able to build the successful nation it is today.

Today's Columbian Exchange

Oddly enough, as one of the greatest beneficiaries of the original Columbian Exchange, Australia remains one of its poorest students. Despite the great transference being the foundation upon which Australian economic prosperity was built, most Australians remain apprehensive about its modern day equivalent.

In today's world, a second Columbian Exchange is presently underway in which new agricultural products are available for adoption much like they were 500 years ago. However, unlike those commodities being discovered in one hemisphere and transferred to another, today's commodities are being discovered in laboratories. They are called genetically modified organisms (GMOs).

GMOs are organisms such as food crops which have had their genes altered or enlarged so that they possess new characteristics. Through the process of genetic augmentation, new genes, which are either adapted from another organism or newly created, are inserted into the organisms. This allows the modified organism to exhibit new traits which are of benefit to their producer. Some valued traits include resistance to pests and diseases, different development and ripening speeds, production of larger fruits and seeds, higher nutrient levels, improved post harvest qualities, greater absorption of light, nutrients and water, better resilience for storage and transportation and stronger tolerance for climates previously deemed too dry, high, wet, cold, frost effected, saline or nutrient deficient. Such changes result in higher living standards, stronger productivity, better yields, accelerated cultivar development, increased farm incomes, lower input costs through less use of pesticides, herbicides, fertilisers and water and improved environmental outcomes.

In many ways, this process is a continuation of the selective breeding programmes which humanity has been performing since the Neolithic revolution 10,000 years ago.[373] But whereas in the past it would take several generations through a "hit and miss" approach to breed a sheep with finer wool or a corn stalk with bigger ears, in today's laboratories, the process can take years.[374] Most importantly, it can be done more accurately and be performed in a controlled environment.

While it is hard to imagine, genetically modified plants and animals are best conceptualised as new commodities being discovered on the mythical continent of Labratoria. Whereas 500 years ago the transference of biological products from one hemisphere to another revolutionised the farming methods of the time, in our era, the transference of genetically modified products from the laboratory to farmland is accomplishing the very same thing.

The fundamental difference, however, is that during the original Exchange, commodities were relocated to areas where the climate, altitude, soil quality and moisture levels were best suited to their natural production. In Labratoria's case, plant, meat, fibre, aquatic and forestry products are being developed to suit their planned relocation. Consequently, the latest incarnation of the Columbian Exchange has a far more significant role to play in transforming the agricultural productivity of the entire planet.

How Australia is missing out

Sadly for Australia's future, it is not embracing this agricultural revolution as enthusiastically as it should be.

Despite enjoying the successful fruits of a multi-century history of openness towards new ideas, new products and new science and technology, today's Australia is one where fear of the unfamiliar is turning it into an agriscience backwater. In fact, its approach to foreign ideas in agriculture is so bad that some states even ban the production of natural crops which are not native to Australia. Commercial release bans, suffocating regulations and state based marketing restrictions, unrelated to human health or the environment, all presently work to undermine Australia's embrace of the world's next Columbian Exchange. What's worse is that many of these approaches are not driven by science, but by political indecision and fear.

In total, only 0.7mha of Australian farm land hosts genetically modified (GM) crops.[375] This represents 0.0041 per cent of the total amount of land used for GM crops worldwide. South Australia and Tasmania presently have commercial moratoriums on GM crops. And to date, only two GM crops have been granted government approval for commercial production in Australia – GM cotton and GM canola.[376]

GM cotton

GM cotton has been grown commercially in Australia since 1996. It is Australia's first and best GM success story with 95 per cent of Australia's cotton crop now comprised of some form of GM cotton.[377] Over the past decade, cotton producers have reduced their insecticide use by approximately 80 per cent.[378] Moreover, since 2010 it has lifted farm income by $395 million – an average of approximately $180 per hectare.[379] In short, it has revolutionised Australian cotton production.

GM canola

GM canola has been in commercial production since 2008. However, it is only grown in New South Wales, Victoria and Western Australia as bans exist elsewhere. Approximately 8.2 per cent of Australia's canola crop is GM.[380] Since 2008, GM canola has increased incomes by $13 million – an average of approximately $73 per hectare.[381]

Other GM crops

Outside of these two crops, wheat, sugar cane, barley, pineapple, grape vines and white clover are currently in trial around Australia, several of which could also revolutionise production.[382] Australia also allows the use of GM products to complement domestic stock feed and processing. At present, GM soybean and GM canola are incorporated into the supply chain. Oddly enough, Australia farmers are allowed to buy GM products (stock feeds containing GM material)[383] but face restrictions in competing with them domestically. As a result, despite some modest progress on the GM front, Australia remains a GM transference laggard, especially compared to our major trade competitors.

The international scene

Since 1996, biotech crop hectares have increased 100-fold from 1.7 million hectares to 170 million in 2012.[384] The United States of America is the world's largest agricultural exporter and grower of GM crops.[385] It presently has 69.5mha of active GM crop land representing 41 per cent of total GM crop land in use.[386] Current GM crops include maize, soybean, cotton, canola, sugar beet, alfalfa, papaya and squash.[387] It also enjoys a near 90 per cent average adoption rate across all biotech crops.[388] Despite persistent claims that the United States is becoming anti-science, its agricultural community remains fervently pro-technology.

Twenty-eight nations across all other continents embraced the latest Columbian Exchange in 2012.[389] Brazil (36.6mha), Argentina (23.9mha), Canada (11.6mha), India (10.8mha), and China (4mha) all have vast tracks of land in GM crop production.[390] Combined, these five nations represent 51 per cent of global GM production farming a total of 87mha – 124 times Australia's share! As with the United States, the key driver behind these adoption rates has been results.

The race to embrace

Due to these well documented improvements, global interest in producing GM crops has exploded. As a result, 81 per cent of global soybean planting, 81 per cent of global cotton planting, 35 per cent of global maize planting and 30 per cent of global canola is now undertaken with GM crops.[391] Moreover, interest in GM potato, GM papaya and GM rice is also gaining ground.[392]

In 2012 for the first time, developing countries grew a greater share of global GM crops than industrialised ones – 52-48.[393] Unfortunately, Australia's position as a global GM backwater bodes poorly for its long term agricultural future. If attitudes to GM technology don't change quickly, Australia risks "missing out on the most beneficial technological advance the world has ever seen".[394]

What is at stake for Australia

The risks facing Australia in not embracing the latest Columbian Exchange are threefold:

- the loss of international competitiveness for agricultural producers;
- the inability to use GM technology to unlock vast sections of the continent to economically viable agricultural production; and
- the loss of the agricultural industry's best entrepreneurs and scientists.

International competitiveness

Agricultural markets are amongst the most competitive in the world. Therefore, it goes without saying that increasing productivity is essential to maintaining long term market share and growth. As demonstrated above, GM technology is continuing to play a larger role in determining where and how agricultural products are being produced. The best example of this is the vast tracts of land in the Americas and Asia which are presently being converted into GM crop production. Soon, if not already, this trend will spread to Australia's other trade competitors.

Whether the majority of Australians recognise it or not, it is only a matter of time before its place within the agricultural market is affected by its GM myopia. If Australia does not keep pace with its competitors, it risks losing market share to them.

Think about it. Countless scientific studies have established that GM foods available on the international market have had no effects on human health.[395] So if you can buy a product which is healthier, uses fewer pesticides and herbicides, has a longer shelf life and retails at a cheaper price, you would buy it wouldn't you? Of course you would. And so would much of the developing world. By not embracing the latest Columbian Exchange, Australia risks the permanent loss of competitiveness, markets and eventually, businesses, incomes and jobs.

Continental transformation

One of the most important features of GM technology is its ability to change the character of organisms. This is a tremendous power. It can be used to offset weaknesses, enhance strengths and create new potential in plants and animals. For a nation like Australia which is home to 5.9 per cent of the world's land territory, this could be a transformative power.

GM technology can be used to open up new areas to agriculture, lift yields in poor performing areas, extend produce storage life, counteract salinity, help grains fix their own nitrogen,[396] kill pests and disease and augment growing cycles. Imagine the economic benefits of being able to grow what we want, where we want, at the most economically efficient price we can. It would breathe new life into Australia's mendicant communities, unlock the tropical far north and the temperate south to investment, attract new investment to existing agricultural regions, return degraded land to production (especially in Western Australia), assist with the development of vertical farming, redefine the meaning of prime agricultural land and increase national income and economic activity.

Unlike many of the world's nations, Australia has a considerable natural endowment available to it in the form of traditional arable land. In fact, Australia has more than it will probably ever need. GM technology has the potential to transform vast sections of Australia's land mass into agriculturally productive territory.[397] Moreover, it can also ensure that large parts of the Australian environment remain undisturbed by lifting yields in current production areas. Whether it is to expand or protect, enhance or specialise, the possibilities for the continent are limitless.

The talent and brain drain

If Australia wishes to be amongst the most successful agricultural producer nations in the world, it must ensure it plays good host to the best available talent. The easiest way to achieve this is by creating a business and research environment which rewards hard work and encourages innovation. Yet if Australia fails to adopt the latest technological advances in the agricultural sciences field, it risks losing its best home grown entrepreneurs and researchers to nations where such technologies are being eagerly embraced. With field trials, commercialisation and regulatory oversight all geared against the next generation of agri-innovator, it is hard to see how Australia can remain successful at very much for very long.

Opponents of reform

Organised opposition to GM technology is one of the biggest challenges preventing Australia's embrace of the latest Columbian Exchange. At present, opposition to GM technology consists of anti-GM farmers, food advocacy organisations, dedicated organic farmers, environmental activists, religious organisations and even those opposed to the private ownership of life. When change faces multiple opposing arguments, the progression of reform is always harder. And that is what has happened in Australia.

Over the past 20 years, the opponents of GM technology have successfully stalled Australia's embrace of the Columbian Exchange through the promotion of emotive fear campaigns. Whether it is erroneous or unsubstantiated health risks linked to eating GM foods,[398] the release of dangerous GM organisms, the rise of herbicide resistant superbugs, secondary pests, diminishing natural enemies, destabilised insect ecologies, increased chemical and herbicide use or the loss of overseas consumer markets, these groups have effectively derailed Australia's GM embrace. Consequently, Australia is arguably over a decade behind its main competitors, exposing the nation's rural economy and research sector to serious economic risk and decline. How quickly Australia can catch up will depend upon how dramatically it chooses to change its GM policies.

Essential GM reforms

Australia presently trails the world in embracing the latest Columbian Exchange to the point that it now faces the very real possibility of becoming uncompetitive in the world's food, fibre, aquaculture and forest product markets. If Australia is to secure a growing market share in global agricultural markets, unlock the continent's full potential and become a GM technology leader, fundamental policy reform must take place. There are seven key areas where action must be taken:

- reducing the cost of GM commercialisation;
- accelerating GM trial approval;
- removing state GM moratoriums;
- creating a stable regulatory environment;
- lifting segregation tolerance levels;
- repelling GM labelling requirements; and
- boosting community confidence in GM products.

Reducing the cost of GM commercialisation

The cost of developing GM crops for commercialisation in Australia is an extremely expensive process, but it doesn't have to be. The main reason why Australia's GM commercialisation costs are so great is because its regulatory authorities are imposing too high a standard on risk elimination. As a result, only large and often foreign agribusinesses are capable of providing the data necessary to satisfy concerns.[399] While the threats posed by GM technology should not be underestimated, demands for zero risk are unnecessary. The enormous potential benefits far outweigh the remoteness of an adverse event occurring. Further, despite decades of GM trials occurring around the world, not one serious health risk has happened. If Australia's farmers, agriscience companies and consumers are to properly enjoy the benefits of the GM revolution, Australia's commercialisation regulations will need to be simplified.

Accelerating GM trial approval

The trial approval process in Australia is another policy area where changes must be made. At present, approval of trials in Australia lags international best practice. While it is reasonable to argue that Australia does not need to degrade its regulatory regime to keep pace with the developing world, no competitor can regain the lead by running slower than the competitors it is trailing. GM is an important area of science where mistakes should always be minimised. However, overregulation does not necessarily guarantee better outcomes when they are unreasonably complicated. A review of Australia's trial approval process should be conducted to determine why Australia's approval regime is underperforming the global standard.

Removal of state GM moratoriums

Just as a river system doesn't recognise state borders, seeds, animals and winds which carry GM products do not recognise them either. Yet despite this undeniable fact, several Australian states impose GM moratoriums which attempt to thwart the unpreventable from occurring.

According to the Australian Bureau of Agricultural and Resource Economics (ABARE), legislative bans on GMOs have been estimated to have cost the agricultural community over $3 billion. Moreover, existing GM bans have also ceded other important advantages such as market share and technology fees/royalties. Recovering historic financial losses associated with Australia's GM moratoriums will be impossible. However, future losses can be prevented if sensible policy reform takes place. All Australian states must begin lifting their GM moratoriums to ensure Australia's agricultural community is not further undermined by poor scientific reasoning and reactionary scaremongering.

Creating a stable regulatory environment

Bans on GM research and a variety of related practices are undermining the ability of Australian researchers and research companies to attract local investment. Ongoing political uncertainty in regard to GM policy issues and regulation represents a unique form of "sovereign risk" which must be rectified. As research in the GM field takes many years to bear fruit, researchers require a stable regulatory environment in order to conduct their work. At present, such an environment does not exist in Australia as there is little consistency in policy across states or political parties. If Australia is to develop a profitable, sustainable and expansive GM technology sector, regulatory stability must be provided.

Lifting segregation tolerance levels

Australia's ruthless approach to self-discipline and product purity is also an area of concern. The nation's AP (adventitious presence)[400] tolerance levels for the segregation of GM and non-GM crops are presently between 0.5-0.9 per cent. This compares to the majority of Australia's trading partners having official AP tolerances between 0.9 per cent and five per cent.[401] Australia's super-low standard adds costs to the segregation process and undermines consumer confidence when a breech occurs. When considering how we should position ourselves in global GM markets, what is good for the goose is good for the gander. Australia need not create a rod for its back if its competitors are not imposing the same requirements on themselves.

Repelling GM labelling requirements

One of the most effective ways to undermine community confidence in GM brands is by imposing unnecessary labelling requirements upon products which contain GM products. Consequently, insisting upon labelling requirements for foods with GM contents should be repealed. While the requirement to inform the consumer sounds perfectly reasonable, in reality, it imposes a higher labelling standard on one type of food product which does not exist for its competitors. It also adds costs and complexity to the process of bringing GM products to market. Despite the fact that GM food is indistinguishable from non-GM foods, opponents of GM technology still persist with tough labelling laws to impair its appeal. The best way to grow Australia's GM product marketplace is to provide a level playing field between it and its competitors.

Boosting community confidence in GM products

The final reform which must be undertaken is a concerted effort to destigmatise GM products as is presently underway in China.[402] In Wuhan, for example, the government is serving porridge made from GM rice to the public to alleviate community concern. Operating alongside a local education campaign, the nation's scientists and political leaders are working closely with the community to change public sentiment and increase support. The Australian community on the other hand remains apprehensive about GM technology still. In order to turn around such perceptions, a well planned marketing campaign designed to change minds and educate the public should be put into effect. GM technology tours and product tasting road shows which include farmers, scientists and retailers should form the basis of such an effort.

§

Over the past 10,000 years, humanity has almost continuously laboured to improve the quality, adaptability, variability and yield of its agricultural production. This process has transitioned from ancient domestication techniques, to the first Columbian Exchange, to the British Agricultural Revolution,[403] through to the adoption of mechanisation and the Green Revolution.[404] Wherever one looks, humanity has nearly always strived to lift its agrarian operational performance in the pursuit of improved nutrition, living standards, life spans, incomes and poverty alleviation.

In today's world, the latest Columbian Exchange is the successor to this important legacy. While many of its concepts are new, its fundamental character remains the same – it is the next revolution in human agricultural affairs.

As a nation which has largely avoided the benefits of the latest Exchange, Australia is at a critical decision point in regard to its agricultural future. On one hand, it can follow the path trail blazed by Europe, turning its back on the application of the best science in its paddocks, fields and stockyards. Or, it can follow those nations in the Americas which have chosen to put the power of modern scientific achievement to use in all of their agricultural sectors.

For the past 20 years, Australia has chosen to have a foot in both camps, simultaneously conducting research into GM technology whilst effectively sabotaging its commercial application. This situation cannot be permitted to continue. Too much time has already been lost as a result of Australia remaining a GM backwater. The time has come to embrace the revolution.

Resettling migration policy

Across Australia today, different regions are experiencing vastly different immigration pressures. In the major cities along Australia's east and south east coasts, community opposition to immigration is on the increase as a result of inadequate planning and investment. Conversely, in the less populated urban centres in Tasmania, South Australia, the Northern Territory and regional Western Australia, communities are more open to the idea of increasing migration to stimulate the economy and help address local labour shortages. As a result, the Australian community holds no united position on what to do about immigration policy. Despite the external appearance of being a congruent continental country operating under a unified immigration policy, Australia is in fact, a disparate archipelagic one with hundreds of distinctive immigration needs.[405]

At the time of federation, the immigration needs of various parts of Australia were also in conflict. The workers in the burgeoning manufacturing hubs of Melbourne and Sydney were fearful of foreign labourers challenging their job security and standard of living.[406] Conversely, the underdeveloped and labour poor north felt the opposite: they desperately required foreign labourers to work their farms and manage coastal transportation.[407] At the time of this disagreement, political and economic power rested indisputably in the south east. Consequently, while the economic priorities of

Australia's various communities differed, the political priories of the nation's south east mattered more. Within nine months of Australia's first federal election, royal assent was granted for the *Pacific Island Labourers Act 1901* (Cth) and the *Immigration Restriction Act 1901* (Cth), formalising what would become the White Australia policy. Not only did these Bills damage our long term international reputation, but they also torpedoed the next 70 years of economic development for much of northern Australia.

Over one hundred years later, Australia finds itself at a similar crossroads. The mining, energy and agricultural districts which crisscross much of the nation are in desperate need of migrants to infuse their workforces and fuel their business development. Equally, dozens of Australia's urban centres are atrophying as a result of long term population, economic and social decline. Yet just like in 1901, Australia's larger and more dynamic population centres are dictating too much of the nation's immigration agenda at the expense of the nations smaller hubs of activity.

If Australia is to successfully manage its various demographic, economic and labour force challenges, it will need to change the way immigration policy is determined. There are two reforms which must be undertaken:

- introduce a statutory authority to determine the national immigration intake; and
- partially devolve immigration powers to state control.

Introduce a statutory migration authority

Australia's annual migration numbers are currently determined by the Commonwealth based upon advice from the Department of Immigration and Border Protection. This process has served Australia well for numerous decades, but in recent years, government decisions regarding migration numbers have become increasingly disrupted by political imperatives which directly undermine the nation's long term interests. Indeed, there is no better example of this in the past ten years than when Australia's net overseas migration rose to 315,700 in December 2008 and then declined 47 per cent to 166,800[408] in reaction to public policy clashing with perceived community hostility. While it is fair and reasonable for our elected leaders to respond to genuine community concern about current policy settings, the difference between strong and weak leadership is whether decision-makers are prepared to defend policies which advance the national interest. In the case of the 2008-10 "Big Australia Debate", short term populist politics won and the greater national interest lost. Since then, similar debates have occurred in regard to both 457[409] and 855 visas.[410] In both cases, business and community confidence in Australia's immigration regime suffered. If the nation is to successfully manage its many and varied immigration related challenges over the decades ahead, strategic policy setting must not be allowed to become a political football.

The best way for Australia to establish a more durable immigration policy is by changing the way it is set in the first place. Over the course of Australian history, many of the nation's most contentious and politically charged policy decisions have been placed in the hands of learned experts. Australian monetary policy being set by an independent Reserve Bank of Australia (RBA) is one example. On the vexed issue of migration, "a non-negotiable plank of Australia's economic policy",[411] a similar approach should be adopted.

To that end, the Commonwealth should create a new statutory authority which:

- evaluates national, state, local and industry labour needs;
- decides when special migration opportunities warrant adjustments to cap and queue mechanisms;
- administers visa policy;
- steers the nation's migration policy response to the three P's (population, participation and productivity);
- recommends an annual migration intake range; and
- maximises the economic and social benefits for the people of Australia from all forms of temporary and permanent migration.

The new authority should be administered by a board comprised of high quality, independent and knowledgeable experts who are capable of overseeing the authority's extensive responsibilities. Furthermore, it must also be accountable to the Parliament, make half-yearly appearances before the House of Representatives Standing Committee on Economics, and issue regular statements on immigration policy. Finally, the authority must maintain formal and informal contact with the Minister for Immigration and their Department. Just as the RBA makes major economic decisions removed from the sphere of politics; a suitably designed statutory authority can start to do the same for immigration.

Partially devolving immigration policy to state and territorial control

The second stage of reform necessary to modernise Australia's immigration system is to partially devolve immigration powers back to the second tier of government. As highlighted above, due to Australia's size and economic disparity, the nation's respective states and territories face vastly different immigration pressures. Whereas some areas are struggling with the pace of population growth, others are desperate for it. In order to better address these disparities, demographic and labour force determinism should be partially returned to the continent's regional governments.

Prior to federation, Australia's separate colonies enjoyed absolute control over immigration policy. Because each was considered a sovereign entity, they were all able to directly manage their response to local demographic, economic and labour force pressure. However, under Australia's current immigration arrangements, the states and territories have no authority over immigration policy – having been relegated to an advisory and sponsorship (nomination) role only.[412] In order to restore greater immigration control to the states and territories within the confines of existing constitutional boundaries, deferential decision making reforms should be implemented.

During 2012-13, Australia's annual migration programme provided places for 190,000 people to migrate to Australia.[413] This number was split between skilled migrants (129,250), family migrants (60,185), and special eligibility migrants (565).[414] Under the reform proposed above, a partial devolution of immigration policy would work as follows.

Australia's new statutory authority would announce an annual migration intake range for the financial year 2014-15, say around 200,000240,000 places. The lower figure (200,000) would represent the minimum national intake permitted for 2014-15 and the 40,000 places above this amount would represent the optional maximum the states and territories would be able to expand into should they so choose. For example, if the Western Australian Government decided that it was capable of absorbing more than its allocated share of the national minimum intake, it could lodge a submission with the authority requesting an additional quota of the optional 40,000 places prior to the commencement of the immigration year. Such a submission would detail how that additional quota should be allocated and where they would be settled, for example, skilled migrants vs family migrants and Perth vs regional WA. In the event that a state or territory government concluded that a slower pace of population growth was required, it could choose to decline the opportunity for optional places of its own volition.

By combining such an approach with Australia's existing Specified Regional Area restrictions (a visa class [475] which binds the worker to a geographic area) and the best elements of the existing 457 visa programme, all of the states and territories would be better able to manage their pace of growth and unique labour force challenges. Those states desiring a slower pace would be able to do so by accepting a modest yet significant number of new Australians. And those which choose to grow faster would have the option of boosting their baseline migrant intake. A mechanism such as this would ensure that the bigger states would be able to moderate their rate of growth without overriding the migration needs of those seeking the opposite. Put another way, it is an archipelagic solution to an archipelagic problem.

§

Overall, Australian immigration policy makers need to better understand that despite the nation being a continental one, its immigration needs are uniquely archipelagic. As a result, in order to meet the various demographic, economic and labour force challenges facing Australia this century, the nation must ensure its immigration system is capable of managing all of them in their complexity. The reforms outlined above will help to remove politics from policy and centralisation from incongruence. Consequently, it will give Australia exactly what it needs to meet its migration challenge – absolute flexibility.

Pioneering an archipelagic abacus

Despite Australia's predilection for governing itself as though it is a congruent nation spread evenly across a vast continental territory, Australia is, in fact, a disparate, waterless archipelago comprised of small population islands centred around our largest cities and major economic centres. Australia's misapprehension about its true nature is a major problem because it directly undermines the quality of its data collection and subsequent decision making.

The majority of Australia's data collection methods are guided by historic planning decisions and artificial physical boundaries such as roads and rivers. Put another way, they are based upon Australia's various state and municipal borders. While this traditional approach has served us well historically, it no longer provides useful information to decision makers. The use of these borders in data collection results in the generation of information which too broadly generalises Australia's demographic and economic reality. Rather than providing an accurate snapshot of how Australians live, work and generate economic output, it misconstrues how people and markets interact.

The best example of this relates to Australia's economy. At present, Australia's 18 largest cities are responsible for around 80 per cent of our GDP and 75 per cent of all jobs.[415] Yet there is no regular collection of data relating to Australia's cities' economic output, tax contribution, employment market or trade balance despite their primacy to the national economy. Definitions of cities and urban boundaries vary from state to state, non-citizen residents are not accurately counted in population estimates, and employment information is too broadly presented. Instead of providing an accurate picture of the economic health of Australia's most productive economic regions, the statistics which are collected are bundled alongside data from the rest of their state or territory. As a result, the data which is made available to decisions makers is diluted with unrelated information.

Where this becomes a major problem for Australia is the fact that these distortions shape the way its leaders make decisions. What you measure is what you focus on. Consequently, if your data collection is determined by out of date parameters such as anachronistic state borders, and technology and population growth has made those borders meaningless, than the answers you collect are unlikely to be useful for good decision making. Unfortunately for the decision makers of Australia, this is exactly what each level of government does.

If Australia is to perfect a demographic and economic growth model which meets the unique needs of its archipelagic settlement pattern, the ability to glean accurate information about its most important components will be essential. Consequently, the nation will need to reconceptualise the parameters by which it collects data. There are three key areas of reform which will be required. These are:

- cities;
- river basins; and
- exclusive regions, economic clusters and supply chains.

Cities

Despite Australia's proud rural history and romanticised notions about non-urban living, Australia's future will increasingly rest upon the productive health of our cities. By 2050, Australia's cities will come to represent the undeniable heartbeat, brain function and digestive system of Australian society.

Yet despite their centrality to Australia's health, cities continue to hold a position of secondary importance in terms of data collection and decision making. At present, no Australian government, local council or statutory authority collects continuous, comparable or definitive economic or demographic data on our major cities. Instead, what is collected is a shallow and confusing amalgamation of often infrequent data based upon ambiguous metropolitan and non-metropolitan divisions, physically congruent but economically disconnected municipalities, and economically meaningless state borders. Rather than providing data for a 21st century government to make forward thinking decisions, they are instead generating misleading information based on 19th century modelling. As Australia progress further into this century and cities continue to assume a more elevated place in all of Australia's affairs, the inadequacy of existing data collection methods will increasingly become evident.

In order to avoid such a situation occurring, government agencies need to reconceptualise the parameters upon which they collect data. For starters, state governments should be able to track on a biannual basis, economic output, employment data (local and foreign), population shifts (citizen, resident and tourist), workforce movements (travel to work areas), transport and logistical functionality, economic, research and cultural infrastructure, communicative ability and physical changes of all economically significant cities and urban regions, regardless of location (split borders or not). This information should also be able to be broken down into several component parts such as Central Business Districts (CBD), Capital City Zones (CCZ) significant economic clusters (industrial, trade, service, education, research and medical), critical logistic corridors (intermodal hubs, ports, airports and freeways) and geographic regions of rapid economic or population change (Gold Coast).

By collecting such information, governments will be able to improve the way they plan, manage, invest and encourage economic and social development. Moreover, decisions makers within the public, private and non-profit spheres will be better able to set budgets, manage political debates, foresee challenges, establish investment priorities, treat mendicant urban areas, develop policy and plan community growth. Rather than making decisions based on antiquate, abstract and community wide information, decisions will instead be based upon the economic and demographic realities of Australia's most important socioeconomic assets.

River basins

Another area where data collection remains inadequate relates to Australia's economically and environmentally critical river basins. At present, a very significant amount of Australia's agricultural production is generated within the influence of its most significant river basins. These regions in turn help sustain (directly and indirectly) hundreds of thousands of jobs, generate billions of dollars of economic output and provide food and water for millions.

As with Australia's cities and major urban centres, state governments do not readily report on the performance of river basins. Instead, the information which they do gather represents a sectional snapshot of the river components which they independently manage. Where this becomes a problem for Australia stems from the fact that river basins cannot be accurately assessed or managed according to artificial border demarcation. Issues like river functionality, flow, health, pollution, salinity, subsurface flows, infrastructure, catchment rainfall and productivity have little to do with lines on a map. As a result, when it comes to making decisions regarding our river basins, the information provided and responsibilities attached to them do not align with the natural realities of their operability. Consequently, critical basin-wide decisions in the areas of finite resource allocation, infrastructure investment, water rights, water trading, environmental flows and regulated water management practices are poorly made.

In order to improve the quality of outcomes in this area, the type of data collected should be revised in order to reflect environmental boundaries, rather than artificial ones. Moreover, the information collected and definitions used should be standardised across all borders. By reforming data collection in this fashion, all Australian decision makers would be presented with the same set of facts, allowing them to better assess the value and needs of the river basin, invest in its potential, and manage its long term health. In addition to providing comparable information on similar forms of natural infrastructure, basin abusers would no longer be able to hide behind the artificiality of political borders; investment decisions along state borders would be harder to avoid; overall river health would become a more collective responsibility; and 'whole of basin' judgments would become more likely amongst public, private and community stakeholders.

Exclusive regions, economic clusters and supply chains

The final area which requires an overhaul of data collection methodology is that which covers those areas of critical importance to key Australian economic industry sectors. Despite the vast majority of economic activity occurring within Australia's major cities, there are several exclusive regions and economic clusters within Australian territory which make exceptional contributions in output, taxation and employment. Whether it is a mining district like the Pilbara, a strategically vital energy hub like Bass Strait, or even a major transportation node like Sydney Airport, these key regions all make disproportionately high contributions to Australia's success.

Unfortunately, despite their strategic value to the broader economy, the information is often irregularly collected, hard to interpret, overtly complex or lost in obscure reports far from the public eye. Moreover, their direct relationship with key supply chains such as a rail and road networks (shipping ore to port), or the co-dependence they have upon neighbouring industry (logistics companies based in the vicinity of an airport or port), is not presented in a format which is easily understood by the broader community. Where this becomes a problem for Australia and indeed the regions themselves, is that if the strategic value and requirements of these regions is not fully appreciated, then the tax regime, regulatory environment and investment attention they require to perform at their full potential may not be put in place.

If governments, investors, key stakeholders and the broader community are to properly appreciate the importance of these regions to our living standards and overall economic prosperity, then the information which demonstrates what they need must be better spelt out. The best way to accomplish this is by routinely reporting on their economic, taxation, employment, logistics and export/import activity. By providing a timely reminder of their functional wellbeing and the importance of their vitality to the broader community's, then these sectors will be in a better position to receive the public and private attention they deserve.

§

Overall, the collection, presentation and utilisation of data remains a critical component of how societies plan and manage their changing circumstances. Consequently, if the system by which Australia gathers data is poorly designed, or the way it is presented is ineffectively communicated, than the quality of its decision making is undermined.

As Australia makes its way through the twenty first century, the margin of error for poor planning and strategic management will increasingly become smaller. Therefore, it is imperative that it gets the parameters of data collection and information distribution right.

Maximising the skilled workforce

Achieving Australia's productive potential in the 21st century will require it to become more effective at maximising its inherent strengths. One area where this will need to occur is in regard to the participation rates of its highly skilled and experienced workforce.

At present, too many of Australia's workers are not utilised to their maximum potential. This shortfall in capacity manifests in three distinct ways. First, they retire from the workforce early due to their inability to find suitably flexible employment; second, they become devoted full time parents because the financial benefit of returning to work is weak; and third, there is very little compunction for the unemployed or moderately impaired[416] to re-enter the workforce.

As Australia's population ages over the coming decades, the pressure to address the nations worsening workforce situation will intensify,[417] as will the social and economic side effects associated with the underutilisation of its workforce. In order to rectify this, new policy approaches aimed at unlocking Australia's workforce will be required. Three key reforms should be considered:

- providing greater flexibility and incentives for employers to employ and retain older workers;
- encouraging mothers back into the workforce without compromising parenting standards; and
- restoring genuine mutual obligation requirements upon the unemployed and DSP recipients.

Employment flexibility for a downshifting generation

Over the next 36 years, the number of Australians aged 65 and above will nearly triple to over eight million people.[418] As this population cohort increases in size, and its health and activism levels compared to today's cohort improve, the number of Australians desiring employment conditions which accommodate their evolving work-life aspirations will rise.[419] Unfortunately, due to the present rigidity of Australia's workplace relations system, it is very hard for employers to retain existing staff who want to downshift their employment hours, employ older workers at wages which are sustainable or provide reasonable workers compensation income replacement.

If Australia is to maximise the productive potential of its most experienced and knowledgeable generation, as well as help businesses better match their workforces with an ageing consumer market, government at Commonwealth and state levels will need to give employers greater flexibility. In doing so, governments should review existing worker compensation schemes and reintroduce individual contracts for businesses who would like to employ older Australians on more flexible conditions, but can't. Such reforms should allow workplace assessments to be conducted based upon ability, not age, and ensure that maximum flexibility is provided in regard to minimum working hours and shifts outside of the traditional 9-5 work day.

Australia's exorbitant penalty rates also make it harder to offer older Australians the choice of working on weekends. While for many Australians the weekend period remains sacrosanct, for those who are unemployed or semi-retired, it remains a viable employment day which holds a different degree of personal importance. One way Australia could reduce the financial impact of penalty rates on businesses and offer employment opportunities for older Australians would be to abolish penalty rates for Australians based on age. By doing so, the attractiveness of employing older Australians would rise without compromising minimum wage standards for other Australians. If successful, age-based wages could extend to other days of the week as currently exists for workers aged between 11 and 20.

Childcare choice for Australia's working mothers

Another way Australia can maximise its skilled workforce is by encouraging mothers back into the workplace without compromising parenting standards or the functionality of the Australian family unit. "In November 2011, there were 524,300 mothers in Australia with a child less than two."[420] Over two-thirds were employed while they were pregnant[421] and many had either university, vocational or Year 12 or equivalent level education.

Many of these mothers make the highly valued choice to stay at home either full time or part time to raise their children and help manage their households. This is an important choice and one which should always be valued. However, while this is important, a large number are prepared to re-enter the workforce if the cost of child care is available at a more affordable price. Unfortunately, as a result of Australia's high wages and restrictive workplace practices, such options are not available at a price the average family can afford. Consequently, Australia has a female workforce participation rate 'substantially lower' than that found in many other OECD countries.[422]

The best way to deliver improved employment choice to mothers who wish to re-enter the workforce is by changing the way they receive childcare support from the government.[423] At present, parents receive a 50 per cent rebate to offset the cost of placing their child in childcare up to $15,000. Some are also eligible for childcare benefit payments. This approach, whilst institutionalised, is costly, inefficient and inflexible. Moreover, it is a perfect example of a "one size fits all" model which doesn't do enough to provide its recipients with genuine choice.

An alternative approach would be for parents to receive the government rebate as a cash voucher they can use for a range of authorised means. Some examples could include paying their parents a small stipend to look after their grandchildren during the day or pooling their vouchers with other parents to employ a dedicated nanny to care for their child at their place of residence. In both cases, parents would be able to decide:

- how much of their voucher they choose to spend on each service;

- add their own discretionary funds to top up the amount dedicated to childcare;
- choose their preferred child care hours; and
- avoid the built in costs and overheads which the present system currently consumes, such as business profit, regulated work hours and facility hire.

By offering greater choice for parents seeking more affordable childcare solutions, the government can directly increase flexibility for mothers eager to return to the workforce. By doing so in such a fashion, policy makers can help lift female participation rates without needing to increase government expenditure in the process.

Restoring mutual obligation for the unemployed and moderately impaired

The final reform necessary to unlock the Australian workforce's productive potential is the restoration of mutual obligation requirements upon the unemployed and those who are moderately impaired. As of December 2013, Australia is home to 722,000[424] unemployed people (of which approximately half are classified as non-job seekers who are "not necessarily required to look for work")[425] and 825,000 people on a Disability Support Pension (DSP) of which 350,000-400,000 could go back into the workforce with the right support.[426] In both cases, reforms can be made to the welfare system to reduce these numbers without compromising the important principle of compassion.

In regard to the unemployed, after the election of the Rudd Government in 2007, several significant changes were made to the welfare system which wound back the previous government's mutual obligation policies. These included:

- Doubling the time period a person may remain unemployed before they must commence *WftD* activities.

- Weakening the obligations upon Parenting Payment recipients to find employment.
- Shifting the focus towards skills training at the expense of "work first".
- Softening the penalty regime for activity failures, including:
  - Replacing income suspension with "no show, no pay" penalties.
  - Greater discretion for the Job Network to report "participation failures".
  - Softening the enforcement provisions behind the eight-week non-payment period rule.
  - Creating hardship provisions to alleviate the impact of the serious failure penalties.[427]

Further refinements were also made under the Gillard Government.

If Australia is maximise its full labour force, it will need to ensure that as many people as possible are engaged in work they are capable of undertaking. The best way to do that is by reversing these policy changes.

A second area Australia has great potential to expand its workforce is through reforming the obligations placed upon Australians who receive DSPs. Over the past three decades, the number of Australians on DSPs has grown 280 per cent (well above disability growth numbers across the community).[428] With so many Australians on DSPs, huge opportunities exist for expanding the available labour force. Two reforms should be considered.

First, mutual obligation requirements for DSP recipients should be modified to ensure that those capable of returning to work do so. According to Mission Australia, over 200,000 DSP recipients who experience mental health issues could return to work with the right assistance.[429] As a result, new assistance measures should be provided and their DSP eligibility requirements amended to encourage them to begin looking for work. Second, the government should modernise DSP eligibility requirements and compel all existing recipients to reapply. By performing this reform, the government can better identify those who have the capacity to return to work in some form as well as shake loose those who should be on another form of welfare assistance (preferably one with greater mutual obligation requirements). While such an approach will undoubtedly be controversial, the experience in the United Kingdom has seen 750,000 DSP equivalent recipients being found to have capacity for work with a further 878,000 choosing not to reapply.[430] It is entirely possible Australia could enjoy comparable labour force benefits if it chooses to manage its DSP arrangements in a similar fashion.

§

Overall, if Australia is to make the most of the opportunities this century presents, it will need to ensure its skilled workforce is as liberated and engaged as possible. By introducing greater workplace flexibility, increasing employment choice for stay-at-home mothers, and by compelling underemployed workers to look for work, Australia can ensure its full potential is not left underutilised.

Upgrading our foreign intuition

Understanding the complex internal cultures of the world's nation states will be crucial to our ability to become a more diversified trading nation this century. With global consumer markets forecast to explode in size over the coming decades, especially in the area of internationally traded services, nations with the most intuitive understanding of foreign cultures will be the best placed to successfully penetrate them.

As a nation that is home to over 300 different ethnic groups, speaking hundreds of different languages and practising thousands of different customs, Australia enjoys a unique advantage few nations possess. However, just because a large percentage of Australia's population was born overseas, practises distinctive customs, or speaks a language other than English,[431] doesn't mean it is a service and product export machine ready to go. Trade, especially international trade, is infinitely more complicated than that.

If Australia is to successfully secure its fair share of global markets beyond commodities, tourism and tertiary education, its future entrepreneurs and workforce will need to possess a deep and intuitive understanding of the needs, aspirations, cultural values, customs, politics and market preferences of the overseas markets they wish to secure.[432]

Traditionally, the method for achieving this national ambition has been pursued by teaching foreign languages in our primary and secondary school systems. Unfortunately, while this ambition has been well intended, it has also been an abject failure. This situation is best illustrated by the nation's foreign language enrolment rates. In 2000, 767,281 students were enrolled in a Chinese, Indonesia, Japanese or Korean language programme of some kind. By 2008, the number of students enrolled in Year 12 studies of these languages was 11,654.[433] Of those who studied the languages of our first and third most important trading partners, China and South Korea, less than five per cent studying Chinese came from a non-Chinese background and no one studying Korean came from a non-Korean background.[434] Similar trends also exist for other Year 12 LOTE subjects such as Japanese, Indonesian and Hindi where the majority of students have an ethnic relationship with the language. Put simply, rather than increasing the depth of our nation's foreign culture knowledge base, our LOTE programmes are only succeeding at helping students retain their parents' first language.[435] As a result, LOTE programmes as they currently operate are failing to accomplish their primary goal – to broaden Australia's language skills and help the nation become a more diversified trading nation.

If Australia is to achieve its full potential in this area of critical skill development, its methods for educating children will need to change. Outlined below are two reforms which should be considered.

Cultural education

Understanding the sharp and subtle differences between Australian culture and foreign ones is essential to Australia's ability to become a more dynamic, insightful and responsive trading nation. Generally speaking, there are two areas where Australia's knowledge of foreign cultures needs to be further developed.

The first and least discussed area is that of the established world. While irresponsibly ignored in trade documents such as the *Australia in the Asian Century* White Paper, the consumer markets of the established nations in North America, Europe and North East Asia represent some of the most promising opportunities for Australian product and service export. Over the next few decades, the number of middle class and upper class consumers within these markets is forecast to grow substantially. This fact, combined with the market access that Australia already enjoys as a result of functioning free trade agreements makes them prime targets for increased trade and investment attention. Consequently, it is vital that more Australians become familiar with the subtle cultural differences between Parisians and Marseillais, Floridians and Hoosiers, and Mancunians and Brummies.

Understanding the infinite complexity of the developing world will also be critical to Australia's efforts to diversify its existing trading patterns. Consequently, Australia can no longer engage with the developing world "based on old information and outmoded prejudices."[436] More than 2.5 billion people are forecast to enter the middle class within the developing world by 2030, resulting in the creation of thousands of diverse and complex consumer markets. At the same time that this is occurring, new technology, social freedoms, personal wealth and women's rights will each be challenging the traditional values, the importance of hierarchy, and religious and racial relationships which have defined these nations for millennia. These markets will be extremely difficult for the enterprising outsider to understand and even harder to penetrate. Ensuring that Australians have an appreciative understanding of the national histories, present day tensions, internal social diversity and regional and national economic realities of these markets will be critical to their ability to succeed in business with them.

In order to boost Australia's knowledge base of these vastly different, but essential market opportunities, existing primary and secondary school subjects on foreign culture will need to be modified to reflect the aims of Australia's redefined challenge. Ideally, foreign culture subjects should be taught throughout secondary school with a strong emphasis on the day to day life, living standards, diet, cultural customs, technological standards, history of engagement with Australia, colonial history, existing institutions (or lack of), trading patterns, working week parameters, economic outlook, and short and long term prospects of Australia's most important existing and future trading partners. In doing so, all students undertaking these courses should be left with a greater understanding of the social, economic and commercial reality of the nations that interact with us in trade and commerce. Decisions about which nations' cultures are prioritised should be determined by the local community based on advice from their respective state and Commonwealth Governments.

Overseas exchange/hosting programmes

Of course, learning about foreign cultures in a classroom will only take students so far in terms of developing a thorough and practical understanding of the world beyond their borders. In order to acquire a deeper insight into the differences which exist, and change the way the next generation of Australians conceptualises foreign marketing, business strategies and service and product innovation, it is imperative that secondary students experience these cultures firsthand.

One of the easiest methods for achieving this aim is by providing all students with the opportunity to participate in student exchange and hosting programmes during their secondary schooling. Student exchange programmes provide students with exposure to different environments, curriculums and cultures as well as the opportunity to further develop their linguistic skills.[437] Importantly, they open impressionable and developing young minds to the opportunities and challenges which exist within the other nations of the world.

Unfortunately, too few secondary students participate in foreign exchange programmes with an unsatisfactory number hosting in-bound students in return. If Australia is to meaningfully expand its international trade footprint over the decades ahead, the next generation's exposure to foreign cultures and lifestyles will need to substantially change.

To achieve this, Australia's current exchange and hosting arrangements should be revamped to better link a student's academic performance, cultural studies uptake and LOTE course completion with the opportunity to travel abroad rather than simply that student's socioeconomic status. In order to broaden foreign trade in the 21st century, Australia must ensure that it provides the opportunity for all of its brightest and most dedicated students to experience foreign culture first hand. This can be achieved through an expansion of government subsidised exchange programmes. The following reforms should be considered.

Out-bound foreign exchange (non-language skill)

All students who achieve a predetermined grade in the cultural education subjects discussed above should be eligible for a government subsidised out-bound exchange trip of between one and 12 months' duration. If the student cannot speak a second language, their exchange should be restricted to a secondary school overseas where English is widely spoken. The United States, the United Kingdom and Canada for example are home to the world's largest, sixth and tenth largest consumer markets. Consequently, subsidised cultural exchange to any of these nations should never be mistaken as a holiday. Opportunities in Asia should also not be forgotten. As home to approximately 800 million English speakers (more than the entire Anglosphere), exchange choices must be considered there as well.[438]

Out-bound foreign exchange (language skill)

All students who achieve a predetermined grade in the cultural education subjects discussed above and have formally assessed LOTE skills should be eligible for a government subsidised out-bound exchange trip of between one and twelve months duration to any of the above nations plus any nation where the LOTE is in regular use.

Out-bound LOTE foreign exchange

All students who achieve a predetermined grade in LOTE should be eligible for a government subsidised out-bound exchange trip of between one and twelve month duration to any of the above nations plus any nation where the LOTE is in regular use. Along the same lines as industry placement programmes in university, out-bound student exchange should form a core element of Australia's LOTE education curriculum.

In-bound student hosting

Students who do not qualify for out-bound student exchange should be eligible for government subsidised support for in-bound student hosting. Though on a lesser scale than an out-bound exchange, hosting an in-bound exchange student still provides the benefits of exposure to foreign concepts, customs and practices. If one cannot bring the student to a foreign culture, then a microcosm of foreign culture should at least be brought to the student.

§

In a world which is becoming increasingly competitive and complicated, it will be vital to host a workforce and entrepreneurial class which intuitively understands foreign markets and the cultures which host them. By revamping Australia's student exchange and hosting programmes, the nation can dramatically expand the knowledge, experience and capability of the next generation of Australian workers and businesspeople. This kind of reform has the potential to unlock vast economic and social benefits for Australia. Hopefully Australia's leaders have the intuition to make the change before any of our competitors do.

Economising municipal operations

Local municipalities are the weakest, poorest and least scrutinised level of government in Australia.

This is an immense pity because they not only collect over $13 billion of tax revenue each year,[439] but they are also responsible for a wide variety of community services which are essential to Australia's liveability, functionality and competitive performance.

If Australia is to punch above its weight during this century, all tiers within its government sector will need to be functioning at peak efficiency. In order to achieve such an outcome at the municipal level, three types of reform will need to be instigated:

- centralising revenue collection;
- regionalising service delivery; and
- amalgamating infrastructure tendering.

Centralising revenue collection

At present, all 562 local municipalities in Australia[440] engage in tax collection as autonomous financial entities. In doing so, they conduct all the necessary procedural actions related to revenue collection such as rate assessment, notice distribution, payment management and customer service.

In order to perform such services, each municipality requires its own team of financial specialists to manage their operations. This typically includes a collection of managers, accountants, auditors, lawyers, assessors and of course, the relevant support staff necessary to assist.

Where this is a problem for Australia is the fact that the current approach is unnecessarily bureaucratic, decentralised and costly. The best way to illustrate this problem can be achieved by highlighting the perverse incentives within Australia's current tax collection arrangements.

Across Victoria and New South Wales for example, 231 autonomous municipal level offices collect $7.1 billion[441] through one form of taxation – rates. At the same time however, the Victorian and New South Wales State Governments utilise just two autonomous offices to collect over $36 billion dollars[442] across dozens of forms of taxation.

In other words, under Australia's current tax collection arrangements, if your tax regime is simple, the government sector responds with a form of decentralised over management. However, if your tax collection arrangements are complicated, the government responds with centralised efficiency. For a nation with a population of just 23 million people, this is not the most efficient model Australia could be operating.

In Canada, for example, operational responsibility for tax collection is managed in a much more centralised fashion. Despite all provinces (states) enjoying policy autonomy in regard to their respective tax regimes, several provinces utilise a national tax collection body to administer their policies. Entitled the Canadian Revenue Agency (CRA), the CRA partly administers taxation policy on behalf of several of Canada's provinces, territories and the

Federal Government. In doing so, it performs this service through a centralised collection system with identical service standards, procedures and information technology. Moreover, having developed suitable training systems, it does so without the need for a highly localised model.

With Canada having successfully functioned with a semi-national model of tax collection for decades, there is no reason why Australia cannot accomplish the equivalent at a state level in regard to its municipal councils.

Ideally, each state's respective councils could have their revenue collection operations bundled together into larger regionally based collection authorities which report directly to them. Operating in a similar structure to Victoria's State Revenue Office (SRO), these authorities could maximise their operational efficiency and workforce productivity by rationalising their management structures, reducing overheads, in better recruitment and remuneration, and through the achievement of economies of scale in regard to automation, printing, distribution and customer service. Better still, municipalities could even outsource their tax collection operations to the SRO for a minor service fee.

Overall, if Canada's respective states can function independently within a national model of tax collection, then Australia's municipalities can do so as well under a centralised state based model.

Regionalising service delivery

Regionalising municipal service operations is another area where improvements can be made to conserve the resources of local municipalities.

In metropolitan Sydney at present, hundreds of ticket inspectors are employed across dozens of municipalities to enforce municipal regulations on street and allocated car space parking. This service requires them to wear uniforms, carry electronic processing equipment and report back to their respective municipalities. While the individual services themselves are relatively efficient, when viewed through the prism of a regional service delivery model, the system is far from effective.

In spite of the similarity of their roles and the uncomplicated nature of their service, Sydney's numerous ticket inspectors wear different uniforms, utilise different ticketing devices and report to different internal management structures under different remuneration systems. Given the unnecessary cost and inefficiency this generates, there is no reason why all of Sydney's municipalities could not merge their ticket inspection services into larger regional entities accompanied by suitable neighbourhood training.

Called Ticket Inspection Sydney for instance, such an approach would free up limited municipal resources by rationalising labour costs, bundling equipment and uniform purchases and reducing fixed overheads. Moreover, it would allow municipalities to divert those resources into more beneficial areas such as equipment modernisation, computerisation, expanded service provision or rate relief.

It is worth noting that some municipalities have already progressed some way towards regionalising their operations. Banking, telecommunications and waste management each enjoy a higher level of centralisation. However, much more can be done. Put simply, there is little reason to believe that the above approach couldn't be applied to the regional management of swimming pools, child care centres, call centres, garbage tips, websites, license issuing, town planning, permit processing and the enforcement of local regulations and codes of practice. In much the same way that the Victorian Electoral Commission (VEC) provides electoral services to all municipalities in a centralised and uncontroversial fashion, each of these services areas could easily be delivered on a regional basis.

Amalgamating infrastructure tendering

Each year billions of dollars are spent by municipalities on the construction, maintenance, repair, refurbishment and expansion of public assets across Australia. These resources are expended by municipalities in order to maintain and improve the standard of living enjoyed and expected by their constituents.

However, with the rate base of many municipalities declining, the cost burden of maintaining public assets appreciating, and population pressures in almost all communities intensifying (through both population growth and population decline), municipalities are increasingly finding it harder to meet their community's infrastructure expectations.

At present, most municipalities request tenders for the above infrastructure services on a municipality wide basis only. Naturally parochial, this is an unsurprising and arguably inevitable side-effect of Australia's system of regional governance. However, while such an approach ensures that local small businesses are given the opportunity to tender for local work, it also means that fewer businesses tender for projects due to their relatively small size. As a result, the ratepayer and the municipality are both worse off.

If municipalities are going to be able to achieve savings in their growing infrastructure budgets, then they will need to increase the level of interest in their local tenders. One method which has proven effective for achieving this has been the bundling of tenders across municipalities. Rather than offering road maintenance work on one local road for a measly $900,000 dollars, three municipalities would instead pool their tenders together and seek out commercial interest for a combined project valued at $5 million. By increasing the size of the project's scale, more businesses will be attracted to making a bid. Consequently, with more businesses competing, the cost of funding the project should decline.

Perversely, almost all municipalities are aware of the benefits of tender bundling, but few actively engage in it. The reason this is the case is because while responsible budgets are popular, business favouritism tends to secure the support of the loudest local voices. As a result, ratepayers pay the price for the absence of responsible political leadership. In order to overcome this political hurdle, state governments will need to become involved. Whether it is through the provision of financial bonuses rewarding financial astute behaviour (the carrot approach), or, regulatory reform forcing municipalities to bundle their projects (the stick approach), tendering reform of some kind should be encouraged.

§

Overall, economising the operations of local municipalities remains one of the must do reforms for the government sector this century. Whether it is their outdated methods of revenue collection, service delivery or tendering practice, the quality of municipal operations have been ignored for far too long.

As with all endeavours reformist, the challenge will always be in managing the politics. However, given the financial benefits on offer, and the possibility of improved social outcomes, proposals like these will surely only need one successful domino to entice the rest to act.

Northern cerrado

One of the biggest reasons why northern Australia has not developed as successfully as the landmasses' other regional areas, is the belief that the task of continental nation building is complete.

This belief is predicated upon an incorrect multi-generational assessment that with the exception of the nation's eastern, south eastern and south-western coastlines and drainage basins, the continent is a mixture of torrid zones[443] and undevelopable territory.

Fortunately, as a result of soaring global demand for food, energy and raw materials; rapidly evolving technological advancement in genetic modification, hydrology, edaphology,[444] pest management and extreme climate construction; and the timely reversal of Australia's century old north-south economic and political relationship,[445] this misguided assessment about northern Australia's development potential is about to be turned on its head.

To ensure Australia is primed to maximise this grand development opportunity, four major reforms must be undertaken to ready the north for long term success. These are:

- developing a multi-decade plan for northern economic development;
- establishing growth zones with special rules for business, labour and investment;
- investing in infrastructure to attract development; and
- removing the obstacles preventing increased foreign involvement

A new economic strategy for Australia's rediscovered frontier

Unlocking the full potential of Northern Australia will require a fresh approach towards national economic development.

First, all Australian governments would need to recognise that vast tracts of northern Australia remain in a different stage of development to that found in the more populated southern and eastern regions. By acknowledging the underdeveloped and frontier status of northern Australia, national and interstate policy settings can be recalibrated to reflect the unique challenges the region faces.

Second, a new government department overseen by a minister dedicated to the north's long term growth and administration should be created. This department would be given responsibility for drafting a 30 year cross border development plan with the expressed intention of bringing northern Australia to a position of economic self-reliance. Importantly, unlike many of the Commonwealth's other government departments, the new department would be located in a major capital city where decision makers in the mining, energy, agriculture, infrastructure and foreign capital investment sectors can be easily engaged with.

Special enterprise zones

Unlocking the full potential of northern Australia will also require the region to be treated as a unique sub national entity.

This differentiation will be vital to the region's success as the isolation, transport costs, environmental and infrastructure challenges and capital required to achieve socioeconomic progress in this part of Australia is much greater than that found elsewhere.

To begin with, selected parts of northern Australia should be granted special exemptions to the regulatory standards and investment delays which presently discourage business activity from occurring elsewhere. In a fashion similar to the Free Trade Zones found in China,[446] northern Australia should enjoy a different and temporary set of rules to attract development and foreign investment. Ideally, the region's investment environment should be positively pro-development, low tax and light on non-tangible regulatory compliance. OHS and environmental laws should continue to be consistent with national standards, however, rules regarding foreign investment; foreign labour and genetically modified organisms should be designed to encourage accelerated deployment.

Investing in economic infrastructure

One of the biggest obstacles to attracting investment in northern Australia is the absence of large scale infrastructure necessary to support private development.[447] For example, "there are hundreds of major dams in the southern part of the country, but just three in the top third".[448]

Where this becomes a problem for Australia's northern development is that for any resource, food, fibre or energy business considering the possibility of an investment, they must also factor in the cost of building their own infrastructure base. Consequently, the capital outlays required to undertake business activity in the north is cost prohibitive for all but the largest of investors, both foreign and domestic.

If Australia is to unlock the full potential of the north, it will need to change the way it thinks about infrastructure investment in the region. States cannot and should not be solely relied upon to invest in major infrastructure projects for the nations long term benefit. Not only are they incapable of doing so financially, but the political reality of state politics dictates that the infrastructure needs of their major population centres will nearly always prevail.

Consequently, two other parties must be leaned upon to fund and fulfil northern Australia's economic promise – the Commonwealth and those not based in Australia.

In the case of the Commonwealth, more resources will need to be deployed into building infrastructure which can help attract business investment. Whether it is power stations, dams, roads or rail lines, the Commonwealth needs to assume a more active role in the development of the north's primary infrastructure base. Just as New York's long term public investment in the Erie Canal unlocked the American Midwest,[449] selective and sensible infrastructure investment can do the same in Australia's north.

Such an approach will require changes to federal environmental regulations and a mixture of public and public-private funding initiatives mirroring the best which exist overseas. Critically, this approach must be done in conjunction with a more rigorous assessment process for determining future tax revenues. If the Australian public is being asked to fund infrastructure in a region few will ever visit, then the case for justifying it must be watertight.

The other grouping vital to infrastructure development in Australia's north is that which can be found outside of its borders. As the developing world pursues economic growth, their hunger for food, raw materials and energy will continue to intensify. One of the fascinating trading changes resulting from this process has been the unexpected substitution of supply affordability with that of supply reliability. Throughout continental Africa for example, Chinese state-owned enterprises (SOEs) are funding the development of railways and ports to improve the reliability of their supply chains. In many cases, China has begun bankrolling the infrastructure needs of foreign nations in exchange for reliable access to their strategically vital resources. With such arrangements presently in operation in several nations, there is no reason why Australia could not negotiate an equally beneficial outcome for itself. Exploration of such an approach must be considered essential to any effort to develop northern Australia's infrastructure base.

An embrace of all things foreign

The final area of reform necessary to unlock northern development is the removal of government created obstacles to foreign involvement. Whether it is foreign investment controls restricting the influx of overseas capital, domestic business opposition to foreign involvement in selective industries, or community apprehension about foreign labour, each in its own way is sabotaging Australia's ability to unlock the north's full potential.

In order to turn this situation around, all levels of government need to adopt a more welcoming approach to foreign involvement throughout Australia's frontier. For starters, restrictions on foreign investment will need to be loosened. At present, Australia's foreign investment regime is considered to be more restrictive than the OECD average – a standard deemed tougher than that found in the United States, Britain, Canada and New Zealand.[450] If Australia is to secure the billions it requires to maximise its response to the commodity boom of the 21st century, its foreign investment regulations will need to change. Recent reforms included in the Korean and Japanese free trade agreements which lift the screening thresholds fourfold[451] are a positive start. However, improved access must also be granted for the agricultural land and agribusiness sectors as well.

Community concerns about foreign ownership of Australian farm land and the possibility of a food security crisis must also be aggressively put to rest. "According to the Australian Bureau of Statistics, 99 per cent of Australia's 135,600 agricultural businesses and 89 per cent of our agricultural land is held entirely by Australian interests."[452] Further, Australia presently produces enough food in a single year to feed over 60 million people every single year. Yet despite Australia's high proportion of national farm ownership and food self-sufficiency, too few Australians are aware of how strong the nation's strategic position actually is. In order to turn around public perception on this critical trade and investment matter, a coordinated information campaign should be launched to ensure that the public remains appropriately informed.

The final policy area which requires modification is Australia's approach to sourcing foreign labour. As northern Australia will remain one of the continent's most isolated economic regions for the foreseeable future, it is crucial that sourcing labour to maximise its potential is made as easy as possible. Unfortunately, the present process of recruiting foreign labour remains extremely complicated, time consuming, political and costly.

In order to better unlock the full potential of Australia's northern frontier, governments overseeing foreign labour laws and international recruitment regulations should gear the system towards one which favours liberalisation, affordability and speed. Increased flexibility in management, recruitment and the processing of foreign workers would also be of benefit.

§

In conclusion, the time has finally arrived for northern Australia's full potential to be realised. With economic, technological and political factors each aligning its favour, Australia's governments need only get on board, or get out of the way. Time will tell if they do. But if that day comes, the north's future will definitely be one too exciting to ignore.

Archipelagic amalgamations

As Australia changes as a result of population growth, evolving settlement patterns, and demographic, economic and technological transformations, it is inevitable that the methods by which it governs itself will become less effective.

In the corporate sector, this reality is recognised every day through the near continuous evolution of business. Driven by the pressures of fickle customers and breakneck product and service delivery innovation, business structures are constantly in a state of reform. Whether they are big or small, or local or multi-national, businesses periodically change their shape and size to best meet their needs (and those of their customers).

Unfortunately, in the realm of government, such pressures for constant evolution do not exist. While it is correct to state that government can be booted out by the voters (their electoral customers) if their policies are out of touch, the physical boundaries which determine where governments begin and end rarely change. Parties and policies evolve, and seat divisions may shift, but the physical borders of their authority rarely do, if ever. This is one area where the Australian public has been consistently let down and where valuable improvements can be made.

There are two areas where boundary changes in Australia should be investigated. These are:

- local municipalities within state borders; and
- state conurbations across state borders.

Local municipalities within state borders

One of the biggest flaws of current municipality level boundaries is their insensitivity to areas of natural economic integration. Far too often, community economic activity zones are split across different municipal borders. Moreover, vital transport assets such as major roads, rivers and highways are utilised as borders to politically divide municipalities, rather than bind them together as these assets often do.

In central Melbourne for example, its medical, tertiary and corporate assets are each split across separate municipalities. Its world class medical precinct and internationally recognised university cluster are split between the City of Melbourne and the City of Yarra, and its Capital City Zone is split between the City of Melbourne and the City of Port Phillip. Even Melbourne's recent Fishermans Bend expansion which sees the CBD grid grow by two-thirds its present size will be split across different municipal boundaries.

In each of these cases, long term development outcomes are undermined as a result of unnecessary bureaucracy; inconsistent long term planning; contradictory tax, investment, mobility and growth priority settings; and differing rules of operation for entities located in the same market a short distance from each other. In essence, you can have two businesses selling the same product to the same customer paying different council rates, complying with different council regulations whilst reporting to two very different bureaucratic cultures. While such an approach may represent the pinnacle of local governance, it also runs counter to the very economic and operational benefits derived from clustering similar sectors together. Whereas much of the world is desperately trying to concentrate such development in close proximity, Australia has voluntarily sought to create barriers.

Luckily, there is an easy solution to this problem. As local government is not recognised within the Australian Constitution, their physical borders and the numbers in which they exist can be changed via ministerial direction and/or legislative change.

In order to reduce the number of political divisions intersecting Australia's economic activity zones, a redrawing of existing municipal boundaries should be undertaken. This could be achieved by amending the criteria by which municipal borders are determined by stipulating that political boundaries may not divide areas of natural economic integration. Once such an amendment has been made, the orderly redivision process driven by population growth should be able to take care of the rest.

State conurbations across state borders

One of the greatest and perhaps most unforeseen changes to occur in Australia since its federation has been the growth of conurbation zones along its state borders. At the time of federation, personal travel and goods transportation between Australia's major cities was still dominated by boat (due to cost and time efficiency reasons). However, as the population has grown and economics of air and land transport have changed, Australia's population footprint has dramatically altered.

The most significant side-effect of this has been the development of conurbation zones across state borders where population settlement has been driven by the unifying force of economic activity. In Australia at present, there are two distinctive forms of conurbation zones which warrant further attention. These are:

- the sister city developments which have sprung up either side of the Murray River; and
- the vast conurbation zone which links the Queensland Gold Coast with the New South Wales Tweed Coast

(the largest non-capital urban conurbation on the continent).

What makes these two conurbations unique is that the present model of Australian governance does not serve their economic interests well. There are four areas of concern:

First, these conurbated zones are overseen by two state governments. This results in competing state interests, differing ideology towards strategic planning and inconsistent levels of taxation, regulation, environmental standards, operating hours, development contribution plan levies and labour laws. The Gold Coast-Tweed for example, is governed by two separate strategic planning documents, the South East Queensland Regional Plan 2009-13 and the far North Coast Regional
Strategy.[453]

Second, each zone is also overseen by multiple local municipal authorities. Even in the cases where amalgamations have taken place on one side of the state border, different laws still exist on the other. Local government laws in the areas of planning approval, rates, infrastructure charges and local by-laws are often different for the local businesses competing with each other within different jurisdictions. This makes economic growth and operational efficiency within the zone harder to achieve.

Third, conurbations which are located at distance from the centre of a state jurisdiction's political heartland have a history of being let down. In the worst of cases, priority is given to other competing centres, typically the capital itself. The best examples of this occurring can be found in the historic competition between Melbourne and Portland over Victorian port primacy and Melbourne and the Victorian Goldfields over managing labour shortages. In both cases, the bigger economic centre acted against the interests of the smaller one. This problem continues to occur today at the expense of regional centres, regardless of their economic growth prospects.

Fourth, when economic and political integration have failed, the region within which it occurs inevitably suffers. The best example of this in Australia can be found in the Riverina which is home to one of Australia's most productive agricultural regions. As with all major agricultural produce, exports which need to be sent to market are shipped to the coast for maritime transport. Subsequently, as a result of the Riverina's location and its absence of navigable waterways, the most logical destination for this to occur is its closest coastal port. However, in the Riverina's case, this is not within the state in which it resides. Originally it was South Australia and today it is Victoria. As a result, over the course of more than century, the Riverina has either integrated westwards or southwards towards its economic interests rather than eastwards towards its political capital.

As things stand today, over 100,000 TEU travel from the Riverina to the Port of Melbourne each year;[454] the Victorian Government continues to own property and rail assets in the region (VicTrack) and many of its towns play AFL, not NRL (which is not the dominant football code in greater NSW). Consequently, the people of the Riverina are New South Welshman by citizenship, but are actually economically and culturally Victorian. Put another way, the people of the Riverina are Victorian refugees caught on the wrong side of the border!

The main consequence of this is that the Riverina's economic imperatives and political imperatives exist at cross purposes. State investment in the region disproportionately benefits Victoria, even if they don't pay for it. Further, heavy transport infrastructure built in the Riverina primarily benefits travel into and out of Victoria, rather than for the broader benefit of greater NSW. This unfortunate reality means that decisions made by the NSW Government are always overshadowed by the fact that the Riverina is an economic orphan within its own political territory.

Fixing political problems associated with changed economic realities on the ground is one of the most challenging governance issues facing Australia today. Often deemed too difficult to resolve politically, successive political leaders have either misunderstood the extent of the problem, or have failed to act decisively. Broadly speaking, there are two key avenues for reform which should be explored in regard to rectifying these problems.

The first and least complex solution is to merge the cross border conurbation zones under one regional local government authority. By doing so, a combined regional municipal authority would be able to bring all local regulations, rates, by-laws, strategic planning and investment and all other government processes under one consistent policy regime. The benefits of this to local businesses would be significant as similar businesses (and farms) would no longer be forced to compete on uneven playing fields. Ratepayers and local service and infrastructure consumers would also benefit as a result of the greater economies of scale. With a larger combined economic and political footprint within the one municipal boundary, the divisions which set neighbouring communities against each other would be eased in favour of common collective interest.

In seeking to achieve such a merging of separate interstate entities, support would be necessary from each respective state government. Ideally, to maximise the benefits to the local community, state laws affecting the region should be brought into alignment to further improve local efficiencies. However, this step need not be necessary for a successful outcome. Policy setting powers in a number of areas could be devolved to the local authority with the municipality deciding which state regime they wish to adhere too. This approach would be ideal for the Gold Coast-Tweed and the Murray River communities.

The second solution applicable to this problem would be to commence the process of conducting a local referendum to have the political borders shifted to reflect the economic and cultural reality on the ground. The first stage in this process would be to instruct the Productivity Commission to investigate the merits of the idea. Their findings would then be circulated to the local communities for their own objective assessment. With a sufficient socioeconomic case put before voters, local communities could then be given the power to decide their own political destinies. Such an approach would be an effective proposition for all of Australia's interstate conurbations.

It is worth noting that many will argue that such divisions will eventually be resolved through the process of harmonisation and that eventually, Australia will essentially become internally borderless. To the advocates of this prognosis, I would simply point out that, over a century after federation, the vexed public issues of water, labour standards and taxation continue to be points of considerable interstate tension and competition. While it is correct to state that some progress has been made, the cohesive nirvana which many forecast to be around the corner is in reality nowhere to be seen. Total harmonisation, despite its clear and indisputable benefits, remains contrary to historical state government behaviour.

§

Over the past two centuries, Australia has changed dramatically as a result of population growth, evolving settlement patterns, demography and economic and technological transformations.

If Australia is to remain home to hundreds of dynamic, innovative and responsive government entities, it will need to ensure that these entities accurately reflect the rapidly changing communities they seek to represent. Internal boundary reform is the surest way to improve the current standard – it needs only governments' willingness to self-assess.

A bigger Australia, demanded by the people

By the middle of this century, Australia will be home to a significantly larger population.

This eventuality will occur not simply because its resources, wealth and environment are capable of doing so at a sustained and enviable living standard, but because the achievement of this outcome will be vital to the nation's long term prosperity.

Due to a combination of factors such as rising taxes, an ageing population, acute labour shortages and unprecedented demand for infrastructure, markets and capital, structural problems within the economy will trigger a seismic shift in public attitudes in favour of population growth.

Whereas in the past community debate has revolved around how many people Australia can host sustainably, in the future, discussion will focus upon which methods the public is prepared to accept in order to increase migration as quickly as possible.

This remarkable shift in public attitudes will no doubt come as a surprise to many Australians. Outlined below are the primary reasons why this shift will occur.

More migrants means lower taxes

Keeping Australia's tax base low for individuals will be vital to maintaining the nation's long term prosperity. In fact, keeping income taxes at rates which are internationally competitive will be amongst the most important tasks facing all nations this century, especially those with high cost bases such as Australia.

It is for this reason that increasing Australia's population will be so important.

Since the early 2000s, Australia's largest population cohort (the baby boomers) has slowly begun to depart the workforce. While incremental at first, this shift is resulting in Australia's greatest economic dividend – a large and productive generation of workers evolving into Australia's greatest economic liability: a large, savings poor and ageing retirement class. Over the space of three decades, the largest income tax contributing generation in history will transform into the largest tax consuming one.

Between 2010 and 2050, the ratio of workers to retirees is forecast to decline from five-one to 2.7-one.[455] Further, the number of Australians aged 65-84 will more than double and those aged over 85 will quadruple.[456] As these participatory and ageing changes ripple through the community, the beginnings of Australia's tax crisis will commence.

At present, approximately 45 per cent of Australia's Commonwealth tax revenue is collected from income taxes ($151 billion).[457] This money is raised from Australia's 11.5 million person workforce. Over the next 36 years, millions of people are forecast to retire from full time employment with the proportion of working-age people declining more than ten per cent from current levels.[458]

Where this becomes a major problem for Australia is through the fact that at the same time that the nation's tax base will be shrinking proportionally, community spending on healthcare, aged care and age related pensions will be rising dramatically (from 25 to 50 per cent of all Commonwealth spending).[459] Worse still, less than half of Australia's retirees will have enough superannuation to fund their retirements.[460] In combination, this trio of fiscal challenges will push the Commonwealth budget beyond its sustainable limits. As a result, governments will be forced to make one of three choices: raise taxes, cut public service support or broaden the tax base. If history is any guide, than the latter will be the most probably outcome.

For over 200 years, Australia has routinely used mass migration to overcome its myriad of strategic weaknesses. Burdened with high capital costs and a small labour base, policy makers have routinely used foreign labourers to alter the nations demographic and economic prospects. Faced with a new challenge of equally daunting importance, migration policy will once again be used to reshape the nation's destiny.

As identified above, Australia's long term fiscal challenge is rooted in a declining ratio of workers to retirees. Therefore, if Australia is going to ease into its demographic destiny and keep its tax rates competitive, it will need to increase the size of its workforce in proportion to its cohort of growing retirees. So how does one do that via migration policy? By reorientating the nation's migration system towards aspiring Australians of early adult age.

One of the great iron laws of demography is that young adults are the least expensive of all a nations citizens. Due to a combination of good health, limited government dependency and high employability, young adults often cost little, but contribute lots. Consequently, when attempting to address a labour shortage in an ageing society, one potential solution is to fill the ageing workforce hole with a youthful workforce plug. According to the Productivity Commission, an increase in Australia's annual net migration by 150,000 people would lower the proportion of those aged 65 and over by approximately three per cent by 2044-45.[461] While clearly not a comprehensive solution, a retargeted migration programme which preferentially targets young adults can go a sizeable way towards addressing the problem. Consequently, it is highly likely that a retargeted migration programme will be adopted as part of Australia's multifaceted insurance policy against rising taxes.

Servicing the baby boomer's retirement

Managing the service provision challenge associated with the retirement of the baby boomers will also demand Australia host a bigger population. As the largest generation in Australian history retires, and the number of people aged over 65 soars, the structure of Australia's economy, workforce and welfare, health and aged care systems will dramatically alter.

As a human being ages, two fundamental changes generally take place.

First, they typically start to draw more heavily upon a nation's welfare, health and aged care systems. This occurs as a result of a reduction in work related income, increasing bone and muscle weakness, rising chronic disease risks and deteriorating organ health such as eyes, heart and skin. The second change they experience is that of growing dependency upon others to perform daily tasks. This occurs as a result of declining strength, mobility, confidence and overall health.

As these two changes take place, demand for workers in the employment fields that provide these services will inevitably grow. Whether it is doctors or nurses; healthcare specialists or home carers; or lawn mowers or cleaners, demand for workers across all of these professions will rise.

Where this becomes a major problem for Australia's largest retirement generation is how these services will be provided. Most if not all presently suffer from labour shortages. Furthermore, many are predicting a decrease, rather than an increase in their workforces over the decades ahead.

If Australia is to avoid the social, service and wage spike implications this unmet wave of service demand will unleash, an aggressive shift in addressing the nation's skill shortages will be required. Historically, Australia has consistently failed to solve its labour shortages through domestic solutions alone. Ineffective career advising techniques combined with weak training programmes and a high degree of job snobbery have often left Australia grasping for workers across the skilled and unskilled divide. As a result, successive governments have turned to the next most palatable and effect alternative – migration.

When attempting to solve this particular problem, Australia will again need to embrace this trusted public policy solution. By adjusting its migration programmes to proactively recruit and entice in-demand workers to Australia, the government can address its service provision problems both quickly and effectively. Moreover, it can do so with new Australians guaranteed to be employed for decades to come.

If Australia is to adequately manage the retirement expectations of its baby boomer generation, it will need to ensure it hosts a workforce capable of meeting their service delivery needs. At present, Australia is not equipped for that challenge. However, as community concerns rise as a result of declining service quality, the development of innovative migration techniques will ensure that growing workforce shortages are eventually overcome.

Overcoming the infrastructure deficit

Increasing Australia's population will be essential if Australia is to begin addressing its massive infrastructure deficit. According to Davis Langdon, total infrastructure sector investment between 2010 and 2050 is estimated to be as high as $3.87 trillion.[462] If Australia is to have any chance of overcoming it, let alone meet the demands of a growing population, the nation will need to ensure it has a capable and affordable construction industry workforce in place.

Over the next three decades, Australia's construction industry workforce will face considerable pressure as a result of a severe mismatch between ageing worker retirements and new industry recruits. If this process unfolds as expected, the inevitable result will be a worsening of the nation's skilled labour crisis and an escalation in the costs associated with infrastructure provision. Put simply, unless something dramatically changes, Australia's ability to resolve its infrastructure deficit will become impossible.

During the past two decades, "Australia's infrastructure trade labour force has increased by more than 70 per cent"[463] with much of this growth occurring in the past decade.[464] However, despite this monumental achievement, infrastructure related labour shortages have continued to undermine projects costs, timetables and investment pipelines. As a result, even with existing recruitment and training efforts operating in overdrive, the nation is still struggling to build a workforce large enough to do the job.

If Australia is to overcome its infrastructure challenge, it will need to find a way to dramatically increase the size of its construction industry workforce. As with the nation's retirement services challenge, the most effective method for accomplishing this will be through a concerted effort to recruit the world's global supply of construction workers. By recruiting foreign trade labourers along the same lines outlined above, Australia will slowly find its infrastructure deficit becoming more manageable. Critically, it will do so with the support of an infrastructure starved electorate.

Boosting the size of Australia's consumer markets and capital generation capability

Growing Australia's local population will also be necessary if the nation is to more effectively overcome its strategic market and capital weaknesses. As a small population scattered across a large and isolated continent, Australia is disadvantaged by modest consumer markets and an insufficient supply of capital. These two factors make Australia's long term economic growth capacity highly dependent upon access to overseas markets and inwardly flowing foreign capital. As evidenced during the Global Financial Crisis, access to both can quickly change if Australia's trading partners deem it contrary to the short term political or economic interests.

If Australia is to do a better job of minimising the risks and limitations of its economic growth model, it will need to do more than simply rely upon the free trade sensibilities of its trading partners; it will need to build alternative markets.

One of the easiest ways to grow larger and pro-Australian consumer and capital markets is through the expansion of its own. By selectively adjusting Australia's immigration quotas, larger consumer markets will naturally evolve over time, generating economy-wide benefits such as greater product diversity and innovation; increased market competition; downward pressure on product, services and living costs; and improvements in economies of scale, especially in the transport and supply chain sectors where costs are globally uncompetitive. Further, for every additional person who comes to Australia, especially highly skilled ones, additional wealth will be generated as a result of their employment activities and long term investment potential. Put simply, in all but the rarest of cases, more people means more consumption and more capital generation.

By increasing the number of consumers and capital generators within its economy, Australia will be able to broaden its economic foundations at the same time as expanding its economic potential. Importantly, it will be able to do so with the added benefit of creating jobs, boosting business opportunities and improving financial liquidity for millions of Australians.

§

Former NSW Labor Premier, Jack Lang, was often fond of saying that "in the race of life, always back self-interest, at least you know it's trying". When it comes to predicting where future public attitudes will be in regard to Australia's population destiny, it is important that forecasters keep this aphorism in mind.

Over the next 30 years, rising income taxes, declining service delivery standards, an underperforming infrastructure base and insufficient markets and capital supplies will each force the public to reassess where their priorities truly lie. In every one of these cases, the public will be asked to choose between accepting a larger population or agreeing to a decline in their living standards.

Throughout Australian history, the public has only on rare occasions opted for the latter – and usually only then during times of war. Over the next 30 years, the only war Australia will be fighting will be the one it has with its demography. As a result, it is highly unlikely that the forces of self-interest will not end up prevailing.

With this fate in mind, the challenge for Australia's policy makers will be to encourage the arrival of this decision point as quickly as possible. Decisive decision makers always enjoy a strategic advantage – and in the highly competitive marketplace of migration, Australia hasn't a moment to lose.

Third world finances, first world infrastructure expectations

Working out how to fund essential state infrastructure is one of the great policy challenges facing Australia at present.

According to Infrastructure Partnerships Australia, the estimated cost of overcoming Australia's infrastructure backlog over the next decade is $800 billion.[465] This figure is comprised of upgrades to roads, rail, ports, airports and essential service infrastructure (sewage, gas, electricity and water). While this figure may seem frightening, what is really scary is the fact that it doesn't include the forecast cost of meeting demand beyond 2019. Total infrastructure sector investment between 2010 and 2050 is estimated to be as high as $3.87 trillion.[466]

Finding a way to fund these projects against the backdrop of a growing population and a widening fiscal gap will be a huge challenge. But it need not be an impossible one. If Australia is to overcome its infrastructure backlog, it needs to be honest about the reality of its present situation. In order to do so, it must come to grips with two simple truths.

First, there are very few significant infrastructure projects within the financing capability of state governments anymore. Through a combination of soaring constructions costs (labour), poor long term planning, an inadequate and declining tax base and a well progressed urban consolidation agenda, almost all essential infrastructure projects now require Commonwealth financial involvement. This means that unless Commonwealth and state government priorities align on investment, as well as politically and philosophically, infrastructure projects which are deemed to be a state priority are unlikely to become anything more than a state aspiration.

Second, there is no way this infrastructure bill can be met through public financing alone: "According to the Bureau of Statistics, government (federal and state) investment infrastructure averaged about 4.5 per cent of GDP from the late 1950s to the late 1970s. This now stands at about three per cent."[467] The notion that state governments are going to restore their infrastructure spending to historic trends against insatiable recurrent expenditure demands on areas such as education and health is unrealistic. They simply do not have the political will or the financial capacity to make such aspirations happen. In essence, they are like third world nations with first world infrastructure ambitions. They have a wish list a mile long, but are unlikely to ever afford it.

So, if the cost of funding infrastructure projects is beyond state governments, and the Commonwealth is unable or unwilling to provide support for every project put forward, how will state governments address the infrastructure backlog and get ahead of forecast demand? The answer is simple. They must find the funding elsewhere.

There are four key infrastructure funding reforms which all state governments must begin investigating in order to get on top of their infrastructure challenges. These are:

- privatisation and corporatisation of existing government assets;
- transfer of government asset ownership;
- user pays; and
- reconceptualising infrastructure wish lists.

Privatisation and corporatisation of existing government assets

The privatisation and corporatisation of government owned assets are two of the simplest and most effective ways for cash strapped governments to address the financial burden attached to their infrastructure responsibilities.

According to the Infrastructure Australia, Australia's nine governments presently retain full or partial ownership in dozens of separate infrastructure assets and statutory organisations which could be privatised, corporatised or leased in the public's interest. Assets and services such as energy generation, transmission and distribution, water collection and distribution, ports, airports, rail, government land, public housing, government buildings, plantation forests and health insurers could all be sold into private ownership to generate finances for infrastructure investment and/or to reduce the maintenance burden of their upkeep on the taxpayer. Current estimates of energy, port, airport, water, freight and plantation forestry assets alone range from $116-$140 billion dollars.[468]

Furthermore, local government authorities which have so far avoided any serious debate in this policy area also have a similar suite of smaller assets which could be privatised and/or corporatised because they do not need to be publicly owned in order to provide affordable quality service delivery outcomes to the community. Assets and services such as airports,[469] town halls, sporting grounds, swimming pools, council offices, early childcare centres, kindergartens, waste management[470] and meals on wheels services are all potential sources of funding and/ or expenditure savings. Moreover, with many of these assets shifted off council balance sheets, the operational savings can also be of use in managing strategic planning and/or undertaking infrastructure investment.

In total, the combined value of these assets is estimated to be worth hundreds of millions of dollars. If a dedicated privatisation/ corporatisation programme with an accompanying regulatory and service quality preservation regime could be devised, the vast majority of these assets could be sold before the end of the decade. Such action would ensure that all levels of government are better placed to build the next generation of public assets and statutory authorities needed to improve living standards, manage growth and keep pace with economic, social and technologically change. In a nation which is likely to remain both capital poor and capital hungry for the foreseeable future, this avenue of capital accumulation and liberalisation is a funding path definitely worth pursuing.

Transfer of government asset ownership

Meeting Australia's infrastructure bill on the back of public financing alone is not realistic.

Another policy response which should be utilised more readily is the transfer of ownership of public assets to the private sector in exchange for infrastructure development or enhancement. To date, this approach is most commonly used in the area of private road construction whereby all or part of a public road is transferred to private control in exchange for its upgrade and/or the development of a major road project nearby. Melbourne's CityLink motorway is the best Australian example of this whereby the private sector has funded the construction and management of 22 kilometres of formerly public roads, private roads, tunnels and bridges in exchange for a 34-year concession on road operation. While controversial at the time, after almost 15 years of operation, CityLink and its accompanying asset transfers have proven to be a stunning success. Not only does it host an average of 768,000 vehicles per day[471] but it also successfully links three public freeways in a continuous, high capacity route servicing the central business district. Put simply, CityLink has evolved to become an essential component in Victoria's transport network.

Beyond the CityLink example, there are countless other opportunities throughout Australia where this approach could be applied. Indeed, many of Australia's major arterial roads, cross city bottlenecks, railway stations and thoroughfare bridges and freight routes to logistic hubs are ripe for private interventions. Greater attention should be devoted to extending the CityLink model of asset ownership transfer throughout Australia. While not applicable in every transport scenario, it remains a proven alternative to publicly funded financing models.

User pays

The use of user pays or tolls to attract private investment in infrastructure and/or pay for public infrastructure construction is another essential pathway worth considering. Importantly, it does so by not imposing construction or maintenance costs on non-users.

At present, there are over a dozen Australian roads and bridges which levy tolls on its users. One of the most attractive attributes about tolls is their ability to create infrastructure markets for investors. Through the introduction of revenue streams for infrastructure usage, governments are able to attract private investment in project areas they are not able to fund. By adopting tolls in this fashion, governments are able to manage their infrastructure pressures more strategically, especially when their financial capacity is constrained. A second important quality of toll imposition is the fact that they can allow governments and/or private operators to directly target infrastructure consumers to fund infrastructure projects. By adopting a user-pays approach, tolls allow governments to minimise the cost impact of projects upon the broader community, especially on those unlikely to use it. Through the possession of these two qualities, tolls can be a remarkably useful tool for managing Australia's immense infrastructure challenge. Outlined below are two tolling approaches which should be considered.

First, governments should consider granting private sector operators the right to impose tolls for a pre-determined period of time on an agreed piece of infrastructure which they must build out of their own expense. At present, this occurs on a number of toll roads and ports around Australia. In exchange for the private sector building or maintaining the asset, the government would grant the private company the right to draw revenue from the asset's users.

To date, this approach has resulted in the attraction of billions of dollars of additional infrastructure investment (capital which would have gone elsewhere). Moreover, it is responsible for easing traffic congestion for the community, improving economy wide logistics and reducing road maintenance costs imposed on the tax payer. While not all toll road have enjoyed financial success, the investment model is financially proven, is in use in over 30 foreign nations and is essential for Australia's long term economic development. Consequently, there are dozens of potential projects around Australia which could be suitable for toll type investment models. If governments are serious about overcoming their infrastructure backlog, every single one should be investigated.

The second area where the imposition of tolls should be explored is for the funding of small scale infrastructure projects. All around Australia at present there are hundreds of small scale infrastructure projects which are patiently awaiting government funding which will probably never arrive. These can range from bridge capacity upgrades and country road overpasses, to arterial road widening projects and level crossings. In each of these cases, an opening presently exists to take the project off the waiting list and place it immediately into the "design and construct" queue.

In order to achieve such an outcome, state government should directly fund the infrastructure project out of consolidated revenue, but seek to recover all or part of their investment through the imposition of micro-tolls on the asset's future users.

Such a system for funding infrastructure would work as follows. Greater Melbourne is presently home to over 170 railway level crossings which routinely disrupt traffic flow and increase transport costs. In some of the worst cases, key roadways are blocked for up to 50 per cent of the peak hour.[472] In an effort to eliminate their impact upon suburban congestion, the government would design, tender for and fund the grade separation at the point of the roadway-railway intersection. As part of the construction contract, a radio based micro tolling system would be installed (similar to the CityLink system) to collect a small usage fee (0.50 cents-$1) on all vehicles which pass through the former intersection point. Through the introduction of such a funding arrangement, the congestion impacts of level crossings could be eliminated for a relatively small financial cost to the taxpayer. Indeed, it is the small cost to the taxpayer which is key. For the price of a packet of chewing gum, significant daily time savings in road transport could be achieved.

With so many projects languishing in a similar financial predicament, the application of micro tolls to activate them should be a policy response which is seriously considered.

Reconceptualising infrastructure wish lists

The final area where governments can secure additional funding for infrastructure investment is through inviting the private sector to reconceptualise their infrastructure aspirations.

At present, all governments across Australia have extensive public and private lists of infrastructure projects which they would like to develop, but lack the financial or technical know-how to deliver them. One approach by which more of these projects could be realised is through their advertisement on a publicly available register which invites the private sector to pitch innovative solutions and unsolicited proposals at their construction and/or funding.

In order to attract interest, governments would need to offer confidentiality on all submissions, guarantee protection of intellectual property and confirm that no pre-determined criteria exist. By establishing the criteria in this way, governments would ensure that the investment drivers which motivate the private sector – air rights, advertising, user pay income, mixed use development and other business and revenue streams – are not constraining creativity in any way.

In all likelihood, hundreds of submitted ideas would not be acceptable for a mixture of political and financial reasons. However, dozens of them would be, thereby opening up a new stream of funding for addressing their extensive infrastructure backlogs.

As highlighted above, state governments cannot afford to fund all of the infrastructure projects that they would like. However, with the right kind of motivation, they can entice the private sector to find a way to help them pay the bill.

§

Overall, the task of finding a way to fund essential state infrastructure is a difficult one. Confronted by weak balance sheets and huge infrastructure expectations, state governments are in an unenviable position.

Luckily, several options exist which most other nations are incapable of pursuing. Privatisations, asset transfers, user pays and reconceptualising infrastructure projects each offer state governments innovative ways to fund their infrastructure backlog. They need only the courage to try.

Population poaching

Australia is one of the most attractive places in the world to live.

Its warm weather, clean environment, welcoming community and high standard of living are all features which people from almost every culture on Earth desire. Additionally, its relatively low unemployment rate, educated workforce, elaborate social services and boundless opportunities all make settlement extremely attractive.

Yet despite these desirable traits, Australia does very little to leverage them when attempting to attract the world's best to resettle. In fact, in terms of marketing itself to the world, Australia does little more than promote itself as an interesting holiday destination rather than an appealing place to relocate, invest and raise a family.

As Australia's labour challenges worsen over the decades ahead, a reappraisal of this approach will be necessary.

The marketing dilemma

It goes without saying that immigration marketing is not the same as tourism marketing.

Tourism is about attracting people to Australia's most interesting locations. Whether they are cities or beaches, or cultural icons or natural ones, the goal is to attract a foreigner for a temporary visit and maybe a return trip, but little more.

Immigration, on the other hand, is about convincing people to make Australia their new home. In order to do so, the foreigner needs to be convinced that factors such as climate, lifestyle, employment, service delivery and culture are better than where they presently reside.

Luckily for Australia, it is no hard task to win those contests against the vast majority of the world's nations. Certainly, Australia's standard of living and the opportunities it provides are far greater than anything offered in the developing world. But what about the established world? How does Australia compare against those nations which share very similar living standards? You may be surprised: very well in fact.

The great northern malaise

In Europe at the moment, millions of young, educated and multilingual 20-somethings are living their lives with little prospect of employment. Having graduated from university with personal debts and genuine employability, they have found themselves entering a continent-wide economy beset by weak growth, hesitant employers[473] and a youth unemployment rate more than twice the adult one.[474]

Prospects for business starts in Europe are also equally depressing. Tight capital markets and depressed domestic spending have combined to create the worst economic conditions in a generation. As a result, an entire cohort of young Europeans are missing out on their dream of economic prosperity.

North America isn't faring much better. With economic growth only slowly recovering, youth unemployment and underemployment problems continue to linger. Moreover, for those who own their own homes, housing debt in too many cases outweigh the property's market value. As with the nations of Europe, North America also is suffering its worst economic malaise in a generation. As a result, the talented youth of this continent are also facing a long winter in regard to their career prospects and wealth ambitions.

The opening

As crude as it may sound, young adults are the best kind of citizens to have. With the public and private cost of raising and educating them having concluded, most young adults are on the cusp of their most healthy, independent and productive working years.

Viewed within such a context, there is only one thing better than young adults from one's own country: young adults from someone else's. Why? The answer is simple: someone else has paid the bill.

With much of the northern hemisphere now locked in a decade of unrealised dreams, Australia is perfectly placed to resolve many of its skilled labour shortcomings. Put another way, the time is ripe to enact a new model for international talent recruitment.

Broadly speaking, there are two reforms which should be initiated:

- the creation of a government approved migrant recruitment business model; and

- the development of targeted recruitment campaigns.

Migrant recruiters

The development of a migrant recruitment business model which enjoys government support will be an essential first step in Australia's efforts to build significant migrant poaching power.

At present, a substantial number of migrants who successfully migrate to Australia do so without any attempted persuasion at all. Rather than having an immigration official convincing them to trade one kind of citizenry for another, Australia instead passively awaits the arrival of certified migration requests. If Australia is to seize the moment and recruit the best that Europe and North America have to offer, this laconic approach will need to change.

In order to upgrade Australia's migration processes, a new business licence should be created for Australian migration recruiters to officially venture overseas and seek out new Australians for resettlement. Initially targeting the depressed economies of Europe and North America, these recruiters should be given significant latitude to advertise, investigate, verify and process migration applications according to specific recruitment criteria, such as age, education, linguistic ability and health and employment history. Much like how the Department of Employment has contracted out employment service provision to the private sector, the Department of Immigration and Border Protection would do the same for a portion of Australia's skilled migration programme. Naturally, government officials would continue to perform the relevant background and security checks.

By shifting a portion of Australia's migration efforts to a proactive recruitment model, Australia can ensure that its migration regime remains globally competitive as well as regionally responsive. Critically, it will help improve the quality of migrants

Australian officials have to choose from. By purposefully seeking out migrants that the Australian community needs, rather than sifting through the applications it receives, Australia's migration managers will be better able to address the nation's myriad of labour force challenges.

Targeted recruitment campaigns

Accompanying Australia's energised recruitment efforts should also be a targeted recruitment campaign.

In the corporate world, aggressive recruitment of staff from your competitors is considered part of the professional game of commerce. While it is costly, disruptive and frustrating, it is also a business reality. Good staff are always in short supply, and if you can attract them away from your competitors, then they should have been taking better care of them.

The competition for labour between nations is no different. While people are obviously not the same as products or services, the rules of international competition still apply. If a nation can offer greater opportunities for people than their host nation can, then the host nation should have offered them better reasons to stay.

For much of the past 100 years, this is a game Australia has played poorly. While it has been successful at attracting millions of hard working people to its shores, it has been just as unsuccessful at retaining its best and brightest. Drawn away to pursue fancier careers, in bigger cities with better education institutions, Australia has been as much a loser as it has been a winner.

In this decade however, Australia has a superb opportunity to turn this situation around. Empowered with a good story to tell and an amazing reversal of attractiveness, Australia is primed to turn the tables.

In order to do so, Australia will need to develop a recruitment campaign which effectively contrasts its strengths against the perceived weaknesses of the regions it is targeting. As highlighted above, Australia has an advantage in liveability, social harmony and employment. It also has a strong economy with an extremely bright future ahead of it. Any campaign designed to recruit the North Atlantic's "lost generation" should ensure that these traits feature heavily. By leveraging Australia's strengths against the north's acute vulnerabilities, Australia should be able to lift its quota of migrants from amongst the most educated corners of the earth.

§

Overall, economic misfortune in the northern hemisphere has gifted Australia with a rare opportunity to address some of its most pressing labour challenges.

Whether Australia's decision-makers appreciate it or not, a discount sale is presently on for some of the world's best talent. As a nation which has perennially been the loser of such global recruitment contests, the time is right to seize the moment and restore some competition to these contests.

Competitive migration, productive settlement

As demand for migrants increases as a result of demographic and economic change, global efforts to attract and retain them will intensify.

This shift in competition will hurt Australia's efforts to tackle its future demographic, labour and productivity challenges.

Consequently, how Australia attracts, integrates and engages with immigrants will require a serious policy rethink.

There are three major reforms Australia should undertake to ensure its migration regime remains competitive and productive in the future. These are:

- enhancing the attractiveness of Australia as an immigration destination;
- accelerating the settlement and integration of new Australians; and
- converting low skilled migrants into high skilled new Australians.

Making them an offer they can't refuse

Enhancing the attractiveness of Australia to potential immigrants will require a fundamental rethink of immigration strategy.

Australia is one of the most attractive destinations for migrants to resettle due to its high standard of living, harmonious culture and wealth of opportunity. However, as living standards improve across the developing world, and the necessity of immigrants for maintaining economic vitality increases within the established world, competition for their attention will grow and Australia's natural advantages will erode. As a result, a key area of migration policy which requires reviewing is that of how Australia markets itself to potential migrants.

According to the OECD,[475] Australia is the third largest foreign education service provider in the world offering services to students sourced from over 160 nations.[476] In 2012, Australia hosted 402,388 individual students in education institutions.[477] Based on OECD estimates, this figure could be as high as 595,000 in just six years.[478]

As a major foreign education provider, Australia is uniquely placed to leverage its market position to strengthen its attractiveness as a resettlement destination, especially in the highly competitive skilled migration sector.

Of the 442,934 students studying in Australia during 2012,[479] 49 per cent pursued higher education, 23 per cent vocation education and training (VET), 18 per cent pursued ELICOS[480] and ten per cent pursued school or non-award education.[481] While these students are not Australian citizens, after three to four years of residency, they are often very familiar with its customs, culture, laws, civil rights, jobs market and language. Consequently, as a by-product of Australia's vast education services sector, the nation has made these highly educated students ideally suited for permanent residency or citizenship.

During President Obama's second inauguration speech in 2013, he announced his plan to offer international STEM,[482] PhD and Masters degree graduates American citizenship upon securing employment.[483] The motivation behind this was to ensure that the world's brightest students, studying at America's best institutions, sought employment and success within America's economy: as Obama later stated, "It's not smart to invite some of the brightest minds from around the world to study here and then not let them start businesses here."[484]

As a nation with comparable aspirations and strengths, Australia should adopt a similar approach and tailor its residency and citizenship programme to meet the nations long term economic and demographic needs. Ideally speaking, the Commonwealth Government should offer permanent residency or citizenship to every international student who graduates from an undergraduate, post graduate or VET course in any area where Australia is experiencing or is forecast to experience a skilled shortage. Qualification for either of these forms of migration should be based upon an agreed level of academic achievement, a suitable background, financial and health check and evidence of local employment. Importantly, the process for awarding the citizenship and residency should be fast, uncomplicated and affordable.

By adopting such an approach to Australia's skilled migration strategy, the nation would not only increase its desirability as a settlement destination, but it would also increase the attractiveness of its education institutions as a venue for study.

Kitchenaid settlement

The success of a new migration boom is often measured by the nation's ability to accelerate the settlement[485] and blending of its new arrivals.

At present, far too many new Australians, especially those who arrive here through its humanitarian migration programmes, suffer from social dislocation, poverty, confusion and high levels of unemployment as a result of the nation's poor resettlement and integration procedures. One of the key factors contributing to these problems is their limited command of the English language.[486]

According to the former Department of Immigration and Citizenship, "an immigrant who cannot speak English as a first language is over five times more likely to be unemployed after six months in Australia than one who does".[487,488] "Twelve months later, this ratio worsens."[489,490] Not only is English vital to securing employment, but it is essential for accessing government services, avoiding social isolation, understanding contractual obligations, reading road signs, improving personal productivity, helping their children with education, understanding one's legal rights and for engaging beyond their ethnic community. "Indeed, language barriers are amongst the greatest obstacles to successful settlement"[491] in any nation. Consequently, eliminating them is a vital step in the process of unlocking the productive and integration potential of all new Australians.

One of the most effective ways of addressing this problem is by mandating English language courses such as the Adult Migrant English Programme (AMEP)[492] for all new immigrants of working age who cannot demonstrate "competent language ability"[493] through a specified language and numeracy test upon citizenship approval. By compelling new immigrants to learn the language of their new home, perhaps by denying future access to the welfare system unless they comply, government can ensure that many of the obstacles they will face later on in life will simply not exist.

To date, governments of all political persuasions have been hesitant about mandating language education for new Australians. They have acted this way because of the dated belief that earlier migration waves did not require such intervention in order to be successful. Therefore, current generations equally do not require government intervention. While this policy position succeeds at keeping the political correctness lobby at bay, the historical application of this experience flawed. The simple fact is, in the 1950s migrants from Southern and Eastern Europe did not need English to settle effectively. At the time of their arrival, language skills were irrelevant to their ability to perform hundreds of thousands of jobs. As a result, poor command of English was of lesser concern. Today, however, language skills are vital for even the most basic forms of employment. If you cannot speak or read English, you cannot drive a taxi, use a computer or even work in a call centre. Consequently, the ability of migrants with poor English skills to settle successfully is far lower than what their predecessor experienced 60 years ago. Regardless of the merits of the argument, accepting low skilled employment which does not require the English language is not the settlement outcome Australians should be satisfied with. Rather, the nation should be working to help all new Australians reach their full productive potential for the length of their working life.

The long term goal of our immigration system should always be about building a community which is not only engaged across ethnic, cultural and religious lines, but one which is also filled with individuals who are settled, productive and fully blended. The pursuit of these essential objectives is always made easier if new citizens are well versed in the language of their new home. Akin to investing in a child's schooling, mandating English language education will result in a valuable return for the individual and the entire community. Any policy which can deliver that kind of outcome is definitely worth pursuing.

Converting low skilled migrants into high skilled Australians

The Australian workforce will always be in need of high and low skilled workers to meet the needs of its growing economy. Unfortunately, while the global supply of low skilled workers is always likely to be plentiful, the supply of high skilled ones will not. As a result, as Australia's domestically grown workforce shrinks in the years ahead as a result of demographic change, Australia will need to begin exploring alternative options in order to avoid a damaging labour shortage and disruptive wage spike.

One way Australia can better manage this challenge is by redesigning its migrant settlement policies with the expressed goal of converting low skilled workers into higher skilled ones. At present, over thousands of low skilled immigrants come to Australia each year aged between 15 and 50 years. With the exception of those choosing to raise a family or enjoy retirement (contributory parent visa), the majority of low skilled migrants will seek to enter the Australian workforce within a few months of arrival. Unfortunately for them and the Australian economy, these people will often begin employment in low paying jobs at a fraction of their productive potential, and usually for life.

Instead of allowing this scenario to happen, it would make much more sense to evaluate their productive potential upon arrival (education level and capacity for upskilling) and directly offer them the opportunity to upgrade their education. Ideally, appropriately identified new migrants would be given the opportunity to undertake a university or VET course with housing and welfare support included. Such a system could be funded directly by the government (via SGP Grants),[494] through a government loan scheme repaid on conclusion of study, through private enterprise (linked to an employment obligation down the track) or a mixture of all three.

By addressing our skilled labour shortage in this fashion, Australia would be able to address its shortages by recognising the productive capacity of its local workforce, and then unleashing its full potential for the betterment of long term economic development. If such a process were able to be perfected, the programme would not only ensure that Australia's best migrants do not fall through the cracks of bad process, but it would also complement the nation's targeted skilled labour programme by developing additional home grown talent.

§

As identified above, Australia faces an increasingly competitive and supply constrained environment when it comes to sourcing its future immigrant population. Consequently, the nation's immigration and settlement programmes will need to be reconceptualised in order to remain effective.

Much like the nation's business sector, Australia's migration programmes will need to constantly innovate in order to remain contemporary, increase global share and maximise the full potential of those who settle here. By adopting the methods outlined above, Australia can establish itself as a global leader before the rest of the world adopts the inevitable. As with all things competitive, first movers often enjoy the greatest strategic advantage. As Australia progresses further into the 21st century, it better make sure that it is one of them.

Archipelagic government

Successfully managing demographic growth across Australia's 100 population islands will be one of the great governance tests this century.

With the population of almost all islands forecast to increase over the next four decades, new governance tools will be required to meet rising community expectations and maximise productivity.

There are three areas where new governance techniques will need to be pioneered. These are:

- forging a new management model for planning, building and servicing the physical expansion of population islands;
- reconceptualising the role of demography related portfolios to better encourage and facilitate urban consolidation; and
- creating new portfolios to oversee the service needs of non-citizens.

Reclaiming the sea

Australia's population islands are growing.

In 2006, the New South Wales Government approved the expansion of Cumberland Island's (Greater Sydney) landmass by 27,000 hectares.[495] Six years later, the Victorian Government did the same by approving a 40,000 hectare expansion of Yarra Island (Greater Melbourne).[496] In both cases, these expansions were driven by strong housing demand linked to population growth.

Over the next five decades, Australia's population is forecast to grow by at least 14 million people.[497] As this demographic expansion unfolds, the majority of these people will settle in the underdeveloped areas outside the boundaries of Australia's existing population islands.

Within development industry circles, these areas are commonly referred to as "growth areas" or "growth centres". However, in the context of a population island model, they are more accurately defined as "foreshores" which are reclaimed from the surrounding sea through the process of urban development.

Reclaiming the sea is a massive undertaking. It not only demands the expenditure of considerable financial resources, but it also requires careful planning and forecasting across of a range of complex fields such as transportation, community infrastructure, employment creation, land use, sustainability and social and economic development.

One of the largest Australian regions reclaimed from the sea during 20th century is Western Sydney. On an area almost 550,000 hectares wide, Western Sydney produces $75 billion worth of economic output and is home to over 1.6 million people.[498] Unfortunately, it is also one of Australia's greatest planning, infrastructure and liveability disasters. Road commuter times are amongst the worst in the nation,[499] urban planning has been poorly thought out, public transport links are sparse and community services are amongst NSW's most stretched. The reason Western Sydney is in such bad shape is because successive governments have failed to effectively manage its development.

Worryingly for the rest of the country, the same mistakes are being made in regard to the next generation of foreshores. Whether it is urban expansion in south eastern Queensland, north western Melbourne or southern Perth, each to varying degrees are experiencing the same growth challenges which resulted in Western Sydney's current predicament – slow and antiquated decision making, uncoordinated long term planning (and internal government communication) underinvestment in infrastructure (road, rail, water, energy and community services), inflexible urban planning, poor rate bases for local government, administrative overreach from statutory authorities and financial neglect from the central government. Yet despite this myriad of problems, it is not too late to change their fate.

In order to get a better handle on the challenges plaguing these foreshores, a complete overhaul of how they are administered is required. As highlighted above, foreshore conversions (developing growth areas) are best conceptualised as sea reclamations. At the beginning of the process, these areas are essentially untouched neighbouring territory, home to little or no urbanisation. However, once they reach full maturity, the opposite is true – urbanisation is their most identifiable feature. In many ways, this progression is similar to that of colony foundation and development. Over the space of many years, an entirely new political and economic entity is slowly created. Consequently, when it comes to the process of managing their development, an entirely new administrative approach is required.

At present, responsibility for these regions rests in the hands of two levels of government spread across multiple lines of authority. At a state government level, almost a dozen ministers across several departments are regularly involved. At a local government level, multiple councils also participate, albeit with slightly different responsibilities. With so many decision makers involved, the quality of administration is often tortuous. Both levels of government work at cross purposes, growth management and investment priorities routinely contradict and each interferes with the core responsibilities of the other. Worse still, administrative decision making is also undermined by a serious imbalance of political power and community interests. On one hand you have existing communities (above the shoreline) arguing for increased resources to improve their overall standard of living, and on the other, you have future communities (the foreshores) requiring the same. However, whereas in shoreline communities the balance of political and economic power is more evenly distributed amongst its constituents, in the foreshores the vast majority of beneficiaries do not yet exist. As a result, government responsiveness to demand for community and economic infrastructure like roads, rail lines and schools almost always lags.

A different approach is required to deliver a better planning, building and management outcome for Australia's future foreshore communities. In essence, a *tabula rasa* of existing arrangements. The following reforms should shape the basis of any revised governance model:

First. Excise the foreshores (growth areas) from traditional state government management along lines similar to "unincorporated areas".[500] State governments need to recognise that they are not just extending their suburbs; they are building communities the size and scale of Adelaide. Excising the foreshores sends a clear message to the community, the private sector and the bureaucracy that the old rules and standards no longer apply;

Second. Establish a new state government department with enhanced and centralised decision making authority for all foreshores (growth areas). The new department should be granted authority to oversee all master planning, service delivery, regulatory control, infrastructure provision and local government activity within the excised area. By centralising decision making authority within one department, a higher level of coordination and consistency will be possible between all decision-makers involved in the excised area. Critically, it will also ensure that all reporting lines for government approvals and activity within the foreshores lead to the same place;

Third. Create a dedicated minister to oversee the new department and ensure he/she is supported by a trio of foreshore specific parliamentary secretaries. e.g. mobility, community development and service provision. At present, the foreshores and the communities they will eventually house lack a dedicated champion in Cabinet and a minister publicly responsible for their fate. The appointment of a committed minister will resolve that problem by simultaneously eliminating the power, responsibility and coordination vacuums; and

Fourth. Form a Board which reports to the minister and consists of representatives from the local community, statutory authorities, private sector stakeholders and the department. In-depth involvement of elected and unelected stakeholders will be vital for achieving a step change in outcomes. Naturally, appointments must be made carefully and enjoy the support of the public.

In the 1990s, the Victorian Government pioneered the management model of "executive" government as an innovative tool to more effectively manage the innumerable governance challenges the state was facing. While controversial at the time, the end result was an undeniable step change in outcomes which continues to echo even today. With Australia's growth areas facing an equally daunting governance challenge, a new and bolder approach is required. A fundamental revamp of existing administrative processes is the only way such an outcome will be possible. As a result, it is time all state governments reconsidered their existing management structures.

Modifying island development operations

The second area where improvements need to be made to Australia's governance models is in regard to encouraging and facilitating urban consolidation.

As highlighted above, the populations of many of Australia's islands are surging. In the space of one generation, the populations of Cumberland (Greater Sydney), Yarra (Greater Melbourne), Oxley (Greater Brisbane) and Swan (Greater Perth) will have grown by more than in any previous generation. This rapid demographic shift will have a profound impact on the effectiveness of present day approaches to infrastructure and service delivery.

In order to effectively respond, initiatives more creative than an increase in public and private expenditure will be necessary. Much like how new ministers and governance approaches in the multimedia and climate change space were pioneered late last century, an overhaul of existing demographic portfolios will be required during this century.

In recent years, many governments have attempted to address this challenge by making minor calibrations to existing appointments and structures. One of the most common reforms has been the merging of planning and infrastructure departments to better coordinate policy. Such reforms have been worthwhile, but sadly, they do not go far enough. If governments are to effectively engineer a marked difference in outcomes, they will need to do more than just tinker at the edges. They will need to completely reconceptualise themselves and their very reason for being.

The most important area where this process must take place is in the demographic portfolio of planning. Planning ministers, no matter their political talent or creed, have a wonderful record of preparing detailed planning blueprints which end up being ignored. In Victoria for example, three separate planning blueprints have been created in just 14 years – all of which have been rewritten by their own creators, rubbished by their political opponents or ignored by their primary facilitators.[501] In essence, not only have they failed to stand the test of time, they have also failed to pass a trial of relevance.

If Australia is to lift its success rate in planning future development across its population islands, it will need to change the way it manages its planning blueprints. Broadly speaking, planning blueprints which outline how cities will manage demographic change fail for two key reasons. First, their objectives lack the support of the community; and second, its authors rarely drive their implementation. Resolving these shortcomings will be essential in order to improve nationwide success rates. Two reforms should be considered:

Marketing urban consolidation

One of the undeniable failures of planning blueprints across Australia has been the inability of their authors to secure deep and wide-spread public support. While extensive community consultation has been engaged in over the years, little genuine goodwill exists in regards to the central tenant of all modern planning blueprints – urban consolidation.

Despite furious agreement between academics, planners, developers and planning department bureaucrats about the merits of urban consolidation policy, communities across Australia's population islands remain vehemently opposed. While the reasons for this resistance is varied and in many cases entirely reasonable, the simple fact is, governments have failed to persuade the public of the policy's merits. As a result, when it has come to the policy's implementation, follow through rarely follows visionary announcements.

If governments are to properly enact their island-wide planning strategies, they will need to modify the way their vision is communicated.

As mentioned earlier, the great strength of planning departments is their ability to develop planning blueprints. They are great on theory, process and design. Beyond that however, their skills are generally limited. In the private sector, this shortcoming wouldn't necessarily be a problem. In a similar situation, a design and construct company would simply pass the planning ideas to their marketing, financial or construction teams for actioning. In the public sector though, those teams simply do not exist. As a result, policy marketing is left to the minister or is not pursued at all.

The easiest way to address this advocacy shortcoming is to create a marketing arm for planning departments. If urban consolidation policy is a must for maintaining living standards and productivity in the face of surging population growth, then more resources should be deployed to encourage its uptake. Historically, multiple governments have expended taxpayers' dollars on promoting the benefits of policy reform. Whether it was been the

GST, workplace relations or border control, governments have recognised the importance of educating the public about complicated but necessary policy reform. If urban consolidation is the most effective pathway for managing population growth, it too should enjoy its own marketing agenda.

Development facilitation

Accompanying any effective marketing campaign must also be a willingness by ministers and their departments to lead a change in public opinion. Leaving hesitant councils to implement a city-wide development strategy which they oppose is akin to assigning emergency room surgery to a hemophobic. Not only will they fail to begin the operation, but they will probably also obfuscate for as long as possible. In order to rectify this mismatch in objectives and responsibilities, two changes must be made.

First, in order to annunciate a clear redefinition of government priorities, the minister and his/her department should unashamedly adopt a title more reflective of their new mission. Rather than playing the role of designer, they should instead assume the role of facilitator. Using the words 'development', 'construction' and 'urban renewal' in their titles would all be good places to start. Rather than focussing internal and external service identification around planning a brave new world, these facilitators would instead be dedicated to actually building it.

Second, governments must assume full responsibility for enforcing their planning blueprints. In the state of Victoria for example, the Government has chosen to accomplish this goal through the creation of a third party – the newly formed Metropolitan Planning Authority (MPA). "The MPA has been created to implement the initiatives and vision set out in the Victorian Government's metropolitan planning strategy – *Plan*

Melbourne".[502] If given sufficient enforcement and planning override powers, the MPA approach could make a sizeable difference in seeing the Government's planning blueprint realised. Without them however, it risks replicating the same delivery failures of the past, albeit using a new letterhead. In order to see a genuine improvement in the area of planning blueprint implementation, all governments must assume a decisive role in policy delivery. The creation of dedicated planning authorities across the nation is one solution which could deliver the breakthrough that is required. The challenge however, will be ensuring that their written mandates end up of matching their public records.

Improving customer service

Addressing Australia's uncoordinated response to rising tourist and foreign student numbers is the final area where major governance reform is required.

While it largely goes unreported in the media, Australia provides a temporary home to millions of foreign nationals each year.[503] Through a combination of tourist visitor arrivals, foreign student residencies and temporary and semi-permanent foreign labour, Australia can play host to well over half a million non-citizens per month.[504]

Just like Australian citizens, these groups exhibit nearly all the same consumption habits. They catch Australia's trains, buses and trams; they reside in the nation's houses, apartments and hotels; they rely upon the nation's safety, health and education services and they frequent the nation's restaurants, retail outlets and entertainment districts. In essence, they are Australians in every way except citizenship.

Where this becomes a major challenge for Australia's governments is in regard to how this form of demand is managed. Over the coming decades, the number of non-citizens in all three visitation clusters is forecast to rise dramatically. And in almost every case, the vast majority of them will choose to reside on Australia's major population islands where tourist attractions, educational services and job shortages are at their greatest. If this increase in demand is handled poorly, more than just Australia's non-citizenry will be affected – voting citizens will be impacted as well.

Despite the obvious infrastructure and service delivery implications of a flexible visitation policy, very few of Australia's planning blueprints address the challenges it inevitably throws up. Worse still, too many areas of government policy such as mass transit ticketing simply ignore the unique service needs these non-citizen consumers create. If Australia is to maximise the economic and social benefits these three visiting demographic clusters will generate over the years ahead, it will need to revise its current approach to managing them.

In order to optimise the quality of customer service Australia's governments offer non-citizen visitors, a dedicated minister should be created. This minister should assume responsibility for understanding, forecasting, overseeing and partially delivering the public service needs of tourists, foreign students and foreign workers. Furthermore, the minister should also be responsible for feeding this information into the broader government policy development process. By appointing a dedicated minister for Australia's non-citizenry population, governments will finally be able to provide the customer service outcomes that their resident non-citizens deserve.

§

In summary, as Australia's population islands grow in size and complexity this century, many will find themselves under increasing pressure to manage their evolving needs more effectively. As demonstrated above, the governance tools presently in use are simply not up to the task.

If Australia wants to avoid a degradation in living standards and island-wide productivity, a new approach will be required. Outlined above are three ideas which should form part of any serious government response.

Responsive, harmonious and flexible workplaces

Ensuring Australian businesses remain competitive in an increasingly interconnected global economy will be one of the toughest challenges facing the nation this century.

Confronted with rising demands for work-life flexibility, intensifying international competition, the third highest minimum wage in the OECD (60 per cent higher than the United Kingdom's)[505] and multiplying sources of product and service acquisition, employers will need a workplace relations system which has flexibility and autonomy at its heart, rather than one defined by outdated social customs and rigid workforce arrangements.

In order for Australia to secure a productive and cost competitive edge, three areas of workplace relations reform must be enacted as soon as possible. These are:

- ushering in the era of 24/7 retailing;
- returning management certainty back to construction, mining and energy businesses; and

- reintroducing EBA's which support growth, creativity and sustainable business activity.

Lamaze for 24 hour retailing

Recognising the end of the traditional 9-5 workweek is an essential first step in helping Australia prepare for the most competitive century in history. Since its conception in the Western world, the traditional 9-5 workweek has helped define normal work hours for millions of Australian workers. At the time of its introduction, it has helped protect the importance of the family unit, personal and recreational time and a workers right to reasonable work hours. For decades, these principles served society well. However, as social standards evolved, technology advanced and international trade accelerated; the primacy of a regulated workweek has given way before society's preference for increased flexibility. Indeed, there is no better example of this evolution than that 1970s shopping innovation, the 7-Eleven. At the time of its arrival on Australian soil, its 7am to 11pm operating hours were unheard of. Yet the idea that you would name a non 9-5 convenience store by the same name today is ridiculous. Whether we like it or not, contemporary consumers now expect service at all hours.

Where this represents a serious problem for Australia's retailers is the fact that the workplace relations system in which they operate remains trapped in the inflexible world of the 9-5 workweek. On one hand, consumers and employees desire greater flexibility in their shopping and employment choices, but on the other, retailers are forced to compete with international and online competitors which enjoy a fraction of their operating costs. If retailers are going to survive being wedged between these competing and complex interests, then new arrangements based around a 24/7 workweek will need to be pioneered.

The most important place to start is addressing the unsustainable rise in penalty rates for workers on weekends and during traditional work hours. In March 2008, the award modernisation and rationalisation process resulted in more competitive state awards being replaced by less affordable ones found in other states. Through the introduction of a "modern award", this process caused considerable economic harm to employers in the retail, hospitality and tourism sectors by increasing the wage outlays for these businesses without balancing it with productivity improvements. This process caused serious economic harm to businesses operating in states where Sunday penalty rates and weekday after 6pm arrangements had historically been more competitive. Indeed, rural operations that depend upon the weekend tourist trade have been particularly caught out.

According to the National Retail Association, "the service sector in Queensland has been a substantial victim of the award modernisation process".[506] Similar impacts have also been reported in New South Wales and South Australia[507] with some industry groups referring to damage done as "extraordinary".[508]

Right across the nation operating costs have risen, retail jobs growth has eased, profitability has declined, domestic tourism has ventured overseas and hard won competitive niches have been lost. Indeed, the situation has become so bad that full time retail business managers on fixed incomes now substitute for casual workers on weekends because the cost to the business is lower. Put another way, the system has grown so out of sync with modern requirements that it is now beginning to distort basic business operations.

With such problems emerging, it comes as no surprise to learn that "two-thirds of tourism operators want penalty rates reviewed",[509] as does the collective memberships of Australia's largest employer organisations – the National Retailers Association, Restaurant and Caterers Australia, Business Council of Australia and the Australian Chamber of Commerce and Industry. In a flat economy facing rising unemployment and intensifying competition from online and overseas, it is hard not to understand why.

If Australia is to secure its place as an international hub for retail trade, host global cities which operate 24-7, offer small businesses cost pressure relief, and provide workplace choice for employees who feel less compunction for working weekends and evenings, than its retail sector will need new methods of managing today's trading expectations. A good place to start would be a comprehensive review of penalty rate arrangements for employees working in the retail sector, especially on weekends and during weekday evenings.

Management with a capital "M"

Restoring management control to businesses operating in the construction, mining and energy sector will also be crucial to efforts to keep Australia's economy competitive.

Over 10 per cent of the Australian workforce is employed in the construction sector, mining and energy sectors, but very few business managers in those sector feel like they have full control over their worksites. The reason for this is because of the disproportionately high level of union militancy in these sectors across Australia. As a result of weak law enforcement, poor workplace leadership and the unique vulnerability of their companies to organised exploitation, a workplace environment has developed in which owners and managers are not in control of their own operations. The end result has been a cost of construction "for high-rise apartments, CBD offices, hospitals, schools and roads"[510] which is amongst the highest in the Western world;[511] an energy and mining sector with globally uncompetitive labour costs; a remuneration structure which is predicated upon employer exploitation rather than mutual corporation and negotiated productivity gains; a highly inflexible work year calendar; and, a workplace environment rife with fear, intimidation and criminal activity.

If Australia wants to host a dynamic economy, perpetuate a modern infrastructure, maximise rising demand for energy and raw materials and maintain pace with population and economic growth pressures, it will need a workplace relations system which is efficient and functioning at peak capacity. To achieve such outcomes against the backdrop of the above mentioned problems, three critical reforms will be necessary. They are:

- restoring "right of entry" provisions;
- reintroducing the "rule of law" and harsher penalties for non-compliance; and
- introducing a higher industry standard for industry participants.

Reasserting managerial control on worksites is a must if productivity and investment is to rise. The surest way to return control of workplaces back to employers is by restoring the Right of Entry (ROE) provisions which existed before the *Fair Work Act* was introduced.

Since the introduction of the *Fair Work Act*, ROE rules have been relaxed considerably leading to increased business costs and workplace disputation and politicisation. At present, union officials are using the watered down ROE rules to enter workplaces and recruit members, conduct non-essential union business and perform their own workplace law breach investigations. Occasionally, this is occurring when there are no union members present, causing considerably disruption in the workplace. Restoring ROE provisions will ensure that site managers can adequately prepare for unscheduled non-workforce visitors (union activists), separate onsite safety matters from industrial disputation, concentrate on business activities and more easily manage who can come onto their sites, how much notice they provide in advance and what they can do when they arrive.

Ensuring that the law is enforced on building sites and that effective penalties are in place to deter reoccurrence will also be essential for changing the behaviour which presently undermines productivity, safety and competitiveness.

The most important reform which can be made to address this would be the reinstatement of the Australian Building and Construction Commission (ABCC) which was replaced by insipid Fair Work Building and Construction Inspectorate in 2012. During its seven years of operation (2005-2012), the ABCC enforced the rule of law on building sites across Australia for both employers and employees. Several studies examining the ABCC's performance have revealed that it was successful in reducing industrial disputation in the construction sector, cutting construction costs and boosting productivity.[512] In 2009 and 2012 however, the Rudd and Gillard Governments weakened the ABCC by amending its Act of Parliament, changing its personnel and by reducing the penalties it could seek for breaches. As a result, Australia-wide industrial militancy on construction sites has risen. Between 2011-12 and 2012-13 workings days lost due to industrial disputation rose from 24,000 to 89,900.[513] Consequently the construction sector presently has the nation's worst record for working days at more than triple the national average.[514]

The surest way to reverse these consequences would be to reactivate the ABCC, recruit new personnel, restore and extend the original penalty provisions and amend its accompanying National Code of Practice and implementation guidelines. As flagged by the current Commonwealth Government, expanding its areas of responsibility into ports and offshore mining and energy projects would also be worth considering.

Securing definitive cultural change in the construction, energy and mining sectors will also require a decade long commitment to higher professional standards. Unfortunately, over the past decade, inconsistent oversight and the resilience of union militancy have made the achievement of lasting cultural change difficult to achieve. In order to secure the cultural wins necessary to clean up the sector, another layer of reforms will be required to change the landscape permanently.

First, efforts must be made to directly confront the number of unsavoury characters who dominate these sectors. Far too many union leaders have criminal records ranging from assault and intimidation, to asset destruction and failure to obey court orders. In some cases, union officials have dozens of different criminal and civil charges to their name. If these sectors are to properly clean up their image, they must first clean up their personnel. The Commonwealth and each state government should begin by imposing good character tests on positions of significant public prominence. If a company director can be banned from assuming a position on a company board as a result of his/her past misdeeds, than there is no reason a similar requirement cannot be imposed on a union official. While everyone deserves a second chance to rehabilitate their reputation, too many senior positions within the union movement are filled by individuals who are too comfortable with criminality. With trade unions recently registering the lowest level of trust amongst Australia's major institutions (at just 49 per cent),[515] it seems the public agrees.

The second level of reform relates to the organisations which consistently engage in illegal behaviour. Far too often, union representatives will gladly break the law if they feel they can justify it politically. In order to deter such behaviour in the future, governments at all levels should legislate to empower the courts to seize assets and/ or delist organisations which continue to defy court orders. In cases of extreme union militancy, the law is effectively useless unless the perpetrators are afraid of the financial or legal consequences. Changes to asset confiscation and delisting laws will ensure that quickly becomes the case.

Lazarien EBAs

The final area where workplace relations reform is necessary is in regard to the enterprise bargaining agreement (EBA) environment which operates in Australia. At present, EBAs are a vital tool for organising labour resources for business operations in the internationally exposed sectors of construction, infrastructure, manufacturing, energy and mining sectors. However, since the introduction of the *Fair Work Act*, a number of changes have been made which restrict their design, content, flexibility and duration.

In order to maximise economic growth and industry competitiveness in an increasingly globalised world, Australia will need to have an EBA environment which supports business expansion and investment, encourages creative workplace practices and promotes sustainable business activity. Two key reforms should be considered:

- reintroducing prohibited content rules and agreement certification standards to avoid the EBA dilution; and

- expand the variability, exclusivity and duration of Greenfield EBAs.

Removing the ability to insert restrictive, costly, unnecessary and overtly union friendly conditions within EBAs is an important first step towards reducing business costs and improving the quality of EBAs in Australia. Since the introduction of the *Fair Work Act*, the number of nuisance provisions within EBAs has soared as a result of the softening of prohibited content rules. At present, Australian EBAs are able to include "trade union training leave, payroll deductions for union fees, right of entry clauses, shop stewards' rights clauses, union offices on site and use of contractors"[516] despite these matters having little to do with the "employment relationship". Further, union friendly content has also been inserted into EBAs which undermines business productivity, breaches Freedom of Association laws and directly challenges the managerial prerogative of employers. Some of the worst examples include:

- restricting the use of on-hire workers and contractors;
- providing the names and contact information of all on-hire workers and contractors the business intends to engage;
- mandatory union consultation on any effort to engage on-hire workers or contactors, including clauses which prohibit greater flexibility/wages in any agreement;
- promoting union membership and activity in the workplace; and
- broadening the circumstances under which strike action may occur.

These changes have severely complicated the employer-employee relationship, increased the cost burden for business, undermined sector competitiveness, deterred investment and undermined managerial control of business entities. They also place in jeopardy any chance of Australian businesses being able to compete internationally. Consequently, putting a stop to these abuses and restoring fairness to the workplace relations systems is a must. In order to do so, the Commonwealth Government should restore the prohibited content rules, reactivate the legislative provisions which prevented the inclusion of invalid terms in EBAs (agreement certification) and close the loophole within the *Fair Work Act* which permits agreements to be Code Compliant even if they breach the National Construction Code and Implementation Guidelines.

The second area of EBA reform which must be instigated is a revitalisation of Greenfield Agreements. Greenfield Agreements are a form of EBAs designed for early stage business operations. Their intent is to allow greater flexibility for businesses in their vulnerable start up stage.

Since the introduction of the *Fair Work Act*, the variability and exclusivity arrangements governing Greenfield Agreements has changed to the detriment of business growth and workplace practice innovation. The biggest challenges in regard to variability exists in regard to the restriction on employers to negotiate only two different kinds of agreements (union elective agreements or union Greenfield agreements),[517] down from six prior to the reforms. Not only is this a severe downgrading of employer-employee choice, the flexibility arrangements are also deficient. Under these arrangements, employers are unable to negotiate on fair terms with unions across a number of distinct areas. The end result is a decline in productivity and workplace practice creativity. This must be rectified.

In regard to exclusivity, Greenfield Agreements may now only be reached with unions as opposed to that not being the case prior. Where this becomes a problem for employers is through the union tendency to increased business costs, complicated negotiations, create wage and condition uncertainty, undermine flexibility and make extortionate and inflationary claims. This approach is particularly harmful during the critical start up phase where absolute flexibility is necessary. A reversion to the old system in this policy space is also required.

The final area where Greenfield Agreements policy should be amended is in regard to their duration. At present, Greenfield Agreements may only run for 12 months. Unfortunately, due to the complex and uncertain nature of business start up, the design and construction process and the global economic environment, this length of time is proving too short to be fully beneficial. Amendments should be made to double the length of time a Greenfield Agreements may run before they transition to normalised agreements. By doing so, the government can help embryonic businesses find their feet more easily, thereby improving their chances of long term success, workforce security and tax generating profitability.

§

In a century where Australia will face the most competitive business environment it has ever know, ensuring its businesses have ultimate flexibility will be essential. The above reforms can help Australia craft a workplace environment best suited to meeting the evolving needs of workers, customers and entrepreneurs. Consequently, consideration of their introduction should be given the utmost attention.

Acknowledgements

This book would not have been realised, let alone attempted without the inexhaustible support of my wife Mary. Her constant feedback, encouragement, personal sacrifice and patience ensured its long gestation concluded successfully. I will forever be appreciative.

My good friend James Matheson provided comprehensive feedback on much of my writings, being supportive and constructive throughout the editing process. I would also like to thank Elizabeth Sheargold, Paul Zennaro, Peter Verwer, Elizabeth Matheson, Rachel Dapiran, Jerome Carslake, Simon Wong, and Megan Gidley for their honest and detailed feedback as well. You have all helped make this a better book.

I am particularly grateful to my original publisher Anthony Cappello whose support for my work never wavered and my editor Michael Gilchrist who was always patient with my edits. I am also indebted to Joe Manariti and Mary Pho at SWIM Communications for their generous help with this book's many maps and James Hooper for the second edition's covers.

A special thank you for the conversations, encouragement, support and words of wisdom from Judy Judah, Chris Sheargold, Marie Sheargold, Brian Welch, Jennifer Cunich, James Atkins, Michael Gidley MLA, Kendall MacDowell, Rochelle Jackson, Peter Seamer, John Roskam, Luke Dixon, Casey Farrell, and Josh van Konkelenberg.

Former employers must also be thanked for the generous gift of knowledge and experience they gave me during my service with them. These include the Hon. Rod Kemp, the Victorian Farmers Federation, the Master Builders Association of Victoria, the

Institute of Public Affairs and the Property Council of Australia. Thank you also to the people at Port Waratah Coal Services for their generous site visit and briefing and the Australia India Business Council and Australian India Institute for their invaluable information sessions.

Finally, a special thank you to George Friedman from Stratfor (now Geopolitical Futures) who through his inspirational writings opened my eyes to the world we live in.

Endnotes

Author's note

1 N. Ferguson, *Empire: the Rise and Demise of the British World Order and the Lessons for Global Power*, New York, 2004, p. 2.

Overture: An introduction to the Australian Century

2 Source: International Monetary Fund.

3 Ibid.

4 Source: World Trade Organization and CIA World Factbook.

5 Source: World Energy Council, US Energy Information Administration and CIA World Factbook.

6 FAO, *World fisheries production, by capture and aquaculture, by country*, Rome, 2008, p. 24.

7 Source: http://nobelprize.org/

8 Source: http://www.olympic.org/

9 Source: Academic Ranking of World Universities (ARWU).

10 Source: H. Laski (1947), British writer, academic and Labour politician.

11 P. Lewis, *The Crisis of Argentine Capitalism*, Chapel Hill and London, 1990.

12 A. Eiras, Ana & B. Schaefer, *"Argentina's Economic Crisis: An 'Absence of Capitalism'"*, Heritage Foundation, No. 1432, 19 April 2001, pp. 1-15.

13 Ibid., p. 1.

14 Source: International Monetary Fund.

15 A. Eiras, Ana & B. Schaefer, op. cit., p. 1.

16 Department of Foreign Affairs and Trade, *APEC and the rise of the global middle class*, Canberra, 2007, p. 4.

17 Source: World Bank.

18 Note: An international dollar has the same purchasing power over GDP as a US dollar has in the United States at a set point in time, in this case 2000.

19 H. Kharas, OECD Development Centre, Working Paper No. 285, *The emerging middle class in developing countries*, Paris, 2010, p. 27.

20 United Nations, Department of Economic and Social Affairs, Population Division (2006). *World Urbanization Prospects: The 2005 Revision*, Working Paper No. ESA/P/WP/200.

21 Department of Foreign Affairs and Trade, op. cit., p. 6.

22 United Nations, Department of Economic and Social Affairs, op.cit.

23 D. Kinch, "Vale confident in China's iron ore appetite", *The Australian* (Dow Jones Newswires), 1 June 2011.

24 C. Elizabeth, "Economy, The Game Changer", *Foreign Affairs*, November/ December, 2010, pp. 142-152.

25 Source: CRU Group.

26 Source: Rio Tinto 2010 AGM, CEO's Report, 26 May 2010.

27 Source: International Energy Agency.

28 McKinsey & Company, McKinsey Sustainability & Resource Productivity Practice, *Resource Revolution: Meeting the world's energy, materials, food and water needs*, Seoul, November 2011, p. 42.

29 R. Komiyama, The Institute of Energy Economics, Japan (IEEJ) – EDMC, *Asia energy outlook to 2030: Impacts of energy outlook in China and India on the world*, Tokyo, 2007, Figure 17, p. 13.

30 Source: Ux Consulting 2009, *Nuclear Power Outlook*.

31 Source US Energy Information Administration. (2025 forecast).

32 Source: US Energy Information Administration.

33 Source: International Energy Agency.

34 N. Varghese & V. Püttmann, IIEP research papers, UNESCO, *Trends in diversification of post-secondary education*, 2011, p. 13.

35 U. Brandenburg, D. Carr, S. Donauer, C. Berthold, CHE Centre for Higher Education Development, Working Paper No. 107, *Analysing*

the Future Market – Target Countries for German HEIs, Gütersloh, 2008, p. 13.

36 Department of Foreign Affairs and Trade, op. cit., p. 19.

37 Source: World Bank.

38 B. Ki-moon (UN Secretary-General), *High-Level Conference on World Food Security*, (SG/SM/11612). Rome, 3 June 2008.

39 Source: United Nations Food and Agriculture Organization.

40 Source: Barclays Capital.

41 Source: United Nations Food and Agriculture Organization.

Chapter 1: The rise of the global middle class

42 Department of Foreign Affairs and Trade, op. cit., p. 4.

43 McKinsey & Company, op. cit., p. 34.

44 Department of Foreign Affairs and Trade, op. cit., p. 6.

45 United Nations Habitat, *State of the World's Cities 2008/2009*, Harmonious Cities, London & Sterling, 2008, p. iv.

46 E. Glaeser, *Triumph of the City*, New York, 2011, p. 1.

47 ANZ, *Earth, Fire, Wind and Water: Economic Opportunities and the Australian Commodities Cycle*, Melbourne, Issue 1, August 2011, p. 46.

48 S. Hajkowicz & J. Moody, (DRAFT DOCUMENT), *Our future world. An analysis of global trends, shocks and scenarios*, CSIRO, Canberra, March 2010, p. 8.

49 ExxonMobil, 2012 The Outlook for Energy: A View to 2040, 2012, p. 11.

50 ANZ, op. cit., p. 46.

51 KPMG, *Insight*, The global infrastructure magazine, Issue No. 1, November 2010, p. 5.

52 Source: Australian Institute of Mining and Metallurgy.

53 McKinsey & Company, op. cit., p. 49.

54 The Hon. P. Costello, *The Costello Memoirs – The Age of Prosperity*, Carlton, 2008, p. 270.

55 McKinsey & Company, op. cit., Exhibit 12, p. 43.

56 Ibid., p. 8.

57 Ibid., p. 5.

58 At 2010 production levels.

59 McKinsey & Company, op. cit., Exhibit 12, p. 5.

60 Ibid., p. 36.

61 International Energy Agency, *World Energy Outlook 2011, Executive Summary*, 2011, Paris, p. 1.

62 ExxonMobil, op. cit., p. 1.

63 Ibid., p. 28.

64 Ibid., p. 30.

65 Ibid., p. 18.

66 McKinsey & Company, op. cit., p. 5.

67 Ibid., p. 37.

68 Ibid., p. 37.

69 ExxonMobil, op. cit., p. 19.

70 Ibid., p. 19.

71 Ibid., p. 19.

72 V. Smil, Department Geography, University of Manitoba, *Energy in the Twentieth Century: Resources, Conversions, Costs, Uses, and Consequences*, Winnipeg, 2000, p. 22.

73 IEA, *2012 Key World Energy Statistics*, Paris, 2012, p. 11.

74 Ibid., p. 13.

75 Ibid., p. 15.

76 Source: http://maplecroft.com/portfolio/new-analysis/2013/12/12/instability-and-conflict-mena-and-east-africa-drive-global-rise-political-risk-maplecroft-bpolitical-risk-atlas-2014b/

77 IEA, *World Energy Outlook 2012 Factsheet*, (New Policies Scenario), Paris, 2012, p. 1.

78 Ibid., p. 1.

79 McKinsey & Company, op. cit., p. 9.

80 Source: http://www.chinasportsreview.com/2009/03/07/beijing-olympicsmade-16-million-profit/

81 Source: http://www.mckinsey.com/insights/consumer_and_retail/capturing_the_worlds_emerging_middle_class

82 Brandenburg, U., Carr, D., Donauer, S., Berthold, C. op. cit., p. 13.

83 Indian Council for Research on International Economic Relations, *Trade in Services: Opportunities and Constraints*, India Habitat Centre, New Delhi, 2001, p. 8.

84 Ibid., p. 8.

85 Source: www.dfat.gov.au/trade/negotiations/services/overview_trade_in_services.html

86 S. Hajkowicz, & J. Moody, op. cit., p. 12.

87 McKinsey & Company, op. cit., p. 5.

88 Department of Agriculture, Fishers and Forestry, *Australian food statistics 2011–12*, Chart C.1, Canberra, 2013, p. 34.

89 Source: http://www.un.org/waterforlifedecade/food_security.shtml

90 McKinsey & Company, op. cit., p. 5.

91 FAO, *100 days to Rio +20, 100 facts* (United Nations Conference on Sustainable Development), Rome, 2012, p. 1.

92 M. Rosegrant, International Food Policy Institute, Testimony for the US Senate Committee on Homeland Security and Governmental Affairs, *Biofuels and Grain Prices: Impacts and Policy Responses*, Washington D. C., 7 May 2008.

93 Ibid.

94 FAO, op. cit., p. 7.

95 B. Ki-moon, op. cit.

96 Source: United Nations Food and Agriculture Organization.

97 Source: Barclays Capital.

98 Source: United Nations Food and Agriculture Organization.

99 McKinsey & Company, op. cit., p. 39.

100 FAO, op. cit., p. 6.

101 Ibid., p. 6.

102 Ibid., p. 3.

103 Ibid., p. 3.

104 McKinsey & Company, op. cit., p. 42.

105 Ibid., p. 51.

106 Ibid., p. 51.

107 Ibid., p. 56

108 US Geological Survey, *Mineral Commodity Summaries (Potash)*, Reston, January 2011, p. 123. http://minerals.usgs.gov/minerals/pubs/commodity/potash/ mcs-2011-potas.pdf

109 McKinsey & Company, op. cit., Exhibit 12, p. 43.

110 FAO, op. cit., p. 6.

111 Ibid, p. 5.

112 Ibid, p. 5.

113 Ibid, p. 8.

114 Ibid, p. 8.

115 R. Trostle, USDA, *Global Agricultural Supply and Demand: Factors Contributing to the Recent Increase in Food Commodity Prices*, Washington D.C., 2008, p. 23.

116 Ibid., p. 23.

117 Ibid., p. 12.

118 McKinsey & Company, op. cit., p. 41.

119 Ibid., p. 9.

120 Ibid., p. 29.

121 Ibid., p. 30.

122 Ibid., p. 30.

123 Ibid., p. 58.

124 Ibid., p. 8.

125 "Indonesia Enacts a Controversial Fuel Subsidy Cut", *Stratfor Global Intelligence*, 19 June 2013, http://www.stratfor.com/analysis/indonesia-enacts-controversial-fuel-subsidy-cut

126 Ibid.

127 McKinsey & Company, op. cit., p. 21.

128 F. Ng & M. Aksoy, World Bank, Development Research Group Trade Team, *Who are the net food importing countries?*, Washington D.C., 2008, p. 6.

129 Note: Using Ng and Aksoy's 'raw food' definition: meats and dairy, grains, and fruits and vegetables.

130 International Energy Agency, *World Energy Outlook 2011, Executive Summary*, Paris, 2011, p. 5.

131 Ibid., p. 5.

Chapter 2: The developing world, triumph and tragedy

132 A Human Development Index ranking between 0.70-0.80 (0.79 being the 2011 dividing line between very high and high human development).

133 A Human Development Index ranking below 0.70 (0.69 being the 2011 dividing line between medium and high human development).

134 HDI ranking below .0.52 (0.52 being the 2011 dividing line between low and medium human development).

135 The Fund for Peace, *Failed States Index 2013*, Washington D.C., 2013, p. 4.

136 United Nations, Department of Economic and Social Affairs, Population Division, *World Population 2012*, New York, 2012.

137 R. Brooks, IMF, Asia and Pacific Department, *Why is Unemployment High in the Philippines?* (Working Paper), WP/02/23, Figure 1, Washington D.C., 2002, p. 6.

138 Ibid., p. 7.

139 Source: http://www.transparency.org/country#PHL_DataResearch

140 K. Chan & T. Cerojano, "Typhoon highlights weak Philippine infrastructure", *The Philippine Star (via Associated Press) (Online Edition)*, Manila, 13 November 2013.

141 The Luzon and the Metro Manila corridor in particular.

142 Such as citizenship and personal freedoms like travel.

143 C. Lee, *Malaysia: Policies and Issues in Economic Development*, In Z. Mahani (Eds), Institute of Strategic & International Studies – Malaysia, Kuala Lumpur, 2011, p. 429.

144 J. Foong, "Extra efforts to improve rural basic infrastructure", *The Star (Online edition)*, Kuala Lumpur, 24 November 2010.

145 Ibid.

146 L. Hunt, "Malaysia initiates another crackdown on illegal immigrants", *The Diplomat (Online edition)*, Tokyo, 3 September 2013.

147 "An amnesty of sorts for illegals", *The Economist (Online edition)*, 3 May 2005.

148 IEA, *World Energy Outlook 2011, Energy for All, Financing access for the poor*,
(Special early excerpt of the World Energy Outlook 2011), Oslo, October 2011, p. 8.

Chapter 3: The supergiants, too big to succeed

149 G. Friedman, *The Next 100 Years, A forecast for the 21st century*, New York, 2009, p. 17.

150 Source: World Bank.

151 Hukou is a form of household registration in China whereby government services are provided to citizens in the regions they are officially registered in. Due to the speed of China's urbanisation, the Government has restricted the number of citizens able to update their hukou after they have migrated internally. As a result, hundreds of millions of people do not have fair access to public housing, education and healthcare.

152 "China warns on growing water shortages", Financial Times (online edition), 16 February 2012, http://www.ft.com/intl/cms/s/0/131bb6dc-588f11e1-9f28-00144feabdc0.html#axzz2pc2cKAsV

153 Source: CIA Factbook.

154 World Economic Forum, *The Global Competitiveness Report 2011-12*, Geneva, 2011, Data Table 2.2, p. 412.

155 M. Lipton, *Why poor people stay poor: Urban bias in world development*, Harvard University Press, Cambridge, 1977, p. 13.

156 Premier Wen Jiabao, *Press Conference*, Beijing, 16 March 2007.

157 S. Koukoulas, "Chinese factories fight a wages inferno", *Business Spectator*, 27 November 2012.

158 Ibid.

159 "China's Achilles heel", *The Economist*, 21/04/12 (Online edition).

160 G. Shilling, *Why India Will Displace China as Global Growth Engine*, Bloomberg Opinion, 17 December 2012 (Online edition).

161 Source: C. Fang, IPLE-CASS, "Market forces and higher productivity the keys for China", 25 September 2011, http://ajw.asahi.com/article/globe/economy/AJ2011092515286

162 *The Economist*, "China's Achilles heel", op. cit.

163 Ibid.

164 WEF, *The Future of Pensions and Healthcare in a Rapidly Ageing World - Scenarios to 2030*, Geneva, 2008, p. 16.

165 *The Economist*, "China's Achilles heel", op. cit.

166 G. Shilling, op. cit.

167 T. Thompson, "Choking on China, The Superpower that is poisoning the world", *Foreign Affairs*, 4 August 2013 (Online edition).

168 Ibid.

169 M. De Villiers, *Water – The fate of our most precious resource*, Toronto, 2001, p. 89.

170 Ibid. p. 89.

171 "China: Protecting food security amid land reform", *Stratfor Global Intelligence*, 22 January 2014.

172 T. Thompson, op. cit.

173 Yale Centre for Environmental Law and Policy, Yale University, & Centre for International Earth Science Information Network, Columbia University, *Environmental Performance Index 2012*, Environmental Performance Index – Ranking & Scores, 2012.

174 G. Shilling, op. cit.

175 Meaning chaos and instability.

176 Source: http://www.irishtimes.com/newspaper/world/2011/0614/1224298864155.html

177 For example, the 1975-77 'emergency' where political opponents were placed in jail, the press suppressed and the judiciary interfered with.

178 Source: Democracy Index 2010.

179 "Australia's Asia Literacy Non-Problem", *CIS*, No. 133, 5 September 2012.

180 M. Thirlwell, "India, the next economic giant", *Lowy Institute Paper 01*, Double Bay, 2004, p. 10.

181 Ibid., p. 11.

182 Source: World Bank.

183 Ibid.

184 Source: CIA World Factbook.

185 A. Dhillon, "Bright lights, tight city", *The Age (Focus)*, 21 February 2014, p. 16.

186 KPMG, *Logistics game changers, Transforming India's logistics industry*, Mumbai, 2013, p. 32.

187 Source: National Highways Authority of India, http://nhai.org/roadnetwork.htm

188 Source: http://www.forbes.com/2006/12/19/india-most-congested-cities-biz-energy-cx_rm_1219congested.html

189 Ibid.

190 "The trouble with India", *Bloomberg Business Week Magazine*, 18 March 2007 (online edition).

191 N. Rangaraj, & G. Raghuram, *Viability of Inland Water Transport in India*, Indian Institute of Technology & Indian Institute of Management, Ahmedabad, 2005, p. 10.

192 A. Maheshwari," The Challenges in Indian Logistics Sector – Infrastructure", *Softlink*, http://www.softlinkglobal.com/resources/Expert%20Opinion/Amit_ TTalkAug10.aspx?Type=resources

193 Source: CIA Factbook.

194 Ibid.

195 J. Hammer, "A prayer for the Ganges", *Smithsonian Magazine*, November 2007 (online edition), Source: http://www.smithsonianmag.com/making-adifference/a-prayer-for-the-ganges-173708201/?page=2

196 World Economic Forum, *The Global Competitiveness Report 2011-12*, op. cit., Data Table 2.2, p. 412.

197 Source: http://www.rediff.com/business/slide-show/slide-show-1-delhihas-the-highest-per-capita-income-in-india/20130913.htm#1

198 N. Nilekani, *Imagining India*, Penguin Press, New York, 2009, p. 415.

199 D. Sharma & A. Kansal, "Current condition of the Yamuna River – an overview of flow, pollution load and human use", New Haven, 2013, p. 15.

200 Yale Centre for Environmental Law and Policy, op. cit.

201 Source: http://www.thehindu.com/news/national/naxalism-biggestthreat-to-internal-security-manmohan/article436781.ece

202 "Update on Global Food Commodities", *Stratfor Global Intelligence*, 19 January 2012.

203 "India: Challenges to Electricity Production", *Stratfor Global Intelligence*, 28 September 2012.

204 Ibid.

205 KPMG, op. cit., p. 2.

206 S. Hajkowicz & J., Moody, op. cit, p. 8.

Chapter 4: The established world, sunset and sunrise

207 Inspired by Halford John Mackinder's Heartland Theory.

208 United Nations, Department of Economic and Social affairs, Population Division, *World Population 2012*; IMF (2012).

209 United Nations, Department of Economic and Social affairs, Population Division, op. cit.

210 G. Friedman, op. cit, pp. 83-84.

211 United Nations; IMF, op. cit.

212 Population Reference Bureau, *The World at 7 Billion*, Population Bulletin 66.2, Washington D.C., 2011, Figure 7, p. 11.

213 Ibid. p. 11.

214 Source: http://www.berlin-institut.org/online-handbookdemography/german-regions.html

215 Ibid.

216 United Nations, Department of Economic and Social Affairs, Population Division, op. cit.

217 Source: http://epp.eurostat.ec.europa.eu/statistics_explained/index.php?titl

e=File:Population_age_structure_indicators,_2011.png&filetimestamp=20130129113545

218 Source: http://epp.eurostat.ec.europa.eu/statistics_explained/index.php/Population_structure_and_ageing

219 OECD, *Providing and Paying for Long-Term Care*, Paris, 2011, Figure 2.2, p. 63.

220 Between 2012 and 2029 the pension age will slowly increase to 67 years.

221 OECD, op. cit., Figure 2.3, p. 64.

222 Federal Ministry of Finance, *An ABC of Taxes, 2011 Edition*, Berlin, 2011, p. 80.

223 Old-age dependency ratio.

224 European Commission, *Pension Adequacy in the European Union 2010-2050*, Brussels, 23 May 2012, p. 68.

225 Source: http://hotair.com/headlines/archives/2013/02/06/despite-hundreds-of-billions-in-subsidies-germanys-birth-rate-continues-to-fall/

226 Ibid.

227 Population Reference Bureau, op. cit., p. 11.

228 Source: http://www.ifr.org/news/ifr-press-release/the-robotics-industryis-looking-into-a-bright-future-551/ Chart: High degree of automation in Korea, Japan and Germany

229 China is presently home to over 20,000 Japanese firms.

230 "Europe: Xenophobia Rising", *Stratfor Global Intelligence*, 3 March 2009.

231 R. Altman, & R. Haass, "American profligacy and American Power", *Foreign Affairs, Volume 89, No. 6*, Tampa, November-December 2010, p. 25.

232 Adjusted Pension Liability Measures for 50 Largest US Local Governments Report,

https://www.moodys.com/research/Moodys-Some-of-the-largest-USlocal-governments-show-outsized--PR_283219

233 Manhattan Institute, D. Di Salvo, "Government Crowded Out: How employee compensation costs are reshaping state and local government", *Civic Report, No. 77*, New York, April 2013, http://www.manhattan-institute.org/html/cr_77.htm#.Utod2hAzFhE

234 United Nations, Department of Economic and Social Affairs, Population Division, op. cit.

235 H. Kharas, op. cit. p. 27.

236 United Nations, Department of Economic and Social Affairs, Population Division, op. cit.

237 Ibid.

238 OECD, *Trends Shaping Education*, Ageing OECD Societies, Chapter 1, Figure 1.6, 2008, p. 19.

239 United Nations, Department of Economic and Social affairs, Population Division, op. cit.

240 OECD, *Trends Shaping Education*, op. cit., p. 19.

Chapter 5: Australia, the undiscovered country

241 United Nations, Department of Economic and Social Affairs, Population Division, op. cit.

242 Cities with populations between 100,000-1,000,000.

243 Department of Infrastructure and Transport (Major Cities Unit), *State of Australian Cities 2013*, Canberra, p. 9.

244 Department of Infrastructure and Transport, (2011) *State of Australian Cities 2011*, Canberra, p. 16.

245 ABS, 3222.0, *Population Projections Australia*, 26 November 2013, pp. 5-6.

246 ABS, 3218.0, *Regional Population Growth, Australia*, 30 August 2013, Table 1, Estimated Resident Population, Significant Urban Areas,

Australia; ABS 3218, *Regional Population Growth, Australia*, Table 1. Estimated Resident Population, Statistical Areas Level 2, NSW.

247 ABS, 3218.0, *Regional Population Growth, Australia*, op. cit.; ABS 3218.0, *Regional Population Growth, Australia*, Table 1. Estimated Resident Population, Statistical Areas Level 2, Victoria.

248 ABS, 3218.0, *Regional Population Growth, Australia*, op. cit.

249 Queensland Government, *South East Queensland Regional Plan 2009-2031*, Brisbane, 2009, Map 12, p. 108.

250 Connecting to Tweed Heads in northern NSW.

251 ABS, 3218.0, *Regional Population Growth, Australia*, op. cit.; ABS, 3218.0, *Regional Population Growth, Australia*, Table 1. Estimated Resident Population, Statistical Areas Level 2, Western Australia.

252 The 2011 Census has Mandurah classified as part of Perth.

253 ABS, 3218.0, *Regional Population Growth, Australia*, op. cit.; ABS, 3218.0, *Regional Population Growth, Australia*, Table 1. Estimated Resident Population, Statistical Areas Level 2, South Australia.

254 Government of South Australia, *The 30-Year Plan for Greater Adelaide, A volume of the South Australian Planning Strategy*, Adelaide, 2010, Map D1. p. 73.

255 ABS, 3218.0, *Regional Population Growth, Australia*, op. cit.; ABS, 3218.0, *Regional Population Growth, Australia*, Table 1. Estimated Resident Population, Statistical Areas Level 2, New South Wales.

256 ABS, 3218.0, *Regional Population Growth, Australia*, op. cit.; ABS, 3218.0, *Regional Population Growth, Australia*, Table 1. Estimated Resident Population, Statistical Areas Level 2, New South Wales.

257 Infrastructure Partnerships Australia, *Re-Thinking Cities: A strategy for integrated infrastructure*, Sydney, July 2012, p. 13.

258 E. Brady, *Unlimited Australia*, Melbourne, 1918, p. 23.

259 PMSEIC, *Australia and Food Security in a Changing World*, The Prime Minister's Science, Engineering and Innovation Council, Canberra, 2010.

260 Ibid.

261 ABS, 4610.0 – *Water Account, Australia 2011-12*, 13 November 2013.

262 NFF, Farm Facts: 2012, p. 10.

263 Source: http://archive.nwc.gov.au/home/water-governancearrangementsin-australia/cross-boundary-arrangements/murray-darling-basin/basin-officials-committee/water-availability

264 Ibid.

265 Of which appropriately 90 per cent directly evaporated back to the atmosphere or was used by plants. Source: http://www.water.gov.au/WaterAvailability/WhatIsOurTotalWaterResource/index.aspx?Menu=Level1_3_1

266 Source: World Resource Institute.

267 J. Marohasy, "There are votes in the Murray", *IPA Review*, September 2004, p. 26. http://www.ipa.org.au/library/56-3-%20there%20are%20votes%20 in%20the%20murray.pdf

268 Source: http://www.bom.gov.au/climate/current/

269 Evapotranspiration is the combined loss of water from evaporation (water loss to the air) and transpiration (water loss within a plant).

270 Source: http://data.worldbank.org/indicator/AG.LND.PRCP.MM; http://www.bom.gov.au/climate/current/

271 Source: http://www.bom.gov.au/jsp/awap/rain/index.jsp?colour=colour&time=latest&step=0&map=totals&period=12month&area=nat

272 Definition: According ANCOLD Register of Large Dans (ANCOLD 2006) large dams are defined as dams with a crest or wall height of greater than 15 metres, or as dams with a dam wall height of greater than 10 metres but meeting other size criteria as follows: having a crest more than 500 metres in length; creating a reservoir capacity of no less than 1,000 ML; the ability to deal with a flood discharge of no less than 2,000 cubic metres per second; or, being of unusual design (ANCOLD 2001). Source:

http://www.abs.gov.au/ausstats/abs@.nsf/Lookup/by%20Subject/1370.0~2010~Chapter~Inland%20 waters%20glossary%20(6.3.9)

273 ABS, 1370.0, *Measure of Australia's Progress*, 2010, 15 September 2010.

274 Source: http://archive.nwc.gov.au/home/water-governancearrangementsin-australia/cross-boundary-arrangements/murray-darling-basin/basin-officials-committee/water-availability

275 ABS, 1370.0, op cit.

276 Ibid.

277 Source: http://www.water.gov.au/WaterAvailability/Whatisourtotalwaterresource/Waterstorage/index.aspx?Menu=Level1_3_1_7

278 Data sourced from ABS Water Account, Australia 2004-05 and ANCOLD.

279 Source: http://www.ga.gov.au/groundwater/basics/what-is-groundwater.html

280 Source: http://www.ga.gov.au/groundwater/groundwater-in-australia/ sedimentary-basins/great-artesian-basin.html

281 Australian Water Association, 2007.

282 Source: http://www.ga.gov.au/groundwater/groundwater-in-australia/ sedimentary-basins.html

283 ABS, 1370.0, op. cit.

284 Source: http://www.water.gov.au/WaterAvailability/Whatisourtotalwaterresource/Alternativewatersources/index.aspx?Menu=Level1_3_1_9

285 ABS, 4610.0, *Water Account, Australia 2011-12*, 13 November 2013.

286 ABS, 4610.0, *Water Account, Australia 2011-12*, 13 November 2013, Table 1 Water supply and use 2011-12 – Australia.

287 Ibid.

288 Media Release: *Australia splashes more cash on water*, ABS 4610.0, Water Account, Australia, 2011-12, 13 November 2013.

289 Newcastle was bad by Australian standards, but globally speaking, minor in terms of casualties and physical damage.

290 P. Collier, *The Bottom Billion*, New York, 2007, pp. 56-7.

291 Source: Geoscience Australia, Table 1. Australia's Mineral Resources and Production – World Rankings 2011, http://www.ga.gov.au/minerals/basics. html; http://www.ga.gov.au/energy/basics.html

292 DFAT, *Trade at a Glance 2013*, Canberra, 2013, p. 31.

293 Ibid. p. 7.

294 Source: www.australian-phosphate.com

295 ABC Radio, *John Faine Show, ABC Conversation Hour Interview (Paul Keating)*, 8 November 2011.

296 Source: http://www.dfat.gov.au/geo/fs/aust.pdf

297 ABS, 6202.0, *Labour Force, Australia December 2013*, 16 January 2014.

298 Source: www.dfat.gov.au/trade/negotiations/services/overview_trade_in_services.html

299 Source: http://www.immi.gov.au/media/fact-sheets/15population.htm

300 Ibid.

301 Source: http://www.censusdata.abs.gov.au/census services/getproduct/census/2011/quickstat/0

302 Source: IMF World Economic Outlook Database, October 2013 (2012).

303 ABS, *5204.0, 2010-11, Australian System of National Accounts*, p. 9.

304 Credit Suisse, Research Institute, *Global Wealth Report 2013*, p. 57.

305 Ibid. p. 57.

306 Department of Infrastructure and Transport, *Our Cities, Our Future, A national urban policy for a productive sustainable and liveable future*, Canberra, 2011, p. 7.

307 Infrastructure Australia, Major Cities Unit, *State of our Cities 2010*, Canberra, 2010, p. 49.

308 SGS Economics and Planning, *Australian Cities Accounts 2011-12*, November 2012, Table 1, p. 2.

309 Source: http://economy.id.com.au/gosford/gross-regional-product

310 Source: http://www.cityofsydney.nsw.gov.au/AboutSydney/CityResearch/GlobalSydney.asp

311 SGS Economics and Planning, *Australian Cities Accounts 2011-12*, op. cit., p. 9.

312 Ibid. Table 1, p. 2.

313 Source: http://economy.id.com.au/melton

314 Source: http://economy.id.com.au/hume

315 After London, Boston and Toyko.

316 SGS Economics and Planning, op. cit., p. 2.

317 Ibid., p. 2.

318 Source: http://economy.id.com.au/kwinana

319 Committee for Perth, *Discussion Paper, Vision Workshop: Perth @ 3.5 Million*, August 2011, Perth, p. 13.

320 University of Western Australia, FACTBase Bulletin, July 2009, *Westward Bound? Perth's Emerging Corporate Power*, Tonts, M & Taylor, M. Figure 1, p. 2.

321 Ibid., p. 5.

322 Committee for Perth, op. cit., p. 5.

323 SGS Economics and Planning, *Australian Cities Accounts 2011-12*, November 2012, Table 1, p. 2.

324 Could not find Gawler's GDP – Have assumed approximately $2b as its population is 20,000.

325 Source: http://economy.id.com.au/mount-barker

326 South Australian Government, Defence SA, *South Australia The Defence State*, Adelaide, 2013, p. 14.

327 SGS Economics and Planning, *Australian Cities Accounts 2011-12*, op. cit., pp. 20-21.

328 Ibid. pp. 20-21.

329 Ibid., p. 23.

330 Western Australian Government, Pilbara Development Corporation, Future development of the Pilbara, Karratha, April 2013, p. 6.

331 Ibid., pp. 6-7.

332 Ibid., p. 27.

333 Source: Geoscience Australia, Reserves Table 1 – Petroleum Reserves by Basin, as at 1 January 2011, http://www.ga.gov.au/products-services/publications/oil-gas-resources-australia/2010/reserves/table-1.html

334 Source: http://www.city-journal.org/2012/22_1_anglosphere.html

335 Markus, Prof. A., "Mapping Social Cohesion", *Scanlon Foundation Surveys, National Report 2013*, Caulfield East, p. 2.

336 Source: Stratfor Global Intelligence.

337 Ibid.

338 G. Johns, *Right Social Justice, Better Ways to Help the Poor* (Chapter 3), Connor Court, Ballan, 2012, p. 49.

339 Source: Stratfor Global Intelligence.

340 John Hirst.

341 C. Darwin, *Voyage of the Beagle*, New York, 1909, p. 470.

342 R. Johnston, M. Poulsen and J. Forrest, "The Geography of Ethnic Residential Segregation: A Comparative Study of Five Countries", *Annals of the Association of American Geographers, Volume 97, Issue 4*, Washington D.C., December 2007, p. 733.

343 As done at the Australian Pavilion at the Shanghai World Expo 2010.

344 Source: http://www.business.nsw.gov.au/invest-in-nsw/sydney-metropolitan-area

345 The Economist Intelligence Unit (EIU) annually conducts a quality of living survey of international cities which consistently places Australia's major cities amongst the world's most liveable. In 2013, Melbourne, Adelaide, Sydney and Perth were ranked in the top ten.

Chapter 6: The Australian Century

346 H. Kharas, op. cit., p. 28.

347 M. Roeder, *The Big Mo – Why momentum now rules our world*, Sydney, 2010, p. 1.

348 Ibid., p. 1.

349 Ibid., p. 1.

350 M. Hooke, Minerals Council of Australia, *The culture of cycles*, Melbourne Mining Club Speech, Melbourne, 6 December 2013.

351 P. Krugman, *The Age of Diminishing Expectations*, Cambridge, 1990, p. 11.

352 ABS, 3222.0, *Population Projections, Australia*, 2012 (base to 2101), 26 November 2013.

353 G. Forster, Manuscript, 20 November 1786. Later republished in Forster, G. Kleine Schriften: Ein Beytrag zur Volker und Landerjkunde, Naturgeschichte und Philosophie des Lebens, gesammlet von Georg Forester, Erster Theil, Leipzig, Kummer, 1789.

354 In 1870 the British wielded considerably more strategic, diplomatic, political and military power than India and China with just 75 per cent and 53 per cent of their respective GDPs. Source: J. Lee, CIS, "Why America will lead the 'Asian Century'", *Foreign Policy Analysis, No. 1*, Sydney, 18 August 2009, p. 3.

Chapter 7: A reform agenda for the Australian Century

355 Source: http://ptv.vic.gov.au/about-ptv/victoria-s-pt-network/networkstatistics/

356 Bureau of Infrastructure, Transport and Regional Economics [BITRE] 2011, Population growth, jobs growth and commuting flows in Melbourne, Report 125, BITRE, Canberra, 2011, p. 269.

357 Ibid., p. 269.

358 Ibid., p. 271.

359 Property Council of Australia (Victoria), *Finding 50, How to solve Victoria's infrastructure backlog*, Melbourne, 2014, p. 11.

360 The Hon. Dr. Denis Napthine MLA, Media Release: *Coalition Government 2013-14 Budget is building for growth for all Victorians*, 7 May 2013.

361 Property Council of Australia (Victoria), op. cit., p. 11.

362 Source: http://www.sydneytrains.info/about/facts

363 Department of Infrastructure and Transport, Major Cities Unit, *State of Our Cities 2013*, Canberra, 2013, p. 111 (Levy 2013).

364 Infrastructure NSW, *State Infrastructure Strategy, The solution, Section 6, Urban Roads*, p. 79.

365 Ibid. Table 6.2, p. 79.

366 Ibid., p. 79.

367 ABS, 3222.0, *Population Projections Australia*, 26/11/13, Series B Assumptions. p. 6.

368 E. Glaeser, op. cit., p. 136.

369 J.M. Duthilleul, *Circulate: When Our Movements Shape Cities*, 2012, Paris, Introduction.

370 N. Nunn and N. Qian, (2010), *The Columbian Exchange" A history of disease, food, and ideas*, Journal of Economic Perspectives – Volume 24, Number 2, New York, Spring 2010, p. 170.

371 Ibid., p. 171.

372 Ibid., p. 178.

373 N. Borlaug, *Ending World Hunger: The promise of biotechnology and the threat of antiscience zealotry*, American Society of Plant Biologists, Plant Physiology, vol. 124 no 2, Rockville, October 2000, p. 489.

374 Ibid., p. 488.

375 ISAAA Brief 44-2012: Global status of commercialized biotech/GM Crops: 2012, Executive Summary, New York, 2012, Table 1.

376 Source: http://www.daff.gov.au/agriculture-food/biotechnology

377 Source: Senate Estimates, May 2011, Supplementary Brief, p. 2.

378 Source: Cotton Australia.

379 Source: National Press Club Address, 20 September 2012, Graham Brookes, Director of PG Economics UK, *The global economic and environmental impact of GM crops.*

380 Source: http://www.daff.gov.au/agriculture-food/biotechnology

381 Graham Brookes, op. cit.

382 Senate Estimates, op. cit., p. 2.

383 Source: http://www.daff.gov.au/agriculture-food/biotechnology/pamphlets/gm_stockfeed_in_australia_economic_issues_for_producers_and_consumers

384 ISAAA Brief 44-2012: op. cit., Executive Summary.

385 Similar upswings in adoption have also taken place for sugar beet, cotton and maize where GM varieties comprise 95, 93 and 86 per cent of commercial crops respectively.

386 ISAAA Brief 44-2012: op. cit., Executive Summary, Table 1.

387 Ibid., Executive Summary, Table 1.

388 Ibid., Executive Summary.

389 Ibid., Executive Summary.

390 Ibid., Executive Summary, Table 1.

391 Ibid., Infographic, http://www.isaaa.org/resources/publications/briefs/44/infographic/default.asp

392 *The Economist*, 14 December 2013 p. 31, Food Fight (genetically modified crops).

393 ISAAA Brief 44-2012: op. cit., Executive Summary.

394 J. Bidstrup, Producers Forum, *History, Policy and Activity Presentation*, 2006, http://www.nuffield.com.au/conferences/06-pdfs/Jeff-Bidstrup-presentation. pdf

395 Source: http://www.who.int/foodsafety/publications/biotech/20questions/en/

396 "Fields of beaten gold", *The Economist*, 7 December 2013, p. 18.

397 Normal E. Borlaug, op. cit.

398 The 'Long term toxicity of a Roundup herbicide and a Roundup-tolerant genetically modified maize' paper published in Food and Chemical Toxicology, September (2012) by Gilles-Eric Seralini, University of Caen, was discredited and retracted shortly after publication.

399 D. Leyonhjelm, "Australia's farming disadvantage", *Business Spectator*, 18 June 2010. Source:
http://www.businessspectator.com.au/article/2010/6/18/european-crisis/australias-farming-disadvantage

400 Refers to the accidental or unintentional appearance of foreign material in a product. Typically happens during production, harvest, storage and marketing. Source:
http://en.wikipedia.org/wiki/Adventitious_presence#Agriculture

401 ACIL Tasman, *Managing genetically modified crops in Australia*, Sydney, 2005, p. v.

402 "Food fight", *The Economist*, 14 December 2013, p. 32.

403 Enclosure, mechanization, 4-field crop rotation and selective breeding (grasses & clover).

404 The Green Revolution revolutionised the productive potential of the developing world through the introduction of new irrigation methods, high yield disease-resistant crops and fertiliser.

405 K. Kukoc, First Assistant Secretary, Migration and Visa Policy Division, Department of Immigration and Citizenship, Speech: Speech to the German Australian media dialogue, 17 October 2012, *Australia's skilled migration programs: from strength to strength and beyond*, p. 6.

406 G. Blainey, *A Shorter History of Australia*, North Sydney, 2009, p. 151.

407 Ibid., p. 154.

408 Source: http://www.immi.gov.au/media/fact-sheets/15population.htm

409 Temporary Work (skilled) – Standard Business Sponsorship Visas.

410 Labour Agreement Visas.

411 C. Wilshire, Chief Executive, Migration Council Australia, "Temporary migration serves national interest", *AFR*, 19 March 2013, p. 47.

412 Source: http://www.immi.gov.au/media/fact-sheets/26state.htm

413 Source: http://www.immi.gov.au/media/fact-sheets/20planning.htm

414 Ibid.

415 Department of Infrastructure and Transport, *Our Cities, Our Future, A national urban policy for a productive sustainable and liveable future*, 2011, Canberra, p. 7.

416 Assessed as having a physical, intellectual, or psychiatric condition that stops an individual from working or being retrained for work within the next two years. Or, if the individual is permanently blind and can meet the eligibility requirements. Source: http://www.humanservices.gov.au/customer/services/centrelink/disability-support-pension

417 Business Council of Australia, *Action Plan for Enduring Prosperity*, Full Report, Melbourne, 2013, Figure 41, p. 77.

418 Attorney-General's Department, *Australia to 2050: Future Challenges*, The 2010 Intergenerational Report (Overview), 2010, Canberra, p. 1.

419 Coming of Age, *BRW Magazine*, October 7-13, 2010, p. 31.

420 ABS, 4102.0, *Australian Social Trends, Nov 2013, Pregnancy and work transitions*, Canberra, 20 November 2013.

421 Ibid.

422 G. Wilkins & C Kruger, "Getting mothers into workforce is no child's play", *The Age*, (Source: Productivity Commission, Grattan Institute Submission), 8 March 2014, p. 10.

423 This is currently being investigated by the Productivity Commission.

424 ABS, 6202.0, *Labour Force, Australia December 2013*, Canberra, 16 January 2014.

425 A. Baker, CIS, *Not Looking for Work: The rise of non-jobseekers on unemployment benefits*, Policy Monograph 136, 2013, p. 1.

426 G. Jones, "The welfare system in Australia is broken", (Toby Hall, Mission Australia), *The Daily Telegraph*, 8 April 2013 (online edition).

427 G. Johns, op. cit., pp. 166-167.

428 T. Hall, "Bailing out the boat with a broken bucket", *The Daily Telegraph*, 8 April 2013 (online edition).

429 Ibid.

430 Department of Education, Employment and Workplace Relations, National Disability Coordination Officer Program, *Disability Education and Employment News: No. 2, Vol. 9*, Canberra, 2013, p. 1.

431 B. Herscovitch, CIS, Issue Analysis, *Australia's Asia Literacy Non-Problem*, No. 133, Sydney, 5 September 2012, p. 1.

432 Source: http://www.heraldsun.com.au/business/future-fund-chairmandavid-gonski-warns-on-cost-of-xenophobia/story-fni0dcne-1226713438719

433 Australian Education Foundation, *The Current state of Chinese, Indonesia, Japanese and Korean Language Education in Australian Schools, Summary Document*, Carlton South, 2010, p. 3-4 Source: http://www.asiaeducation.edu.au/for_school_leaders/research_school_leaders/research_school_leaders_landing.html

434 G. Sheridan, "A nation adrift in Asia literacy", *The Australian*, 27 Mary 2010 (online edition) Source:

http://www.theaustralian.com.au/opinion/a-nationadrift-in-asia-literacy/story-e6frg6zo-1225871765386

435 Ibid.

436 The Hon. John Brumby, Public Administration Today Magazine, 'Views from the outside' edition, p. 20. Speech from the IPAA's National Congress in Melbourne in September.

437 Source: http://www.schools.nsw.edu.au/studentsupport/programs/student exchange/

438 B. Herscovitch, op. cit., p. 8.

439 ABS, 5506.0, *Taxation Revenue, Australia, 2011-12, Total Taxation Revenue*, 30 April 2013.

440 Source: http://alga.asn.au/?ID=59&Menu=41,83

441 ABS, 5506.0, *Taxation by Level of Government*, 30 April 2013.

442 Ibid.

443 The ancient Greek scholar Aristotle referred to region around the equator as the Torrid Zone, a region too hot for habitation.

444 Edaphology is a soil science discipline which studies soils impact upon living things, particularly plants.

445 South eastern Australia's long term economic subsidisation and political domination of northern Australia's standard of living.

446 Such as the Shanghai Waigaoqiao Free Trade Zone in mainland China.

447 "Generous support, some derision, for a new northern state", *AFR*, Bob Katter MP), 14 January 2013, p. 36.

448 Ibid. p. 36.

449 E. Glaeser, op. cit., p. 44.

450 T. Koyama and S. Golub, *OECD's FDI regulatory restrictiveness index: Revision and extension more economies*, Table 1, Paris, 2006, pp. 7-9.

451 Department of Foreign Affairs and Trade, *Korea-Australia, Free Trade Agreement – Outcomes at a Glance*, Canberra, 2014, p. 2.; Department of

Foreign Affairs and Trade, *Japan-Australia, Economic Partnership Agreement – Key Outcomes*, Canberra, 2014, p. 3.

452 ABS, 1301.0, *Year Book Australia*, 2012.

453 Department of Infrastructure and Transport, Major Cities Unit, *State of Australian Cities 2013, Gold Coast-Tweed (Fact Sheet)*, Canberra, 2013, p. 2.

454 Source: Port of Melbourne.

455 Commonwealth of Australia, Australia to 2050: future challenges, The 2010 Intergenerational Report Overview, Canberra, 2010, p. 3.

456 Ibid., p. 4.

457 Commonwealth of Australia, Budget Paper No. 1, Statement 9, Australian Government Budget Financial Statements, Note 3: Taxation revenue by type, 2013-14, Canberra.

458 Commonwealth of Australia, Australia to 2050: future challenges, op cit., p. 4.

459 Ibid., p. 7.

460 R. Burgess, "Breeding a generation of tax slaves won't work", *Business Spectator*, 14 March 2014.

461 Productivity Commission 2011, Submission to the Taskforce on the Sustainable Population Strategy for Australia, Canberra, 2011, pp. 5-6.

462 Davis Langdon, (Michael Skelton, Australia New Zealand Research Manager), http://www.propertyoz.com.au/Article/NewsDetail.aspx?p=56&mid=1685

463 Ibid.

464 Ibid.

465 IPA, *National partnership guidelines will deliver better infrastructure for better value*, 29 November 2008, Media Release.

466 David Langdon, op. cit.

467 J. Wilson, "Congestion to rise with state trapped by rating obsession", *The Saturday Age*, 11 January 14, p. 19.

468 Infrastructure Australia, *Australia's Public Infrastructure, Part of the answer to removing the infrastructure deficit*, Canberra, October 2012, Table 2, p. 34.

469 Karratha Airport in Western Australia is owned by the Shire of Roebourne.

470 Citywide Service Solutions is owned by the City of Melbourne.

471 Source: http://www.heraldsun.com.au/news/victoria/citylink-traffic-onthe-move/story-e6frf7kx-1226552316759

472 Source: http://www.racv.com.au/wps/wcm/connect/racv/Internet/auxiliary/news+_+events/royalauto/news/articles/level+crossings+removal

473 D. Jolly, "Unemployment malaise lingers in Euro Zone", *New York Times* (Online edition), New York, 1 April 2014.

474 Source: http://ec.europa.eu/social/main.jsp?catId=1036

475 OECD, *Education at a glance*, 2011, p. 321.

476 Commonwealth Government, *Educating Globally, Advice from the International Education Advisory Council*, Canberra, February 2013, p. 8.

477 Ibid. p. 29.

478 Ibid. p. 29.

479 Ibid. p. 29. Note: 'The difference between the sum of the number of students studying in each sector (442,924) and the actual number of international students studying in Australia (402,388) reflects those students that are studying in more than one sector'.

480 English Language Intensive Courses for Overseas Students.

481 Commonwealth Government, *Educating Globally*, op. cit. Table 6, p. 29.

482 Science, technology, engineering and mathematics.

483 Source: http://www.washingtonpost.com/blogs/wonkblog/wp/2013/ 01/29/read-president-obamas-immigration-proposal/ and

http://www. firstpost.com/world/us-green-card-for-pg-science-students-indians-to-gainbig-605221.html

484 *The Economist*, 16 November 2013, p. 49.

485 Source: http://www.aph.gov.au/library/INTGUIDE/SP/settlement.htm

486 Functional English is defined as being able to use English well enough to deal with everyday social situations and some work situations. Source: Department of Immigration and Multicultural and Indigenous Affairs, *Report of the Review of Settlement Services for Migrants and Humanitarian Entrants,* Department of Immigration and Multicultural and Indigenous Affairs, Canberra, May 2003, p. 255.

487 Department of Immigration and Citizenship, *Fact Sheet 14 – Migrant Labour Market Outcomes*, Canberra, 2010, Table 3.

488 G. Johns, op. cit. p. 169.

489 Department of Immigration and Citizenship, *Fact Sheet 14*, op. cit.

490 G. Johns, op. cit., p. 169.

491 Ibid.

492 Source: http://www.immi.gov.au/media/fact-sheets/94amep.htm

493 Source: http://www.immi.gov.au/media/fact-sheets/26state.htm

494 Source: http://www.immi.gov.au/media/fact-sheets/92funding.htm

495 NSW Planning & Infrastructure Department, *A Guide to Sydney's Growth Centres*, Sydney, 2011, p. 2.

496 Growth Areas Authority, *Urban Growth Zone September 2012*, Ref 3268-6, 2012.

497 ABS, 3222.0, *Population Projections, Australia*, 2012 (base to 2101), 26 November 2013.

498 Source: http://profile.id.com.au/wsroc/home; http://economy.id.com. au/wsroc

499 Infrastructure NSW, op. cit., p. 79.

500 An unincorporated area is a region of land which is not governed by a municipal corporation. e.g. a small offshore island or ski resort.

501 Property Council of Australia (Victoria), *Submission to the State Government – Discussion Paper: Plan* Melbourne, Melbourne, December 2013, p. 29.

502 Source: http://www.mpa.vic.gov.au/

503 Source: Tourism Australia, Table 1 – Visitors by country of residence, http://www.tourism.australia.com/documents/ABS_arrivals_Jan_2014.pdf (p. 1)

504 Source: http://www.tourism.australia.com/statistics/arrivals.aspx

505 Source: http://www.ceda.com.au/news-articles/2013/11/11/annualdinner

506 Source: http://www.nra.net.au/images/NRASubmissionMarch2012.pdf

507 ANRA, *Economic structure and performance of the Australian Retail Industry*, 2011, pp. 4-5.

508 Source: http://www.nra.net.au/images/NRASubmissionMarch2012.pdf (p. 6).

509 Source: http://www.smh.com.au/federal-politics/federal-election-2013/newattack-on-penalty-rates-in-the-wings-20130906-2taiu.html#ixzz2p1DvGfwK

510 Victorian Government, *Securing Victoria's Future*, Melbourne, 2012, p. 7.

511 Victorian Government, op. cit., p. 7.

512 Multiple reports prepared for the ABCC and Master Builders Australia by Independent Economics (Econtech), 2007; 2008; 2009, 2010, 2012 and 2013.

513 Independent Economics, *Economic Analysis of the Building and Construction industry Productivity: 2013 Update*, Kingston, 26 August 2013, p. vi.

514 ABS, 6321.0.55.001, *Industrial Disputes, Australia*, December 2012; ABS, 6321.0.55.001, *Industrial Disputes, Australia*, December 2013.

515 Prof. A. Markus, Scanlon Foundation Surveys, National Report 2013, *Mapping Social Cohesion*, Caulfield East, 2013, p. 27.

516 Australian Mines and Metals Association, *Finding Fairness*, Melbourne, July 2010, p. 1.

517 Australian Mines and Metals Association, op. cit., p. 10.

Made in the USA
Monee, IL
04 November 2026

67383608R00187